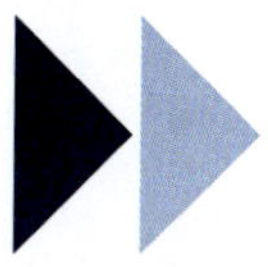

Risk Financing

Risk Financing

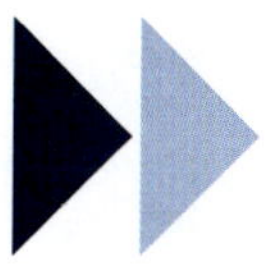

Edited by

Michael W. Elliott, CPCU, AIAF, MBA

6th Edition • 1st Printing

The Institutes
720 Providence Road, Suite 100
Malvern, Pennsylvania 19355-3433

6th Edition • 1st Printing • October 2012

Library of Congress Control Number: 2012948787

ISBN 978-0-89463-620-2

Foreword

The Institutes are the trusted leader in delivering proven knowledge solutions that drive powerful business results for the risk management and property-casualty insurance industry. For more than 100 years, The Institutes have been meeting the industry's changing professional development needs with customer-driven products and services.

In conjunction with industry experts and members of the academic community, our Knowledge Resources Department develops our course and program content, including Institutes study materials. Practical and technical knowledge gained from Institutes courses enhances qualifications, improves performance, and contributes to professional growth—all of which drive results.

The Institutes' proven knowledge helps individuals and organizations achieve powerful results with a variety of flexible, customer-focused options:

Recognized Credentials—The Institutes offer an unmatched range of widely recognized and industry-respected specialty credentials. The Institutes' Chartered Property Casualty Underwriter (CPCU) professional designation is designed to provide a broad understanding of the property-casualty insurance industry. Depending on professional needs, CPCU students may select either a commercial insurance focus or a personal risk management and insurance focus and may choose from a variety of electives.

In addition, The Institutes offer certificate or designation programs in a variety of disciplines, including these:

- Claims
- Commercial underwriting
- Fidelity and surety bonding
- General insurance
- Insurance accounting and finance
- Insurance information technology
- Insurance production and agency management
- Insurance regulation and compliance
- Management
- Marine insurance
- Personal insurance
- Premium auditing
- Quality insurance services
- Reinsurance
- Risk management
- Surplus lines

Ethics—Ethical behavior is crucial to preserving not only the trust on which insurance transactions are based, but also the public's trust in our industry as a whole. All Institutes designations now have an ethics requirement, which is delivered online and free of charge. The ethics requirement content is designed specifically for insurance practitioners and uses insurance-based case studies to outline an ethical framework. More information is available in the Programs section of our website, www.TheInstitutes.org.

Flexible Online Learning—The Institutes have an unmatched variety of technical insurance content covering topics from accounting to underwriting, which we now deliver through hundreds of online courses. These cost-effective self-study courses are a convenient way to fill gaps in technical knowledge in a matter of hours without ever leaving the office.

Continuing Education—A majority of The Institutes' courses are filed for CE credit in most states. We also deliver quality, affordable, online CE courses quickly and conveniently through our newest business unit, CEU.com. Visit www.CEU.com to learn more.

College Credits—Most Institutes courses carry college credit recommendations from the American Council on Education. A variety of courses also qualify for credits toward certain associate, bachelor's, and master's degrees at several prestigious colleges and universities. More information is available in the Student Services section of our website, www.TheInstitutes.org.

Custom Applications—The Institutes collaborate with corporate customers to use our trusted course content and flexible delivery options in developing customized solutions that help them achieve their unique organizational goals.

Insightful Analysis—Our Insurance Research Council (IRC) division conducts public policy research on important contemporary issues in property-casualty insurance and risk management. Visit www.ircweb.org to learn more or purchase its most recent studies.

The Institutes look forward to serving the risk management and property-casualty insurance industry for another 100 years. We welcome comments from our students and course leaders; your feedback helps us continue to improve the quality of our study materials.

Peter L. Miller, CPCU
President and CEO
The Institutes

Preface

Risk Financing is the assigned textbook for the ARM 56 course in The Institutes' Associate in Risk Management (ARM) designation program. This text provides learners with a comprehensive overview of the techniques risk management professionals use to finance, or pay for, the negative consequences of risk events. These techniques usually incorporate a blend of risk retention and transfer.

The first part of the course provides a broad overview of risk financing by explaining how it is one of many risk treatment techniques. It also explains how risk financing alternatives should be examined in light of all of an organization's risks, including both pure and speculative risks. Techniques for estimating losses arising from hazard (insurable) risk are examined in detail.

The middle part of the course concentrates on alternative financing techniques for hazard risk, including insurance, self-insurance, retrospective rating, reinsurance, captive insurance, and contractual risk transfer. The mechanics, advantages, and disadvantages of each technique are discussed in detail.

The last part of the course covers financial risk and capital markets. Various methods for transferring financial risk and hazard risk to the capital markets are discussed in detail. The course concludes with a discussion of how to allocate the costs associated with hazard risk.

The Institutes are grateful to the insurance professionals who contributed to this text, including the individual members of the Risk and Insurance Management Society (RIMS) and the Public Risk Management Association (PRIMA) who gave us feedback on the relative importance of various topics included in the course.

For more information about The Institutes' programs, please call our Customer Service Department at (800) 644-2101, e-mail us at customerservice@TheInstitutes.org, or visit our website at www.TheInstitutes.org.

Michael W. Elliott

Contributors

The Institutes acknowledge with deep appreciation the contributions made to the content of this text by the following persons:

Richard Berthelsen, JD, CPCU, AIC, ARM, AU, ARe, MBA

Pamela J. Brooks, MBA, CPCU, AAM, AIM, AIS

Martin J. Frappolli, CPCU, FIDM, AIS

Douglas Froggatt

Laura J. Partsch, JD

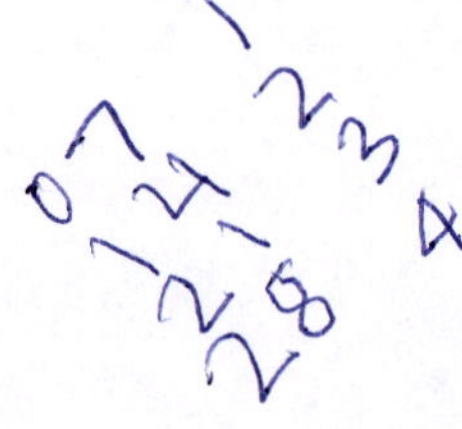

Contents

Segment A

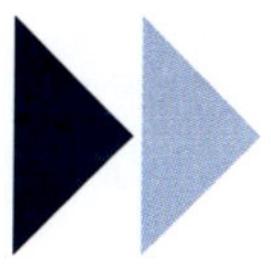

Assignment 1
Introduction to Risk Financing

Assignment 2
Estimating Hazard Risk

Assignment 3
Transferring Hazard Risk Through Insurance

Assignment 4
Self-Insurance Plans

Introduction to Risk Financing

1

INTRODUCTION TO RISK FINANCING

Risk financing enables a risk management professional (any person who has responsibility under an organization's risk management program) to apply techniques that can provide critical resources when needed.

Risk management professionals use **risk financing** to respond to risks that have been identified as a financial threat to the organization.

Risk Financing as a Part of Risk Treatment

Risk financing can be categorized as either risk **transfer** or risk **retention**, both of which are risk treatment techniques. See the exhibit "Risk Treatment Techniques and Risk Financing."

Risk financing
A conscious act or decision not to act that generates the funds to offset the variability in cash flows that may occur as an outcome of risk.

Transfer
In the context of risk management, a risk financing technique by which the financial responsibility for losses and variability in cash flows is shifted to another party.

Retention
A risk financing technique that involves assumption of risk in which gains and losses are retained within the organization.

Risk Treatment Techniques and Risk Financing

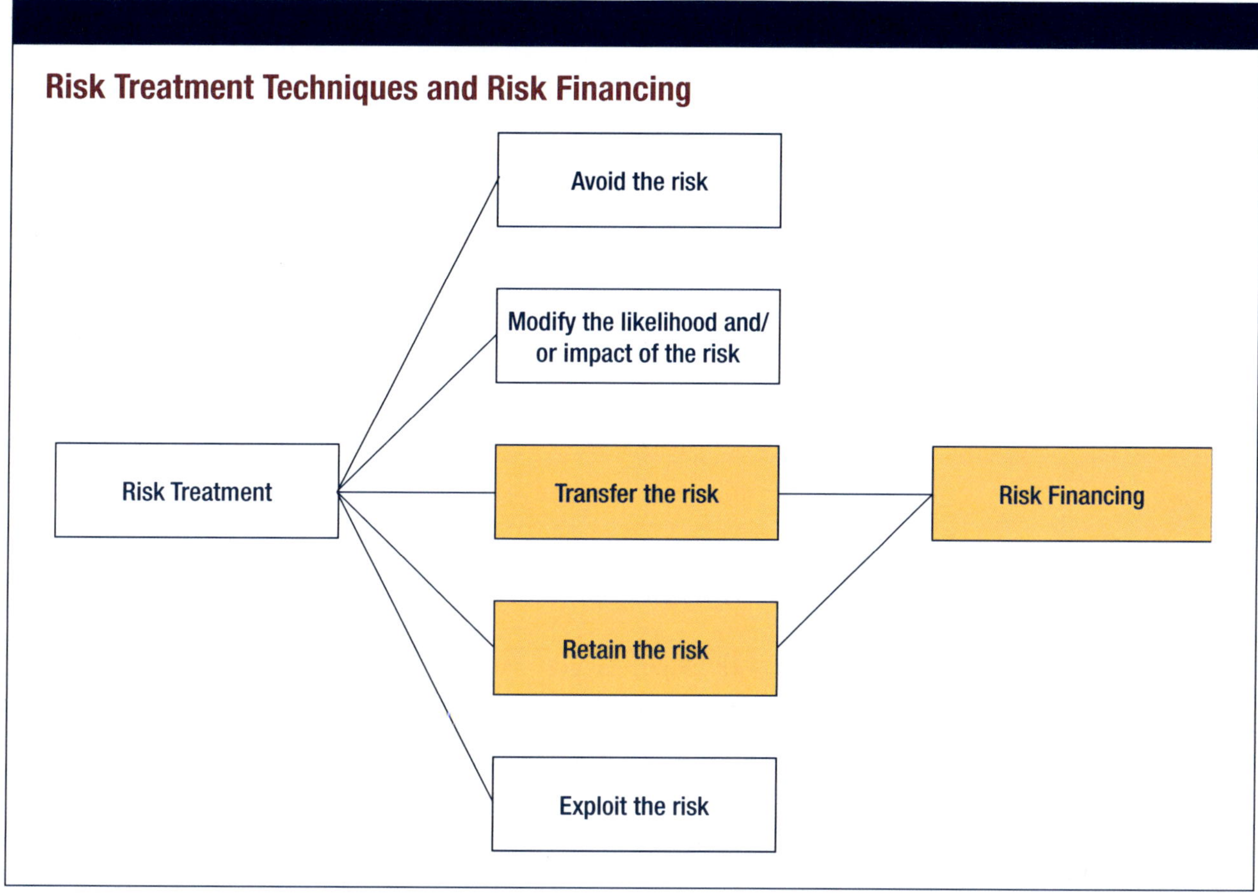

[DA08833]

Hazard risk
Risk from accidental loss, including the possibility of loss or no loss.

Speculative risk
A chance of loss, no loss, or gain.

Risk financing techniques are applied primarily to hazard (insurable) and financial risk. The risk financing techniques for **hazard risk** are insurance, insurance-linked securities, internal funds, and contracts (noninsurance). These techniques involve the transfer or retention of losses. The risk financing techniques for financial risk are futures, forwards, swaps, and options—collectively known as derivatives, or hedging techniques. These techniques involve the transfer of the downside of a **speculative risk** and can result in a missed opportunity for gain. (In some cases, the techniques used for financial risk have been used for hazard risk as well.)

Many risk financing techniques for hazard risk contain elements of both retention and transfer. For example, insurance with a deductible entails retention of the deductible amount and transfer of losses that are above the deductible.

Determining which risk financing techniques are appropriate requires the risk management professional to understand the organization's risk management program goals, which often may be broad and dependent on the successful implementation of both risk financing and other risk treatment techniques. Additionally, risk management professionals must finance risk within the overall context of the organization's financial goals.

Risk Transfer

Risk transfer involves the transfer of risk through insurance and noninsurance techniques.

Insurance

Insurance
A risk management technique that transfers the potential financial consequences of certain specified loss exposures from the insured to the insurer.

Insurance involves providing funds to meet the financial consequences of hazard risk. Insurance transfers the potential financial consequences of certain specified events from the insured to the insurer. The insurance buyer substitutes a small certain financial cost, the insurance premium, for the possibility of a large uncertain financial loss, paid by the insurer. Although insurance is only one approach to risk financing, it is a vital component of a risk management program.

Insurance is essentially a funded risk transfer. By accepting a premium, the insurer agrees to pay for all of the organization's losses that are covered by the insurance contract. The insurer also agrees to provide services, such as claims handling and defense of liability claims.

Contract (Noninsurance)

Risk
Uncertainty about outcomes that can be either negative or positive.

Contract (noninsurance) risk transfer is a risk financing technique that transfers all or part of the financial consequences of an event to a party other than an insurer. Contracts that are not insurance contracts but that transfer **risk** are therefore considered contractual (noninsurance) risk transfers.

These contracts often deal solely with assigning responsibility for an event arising out of a particular relationship or activity and are known as **hold-harmless agreements (or indemnity agreements)**. See the exhibit "Hold-Harmless Agreement for Use in a Lease."

Hold-harmless agreement (or indemnity agreement)

A contractual provision that obligates one of the parties to assume the legal liability of another party.

Hold-Harmless Agreement for Use in a Lease

To the fullest extent permitted by law, the lessee shall indemnify, defend, and hold harmless the lessor, agents, and employees of the lessor from any and all claims arising out of or resulting from the leased premises.

[DA08624]

Hedging

Hedging is practical when it is used to offset the consequences of risk to which one is naturally, voluntarily, or inevitably exposed. It is a form of risk financing for financial risks, which are uncertainties associated with the organization's financial activities. The activities could benefit or harm the organization. For example, currency conversion (converting one country's currency to another's), with the possibility of change in value as a result of the conversion, could either benefit or harm an organization.

Hedging

A financial transaction in which one asset is held to offset the risk associated with another asset.

As another example, a newspaper publisher faces the risk of newsprint price variability. To offset this risk, the publisher might enter into a **futures contract** with its newsprint supplier to purchase a fixed quantity of newsprint over the coming year at a preagreed price. If the market price of newsprint increases over the next year, the newspaper publisher has saved money by buying newsprint below the prevailing price. If the market price drops, the newspaper publisher's risk is still reduced because it has eliminated variability in the newsprint's cost.

Futures contract

An exchange-traded agreement to buy or sell a commodity or security at a future date at a price that is fixed at the time of the agreement.

The same can be said for the newsprint supplier. Whether the newsprint supplier would have made more or less money depends on the ultimate prevailing market price of newsprint, but, in either case, the futures contract reduces the cost's variability.

Risk Retention

For hazard risks, risk retention is often considered to be a form of risk financing when there is an internal fund within the organization to pay the cost of losses. Because retention can be the most economical risk financing technique, it is sometimes preferred even when insurance or contractual (noninsurance) risk transfer is available. Retention can also be the risk financing technique of last resort; the financial burden of any consequences from an event that cannot be insured or otherwise transferred must be retained.

Planned or Unplanned

Retention can be planned or unplanned. Planned retention is a deliberate assumption of a risk (and its consequences) that has been identified and analyzed. Planned retention may be chosen because it is cost-effective, convenient, or the only option.

Unplanned retention is the inadvertent assumption of a risk (and any consequences) that has not been identified or accurately analyzed. For example, many people inadvertently retain flood losses because they do not anticipate the torrential rain associated with hurricanes, against which they would otherwise insure.

Complete or Partial

Retention can also be complete or partial. Complete retention is assumption of the full cost of any consequences that are retained by the organization. Partial retention is assumption of a portion of the cost of a loss by the organization and transfer of the remaining portion.

Funded or Unfunded

Funding for retention differs in this way:

- Funded retention is a pre-event arrangement to ensure that funding is available to pay for the consequences of an event after it occurs.
- Unfunded retention is the lack of advance funding for the consequences of an event that occurs.

Apply Your Knowledge

David is a risk manager of a trucking company with a fleet of trucks that specializes in hauling gravel. Frequently, when a truck is operated on the road by an employee of the trucking company, gravel escapes from the back and cracks the windshield of a vehicle behind the truck. If no insurance or contractual (noninsurance) risk transfer is available for this risk, what risk financing techniques might David consider to pay for these losses?

Feedback: Since neither insurance nor contractual (noninsurance) risk transfer is a viable option, David's employer should consider retaining these losses. This would be a planned retention because it is a deliberate assumption of a risk (and its consequences). Because no risk transfer is available, the retention would also likely be complete, not partial. Finally, it would probably be unfunded, as the cost of repairing or replacing an occasional windshield is minor enough that no advanced funding is needed.

RISK FINANCING GOALS

To manage its risk and maintain a tolerable level of uncertainty, an organization should pursue risk financing goals.

Risk financing goals must support both the organization's risk management and financial goals. Determining how to achieve these goals leads to selection of the most appropriate risk financing techniques.

To achieve the financial goal of maximizing market value, most publicly traded organizations should pursue risk financing goals. (Although their overall goals may differ, privately held and not-for-profit organizations should also do this.) Common risk financing goals include these:

- Pay for negative financial consequences of an event
- Maintain liquidity
- Manage uncertainty
- Comply with legal and regulatory requirements
- Minimize the "cost of risk"

Pay for Negative Financial Consequences of an Event

Risk financing makes funds available to pay for the negative consequences of an event, which can be sudden or gradual. An example of the latter is an organization that suffers a decline in customer loyalty. Risk financing, when thought of in its broadest sense, can provide a source of funds to take action that offsets this decline. However, risk financing is usually related to offsetting the negative financial consequences of a sudden event, such as a flood or an earthquake.

Further, the availability of funds may be important when operations have been disrupted, such as when damaged property must be replaced. However, paying for the negative consequences of an event is also important from a public relations perspective, among others. For example, an organization does not want to tarnish its reputation by not paying liability losses that result from legitimate third-party claims.

Maintain Liquidity

Liquid assets are essential to providing funds to meet or modify the negative financial consequences of events. A **liquid asset** can easily be converted into cash at its fair market value. For example, marketable securities are liquid because they can be readily sold in the stock or bond market. Some assets, such as machinery and equipment, are not liquid because they would be difficult to sell quickly.

Liquid asset
Property that can be quickly and easily converted into cash.

When an organization retains its financial risk, it must determine the amount of cash it needs to pay for the consequences of an event, as well as determine the timing of those cash payments. In deciding how to make financial resources available to pay for its retained risk, an organization must consider its various sources of liquidity: the liquidity of its assets, the strength of its cash flows, its borrowing capacity, and (for a publicly traded organization) its ability to issue stock.

The higher an organization's retention, the greater its need for liquidity. Likewise, organizations that retain risk and experience greatly varying consequences—and, therefore, greater uncertainty—also need substantial liquidity.

Manage Uncertainty

Managing uncertainty is needed to achieve the main financial goal of most publicly traded organizations, which is to maximize market value by maximizing the present value of expected future cash flow. Future cash flow is a projection of the amount of cash that will flow into an organization in a given period less the amount of cash that will flow out of the organization during that same period. The present value of the future cash flow is derived by a calculation (called discounting) that accounts for the time value of money.

In theory, investors value a publicly traded organization by projecting the size of its future cash flow. To estimate the organization's current market value, they use a discount rate to adjust the expected cash flow to the present.

The higher the uncertainty associated with future cash flow, the greater the discount rate. The greater the discount rate, the lower the present value of an organization's cash flow and the lower the current market value that investors assign the organization. Therefore, increased uncertainty in an organization's cash flow reduces the organization's market value.

Achieving the risk financing goal of managing the uncertainties of an organization's cash flow and more can be challenging. For example, an organization often has difficulty determining the maximum level of uncertainty it can tolerate. To do so, it can apply a risk management process that has been integrated into an organization's overall governance, strategy, reporting processes, values, and culture through a **risk management framework**.

Risk management framework
A foundation for applying the risk management process throughout the organization.

Comply With Legal and Regulatory Requirements

Legal and regulatory requirements come from a variety of government entities. For example, the United States Securities and Exchange Commission (SEC) is an agency of the U.S. government that is responsible for enforcing federal securities laws such as the Sarbanes-Oxley Act of 2002. Sarbanes-Oxley sets new or more stringent standards for all U.S. public company boards. Such standards include requirements that senior executives take personal responsibility for the accuracy and completeness of corporate financial reports by certifying and approving the integrity of their reports quarterly. Sarbanes-Oxley also modifies reporting requirements for financial transactions, including off balance sheet transactions, pro-forma figures, stock transactions of corporate officers, and timely notice of material changes in financial condition.

Regulatory entities from other countries have stated that Sarbanes-Oxley could become an international benchmark. For example, the combined code on corporate governance issued by the London Stock Exchange (LSE) is the Sarbanes-Oxley equivalent in the United Kingdom. In contrast with Sarbanes-Oxley, which focuses on financial controls and reporting, the combined code from the LSE covers all controls—financial, operational, and compliance—as well as risk management processes and governance. Also in contrast, compliance with Sarbanes-Oxley is mandatory, but the combined code is voluntary.

Another example of legal and regulatory compliance in the U.S. concerns organizations that raise funds by issuing bonds. These organizations are legally required to purchase insurance. For example, an organization may be subject to a covenant imposed by the bond purchasers that requires it to insure its property for a specific amount. The insurance laws of most states require organizations to purchase liability insurance for their vehicles or, alternatively, to qualify as self-insurers.

Similarly, state workers compensation statutes require most employers to purchase workers compensation insurance or to qualify as self-insurers.

Minimize the Cost of Risk

Cost of risk is a concept applied to hazard risk—that is, the possibility of accidental loss arising from property, liability, personnel, and net income loss exposures. Hazard risk contrasts with business risk (also called speculative risk), which presents not only the possibility of loss but also the possibility of gain.

Managing the cost of risk involves minimizing the cost per unit of risk transferred and retaining risk when a sufficient return would result. The return from retaining risk can be measured by the savings in risk transfer costs, assuming the organization has the option to transfer its risk.

Although managing cost of risk is only one of several risk financing goals, it is the primary measure used by many organizations to gauge the effectiveness of their insurance risk management program. Likewise, cost of risk serves, at least in part, as a personal performance measure for many risk management professionals.

An organization usually seeks to minimize its cost of risk because any reduction in hazard risk expenses increases its net income. The following expenses form part of the cost of risk, regardless of whether losses are retained or transferred:

- Administrative expenses
- Loss control expenses
- Retained losses
- Transfer Costs

Administrative Expenses

Administrative expenses include an organization's costs of internal administration and purchased services, such as claim administration and risk management consulting. Administrative expenses also include any insurance premium taxes paid.

An organization should incur administrative expenses to the extent necessary to properly manage its risk financing program. Often, an organization can save administrative expenses by modifying procedures or eliminating unnecessary tasks. For example, some firms with a loss retention program save expenses by outsourcing the claim administration function.

Loss Control Expenses

Loss control expenses are incurred to prevent losses or reduce the severity of losses that do occur. An organization can best analyze its loss control expenditures by conducting a cost-benefit analysis.

Resources should be allotted to a loss control measure as long as the marginal benefit exceeds marginal cost. However, moral and ethical issues also influence the choice of taking loss control measures—such as equipping corporate vehicles with anti-lock brakes and side-curtain air bags.

Retained Losses

Retained losses are a major part of an organization's cost of risk. When deciding whether to retain a loss, an organization can compare the projected cost of retaining the loss with the cost of transferring it.

Retaining some types of losses that have significant delays in claim reporting and settlement offers an additional benefit. Such losses, which include, for example, workers compensation claims, are known as long-tail losses. Long-tail losses are not paid to claimants immediately but instead are paid over time. Therefore, an organization can invest those amounts until losses are paid.

An organization should measure the value of such deferred loss payments when analyzing the cost of its loss retention program. Deferring loss payments lowers the organization's cost of risk.

When deciding whether to retain or transfer its losses, an organization should also take into account the value of the cash flow benefit from retaining losses. A premium paid to an insurer to transfer losses is usually due at the beginning of the policy period, whereas retained losses are paid at later dates, generating a cash flow benefit to the organization and, therefore, lowering its present value costs.

Transfer Costs

Transfer costs are the amounts an organization pays to outside organizations to transfer loss consequences. In the context of hazard risk, transfer costs often include insurance premiums. In return for the premium, the insurer accepts the uncertainty of the cost of the insured's covered losses and agrees to reimburse the insured for covered losses or to pay covered losses on the insured's behalf.

By minimizing its transfer costs, an organization can maximize the net present value of its cash flow. It can minimize its transfer costs by employing an effective insurance broker or negotiating directly with insurers and other organizations that agree to pay for its loss consequences.

Apply Your Knowledge

Frank is a risk manager for a real estate management company. He has been asked to study whether the company should invest in additional exterior lighting around the buildings it manages to prevent crime. How should Frank decide whether resources should be spent on the lighting?

Feedback: Frank should know an organization can best analyze its loss control expenditures by conducting a cost-benefit analysis. Resources should be allotted to the loss control measure of adding exterior lighting as long as the marginal benefit exceeds marginal cost. Employees, tenants, and customers are likely to feel safer with the additional lighting, which could increase sales and net income. Employees may have fewer workers compensation injuries as well, which would also increase net income. Fewer crime victims could result in fewer liability claims alleging the company should have installed better exterior lighting. Frank should also consider the loss control measure for humanitarian reasons: his employer may allocate resources to install the exterior lighting so that people are not victims of preventable crimes, regardless of the cost-benefit analysis.

SELECTING A RISK FINANCING PLAN

Risk management professionals must consider the characteristics of the losses being managed when selecting appropriate risk financing techniques.

Risk management professionals must consider the effect of risk on an organization's objectives when selecting risk financing plans and the risk management techniques to be used within them. When considering the effect of risk on an organization's objectives, the characteristics of risk must be understood. These characteristics include likelihood, consequences, and variability of outcomes arising from an event. Losses are the financial consequences of hazard risk events.

Hazard Risk

An organization can select a risk financing technique for a loss based on the relationship between its likelihood and its consequences. For hazard risks, the likelihood of a loss is often referred to as its frequency, and the consequences of a loss are often referred to as its severity.

Frequency and Severity Characteristics of Hazard Losses

Characteristics of hazard losses include frequency and severity. The frequency of losses is the number of losses that occur within a specified period. The severity of a loss is the amount of a loss, typically measured in monetary units, such as dollars. Severity can be used to describe the size of an individual loss or a group of losses.

Most large organizations experience numerous relatively small losses. For example, large manufacturers may annually experience many minor injuries to their employees. Conversely, an organization may suffer a catastrophic loss, such as a large fire or a plant explosion, on an infrequent basis. Between these two loss extremes are medium-sized losses that may or may not occur regularly.

The general relationships among losses with different frequency-severity characteristics can be illustrated with the use of a triangle. The width of the triangle illustrates the relative frequency of losses at different severity levels. Usually, the more severe a loss, the lower its frequency. The opposite is also true.

Some categories of loss are not represented by the triangle. For example, organizations often experience losses that are characterized by both low severity and low frequency. Those losses are usually of little financial consequence. Organizations also could experience losses characterized by both high severity and high frequency. These losses are likely to be difficult to transfer and may bankrupt an organization. See the exhibit "Frequency and Severity Characteristics of Losses."

The top segment of the triangle represents catastrophic losses that are characterized by both high severity and low frequency. The cost of these losses is

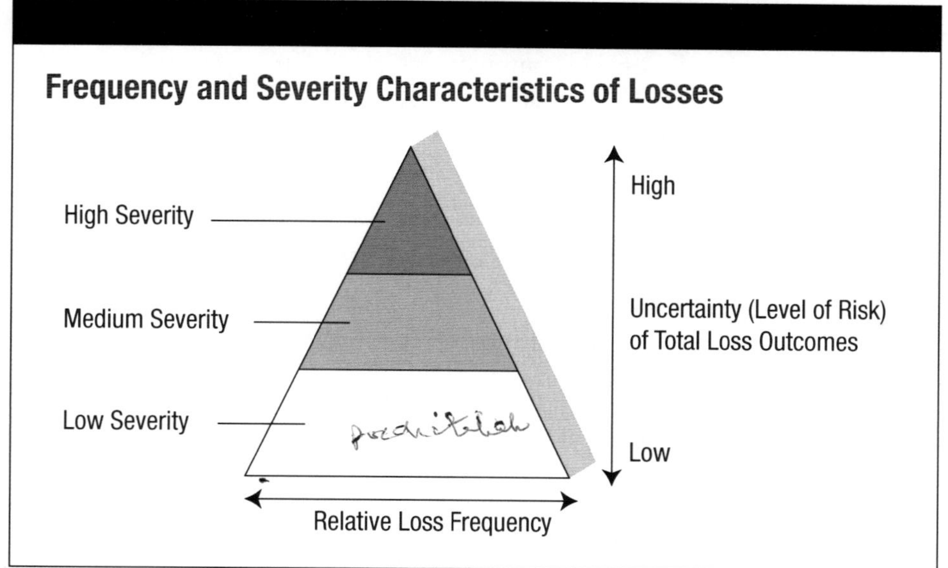

Frequency and Severity Characteristics of Losses

[DA01340]

unpredictable, regardless of whether they are considered individually or as a group. Therefore, they present a high level of risk to organizations. Most organizations arrange to transfer these types of losses before they occur.

"High," "medium," and "low" are relative terms that vary by organization. For example, "low" loss severity would probably be much smaller for a medium-sized organization than for a Fortune 500 organization. "Medium" loss severity for an organization that is financially secure with a high risk tolerance would probably be much larger than for an organization that is financially weak with a low risk tolerance. RIMS defines risk tolerance as "the amount of uncertainty an organization is prepared to accept in total or more narrowly within a certain business unit, a particular risk category or for a specific initiative."[1] Therefore, the placement of the horizontal lines in the triangle varies by organization.

The bottom segment of the triangle represents losses that are characterized by both low severity and high frequency. Organizations with a high frequency of losses find that low-severity losses, taken as a whole or as an aggregate, are predictable. Therefore, organizations usually retain them. It follows that organizations with a low frequency of low-severity losses retain them as well. Because they are low in frequency, such losses are more unpredictable, but because they are also low in severity, when they do occur, an organization can usually afford to retain them.

The middle segment of the triangle represents losses that are characterized by medium severity and medium frequency. Organizations may choose to either retain or transfer these losses, depending on their tolerance for risk and the cost of risk transfer.

The Prouty Approach

One way to analyze all possible combinations of loss frequency and loss severity and apply a method that suggests how to treat risks is the Prouty Approach. In this approach, risks are divided into four broad categories of loss frequency and three broad categories of loss severity. These are the four categories of loss frequency:

- Almost nil: extremely unlikely to happen; virtually no possibility
- Slight: could happen, but not likely to happen
- Moderate: happens occasionally
- Definite: happens regularly

The three categories of loss severity, with suggested risk treatment alternatives, are these:

- Slight: Organization can readily retain each loss.
- Significant: Organization cannot retain the entire loss, some part of which must be transferred.
- Severe: Organization must transfer virtually all of the loss or endanger its survival.

Although these broad categories of loss frequency and loss severity are subjective, they provide risk management professionals with a means of justifying the priority that they believe should be placed on the various risks confronting the organization and a means of providing risk treatment suggestions.

Activities with losses that almost definitely will occur but that are of low severity tend to be accounted for in the annual budget. Consequently, such activities do not need to be avoided. At the other extreme, an activity that happens frequently and generates intolerable loss severity is typically avoided because it is too dangerous to undertake. Therefore, most risk financing decisions concern risk for which individual losses, while tolerable, tend to be either significant or severe and have a moderate, slight, or almost nil chance of occurring. The Prouty Approach is similar in concept to a heat map, which shows risk levels and recommended treatments in a color-coded matrix. See the exhibit "The Prouty Approach."

Relationship Between Characteristics of Hazard Losses and Risk Financing Plans

In general, risk financing retention plans are selected for low-severity losses, while risk financing transfer plans are selected for high-severity losses. Risk financing hybrid plans combine retention and transfer, so they can apply to all losses, regardless of their severity. Hybrid plans combine the elements of both loss retention and loss transfer. For example, a large-deductible insurance plan can be designed to cover all losses that an organization incurs by retaining losses up to the large deductible amount and transferring losses beyond that amount.

The Prouty Approach

		Loss Frequency			
		Almost Nil	Slight	Moderate	Definite
Loss Severity	Severe	Transfer	Reduce or prevent	Reduce or prevent	Avoid
	Significant	Retain	Transfer	Reduce or prevent	Avoid
	Slight	Retain	Retain	Prevent	Prevent

[DA01675]

The selection of a risk financing plan for a hazard risk depends on the level of risk of an organization's aggregate losses and the organization's **risk criteria**. The level of risk is a relative measure of the likelihood or frequency of losses combined with the consequences or severity of an organization's aggregate losses. The higher the level of risk, the less likely it is that the organization would choose to retain losses and the more likely it is to transfer them or at least choose a hybrid combination of retention and transfer. Risk criteria are the benchmark the risk management professional is expected to follow when deciding whether to retain, transfer, or combine the two when selecting a risk financing plan to treat the organization's risks. Risk criteria can be used to assess an organization's level of risk. What may be a high level of risk for some organizations—based on the risk criteria established by its management—may be a much lower level of risk for an organization whose risk criteria allow for a higher risk tolerance because of its management's belief that the lower level is justified based on the organization's larger size and greater financial security.

Risk criteria
Reference standards, measures, or expectations used in judging the significance of a given risk in context with strategic goals.

Another factor to consider when selecting a risk financing plan is the varying cost to transfer risk. In a **hard market**, the cost is relatively high, whereas in a **soft market**, the cost is relatively low. See the exhibit "Characteristics of Losses and Risk Financing Plans."

Hard market
Market conditions in which insurer competition diminishes, buyers have difficulty finding coverage, premiums increase, and insurer profitability rises.

Soft market
Market conditions in which insurer competition is intense and is indicated by widely available coverage, lower premiums, and decreased insurer profitability.

Apply Your Knowledge

Fred is a risk management professional working for a retail clothing store. Store management have told Fred they are concerned about two hazard risks and would like his help in deciding how to treat them. The first risk is a major fire at the store, and the second is shoplifting. What risk financing plan should Fred recommend for each of these risks?

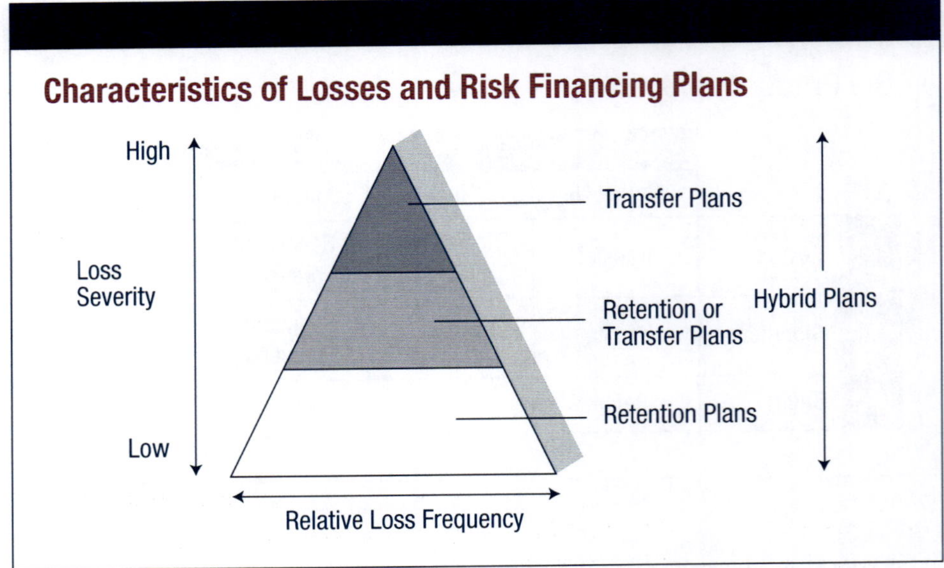

[DA01341]

Feedback: Fred should know that a major fire at the store probably has a low frequency but a high severity. Risks with those characteristics are usually treated by transfer to another party. Fred should also know that shoplifting has a relatively higher frequency but a lower severity than the first risk. Risks with those characteristics are usually treated by retention by the store. However, in the aggregate, all the individual shoplifting losses over an extended period, such as one year, could add up to have the same negative financial consequence as a major fire.

Categories of Hazard Risk Financing Plans

A number of risk financing plans can be categorized as being a retention, transfer, or hybrid plan. These plans fall within the context of traditional risk management and are applied to hazard risk. See the exhibit "Categories of Risk Financing Plans."

Financial Risk

Financial risks are uncertainties associated with an organization's financial activities. As it does for hazard risks, the level of risk for an organization, as determined by its risk criteria, applies in the selection of the appropriate risk financing plan for financial risks.

Hedging is a risk financing plan that includes transfer. It normally requires making an investment to reduce the risk of adverse price movements in an asset.

Categories of Risk Financing Plans

Retention Plans	Transfer Plans	Hybrid Plans
• Informal retention • Self-insurance	• Guaranteed-cost insurance • Insurance derivatives and insurance securitizations	• Large deductible insurance • Retrospective rating • Captive insurance • Pooling

[DA01326]

Risk management professionals use this strategy when they are unsure of what the prices will do in the market for an asset. The benefit of a hedge is that it can reduce an organization's risk of uncertainty over a future price of an asset that it knows it must buy or sell in the future. The cost of a hedge is what the seller of the hedging contract must be paid to guarantee the future price of the asset for the buyer of the hedging contract.

An example of hedging is a contract to guarantee a pre-set interest rate on a future loan. The cost of the asset (capital from the loan), aside from repayment of the principal, is the interest rate charged by the lender. If, at the time the loan is taken out, the interest rate rises above the pre-set rate, the borrower saves the difference between the pre-set rate and the higher current rate. However, if the interest rate falls below the pre-set rate, the borrower loses the difference between the pre-set rate and the lower current rate. In either case, the primary benefit is that the uncertainty is eliminated over what the rate will be when the loan is needed. See the exhibit "Interest Rate Hedging Illustrated."

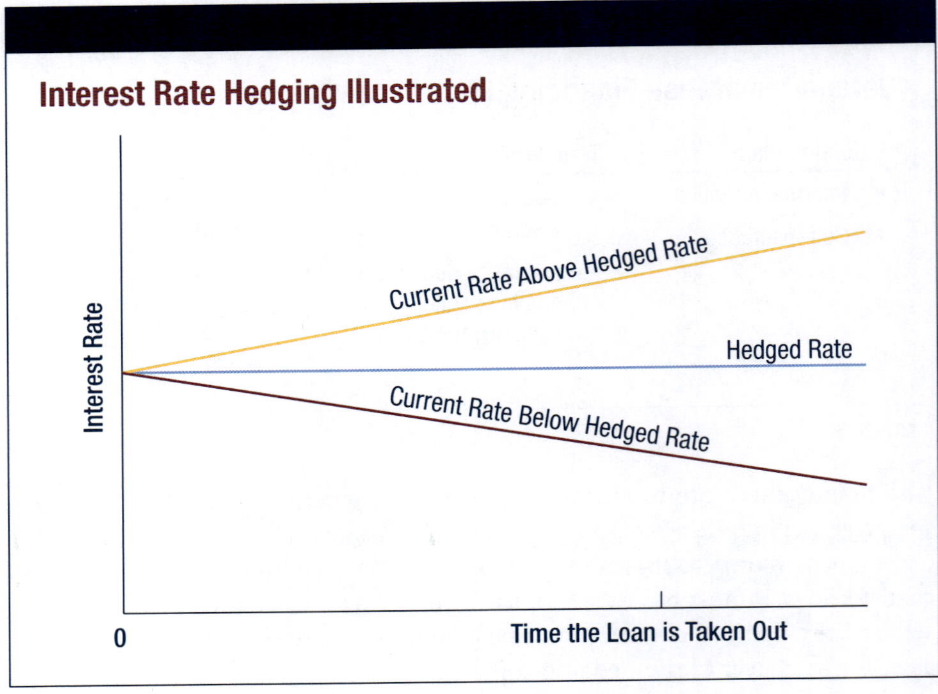

[DA08640]

MANAGING RISK HOLISTICALLY

Many organizations now use a holistic approach to risk management called enterprise risk management.

Enterprise risk management

An approach to managing all of an organization's key business risks and opportunities with the intent of maximizing shareholder value.

Enterprise risk management (ERM) is an approach to managing all of an organization's key business risks and opportunities with the intent of maximizing shareholder value.

Categories of Risk

To realize the goal of maximizing shareholder value, ERM classifies risk into four categories:

- Strategic risks are those uncertainties associated with the organization's overall long-term goals and management.
- Operational risks are those uncertainties associated with the organization's operations.
- Financial risks are those uncertainties associated with the organization's financial activities.
- Hazard risks are those uncertainties associated with the organization's reduction in value resulting from the effects of accidental losses.

Strategic, operational, and financial risks are often called **business risk** because they arise from business activities. Risk management professionals often refer to business risk as speculative risk.

Business risk

Risk that is inherent in the operation of a particular organization, including the possibility of loss, no loss, or gain.

For example, a hardware store owner would be engaging in business or speculative (strategic) risk when he purchases a large inventory of snow blowers in anticipation of a snowy winter season. Likewise, an organization that transfers funds between countries and consequently can incur a gain or loss from the transaction because of exchange rate differences is undertaking a business or speculative (financial) risk.

ERM Versus Traditional Risk Management

ERM differs from traditional risk management in key ways:

- ERM encompasses both hazard risk and business risk; traditional risk management focuses on hazard risk.
- ERM seeks to enable an organization to fulfill its greatest productive potential; traditional risk management seeks to restore an organization to its former pre-loss condition.
- ERM focuses on the value of the organization; traditional risk management focuses on the value of the accidental loss.
- ERM focuses on the organization as a whole; therefore, traditional risk management is both its own discipline and part of the broader enterprise risk management discipline.

Managing Risks as a Whole

Pursuing ERM is a logical step for large organizations that can absorb substantial loss retentions, because different types of losses tend not to occur at the same time. This means that gains in one area of a large organization can offset losses in another.

For example, property losses arising from hurricanes do not necessarily occur at the same time as losses resulting from increases in market interest rates. Therefore, an organization can reduce its costs by analyzing and managing its risks as a whole rather than by managing each source of risk separately.

For example, when using a holistic approach, an organization might analyze the possible outcomes of risk: hazard risk and interest rate risk. Hazard risk is a pure risk, so the possible outcomes are no loss, which is "good," or loss, which is "bad." Interest rate risk (a financial/market risk) is a speculative risk, so the possible outcomes are gain, which is "good," or loss, which is "bad." See the exhibit "Possible Outcomes From Two Sources of Risk."

An organization that analyzes each of its risks separately might transfer its losses that appear in quadrants two, three, and four of the exhibit, because a "bad" outcome is possible for each. However, an organization that adopts a

Possible Outcomes From Two Sources of Risk

		Hazard Risk (Pure Risk)	
		No Loss (good)	Loss (bad)
Interest Rate Risk (Speculative Risk)	Gain (good)	1 good-good	2 good-bad
	Loss (bad)	3 bad-good	4 bad-bad

Neil A. Doherty, adapted from his lecture at the Wharton School of the University of Pennsylvania, April 28, 1999, Philadelphia, Pa. [DA01339]

holistic approach to risk financing might transfer only its losses in quadrant four, which includes a hazard risk loss and an interest rate risk loss in the same period. In quadrants two and three, "good" loss outcomes help offset "bad" loss outcomes, reducing the need to transfer the resulting risk.

When analyzing risk financing across their enterprise-wide risks, many organizations find inconsistencies in their approach to loss retention. For example, an organization that retains millions of dollars of risk on a daily basis in the foreign exchange market may find that it retains only $100,000 per loss under its property insurance policy. Taking a holistic approach to risk financing allows an organization to coordinate and possibly raise its combined overall risk retention level and therefore save money in the long run.

SUMMARY

Risk financing is a conscious act or decision not to act to provide funds to offset variability in cash flows that may occur. Risk financing can be categorized as risk retention or risk transfer, both of which are risk treatment techniques. Risk financing techniques for hazard risk are insurance, insurance-linked securities, internal funds, and contracts (noninsurance). Risk financing techniques for financial risk are futures, forwards, swaps, and options—collectively known as derivatives, or hedging techniques.

Risk management professionals use risk financing goals to guide them in selecting appropriate risk financing techniques. Risk financing goals should support an organization's risk management and financial goals. Common risk financing goals include paying for the negative financial consequences of an event, maintaining an appropriate level of liquidity, managing uncertainty, complying with legal and regulatory requirements, and managing the cost of risk.

Loss characteristics are assessed in terms of frequency and severity. Often, these characteristics direct the risk management professional to use a particular risk financing technique to treat them. Low-frequency/high-severity losses are most appropriately treated through transfer. High-frequency/low-severity losses are most appropriately treated through retention. High-frequency/high-severity losses are best avoided, whereas low-frequency/low-severity losses are usually of little consequence and are retained.

Many organizations use ERM to treat their risk as a whole. ERM is an approach to managing all of an organization's key business risks and opportunities with the intent of maximizing shareholder value. Traditional risk management, which deals only with hazard risk, is one component of ERM.

ASSIGNMENT NOTE

1. Risk and Insurance Management Society, "Exploring Risk Appetite and Risk Tolerance," RIMS Executive Report, 2012, www.rims.org/resources/ERM/Documents/RIMS_Exploring_Risk_Appetite_Risk_Tolerance_0412.pdf (accessed June 1, 2012).

Direct Your Learning

2

Estimating Hazard Risk

Educational Objectives

After learning the content of this assignment, you should be able to:

- Explain how to analyze and evaluate hazard risk.
- Explain how to estimate expected losses arising from hazard risk.
- Explain how to apply increased limit factors to hazard loss estimates.
- Explain how to estimate the volatility of hazard losses.

Outline

Estimating Hazard Risk

2

ANALYZING AND EVALUATING HAZARD RISK

Risk management professionals need to know when it is appropriate to use quantitative and qualitative risk analysis and risk evaluation of an organization's hazard risk to help it better allocate its resources.

To estimate future losses, organizations perform risk analysis on hazard risks. Hazard risk can be analyzed quantitatively and/or qualitatively. Organizations also perform risk evaluation on hazard risks to determine how much of their future losses, as estimated by risk analysis, should be retained versus transferred. Risk evaluation is helpful when making decisions about other forms of risk treatment, such as changing the likelihood or consequences of an event.

Quantitative Versus Qualitative Analysis

Hazard (insurable) risk is a **pure risk** and has only two possible consequences: a loss or no loss. There is no third possibility of a gain with hazard risk. So the analysis of such risk (whether quantitatively or qualitatively) involves only losses and not gains. Specifically, it involves estimating expected total losses and their volatility.

Pure risk
A chance of loss or no loss, but no chance of gain.

Quantitative analysis is based on objective data of past losses. The data are used to calculate probabilities of future losses. It is assumed when analyzing the data that what occurred in the past will occur in the future. Two primary sources of data of past losses include these:

- An organization's internal records of its own past losses
- Insurance industry data

Insurance industry data are often not as useful as the organization's internal records because only insured losses are included. Also, classifications of losses may vary between insurers. However, it is possible they are the only source of data.

Whenever possible, internal data collection should be done consistently on standardized forms. However, even with uniform data collection of an organization's own past losses, concerns may arise over the extent a risk management professional should rely upon it because of these factors:

- Too few a number of loss exposure units
- Too short a time period over which the data are collected
- Lack of diversification of the organization's operations

An organization needs a minimum number of loss exposure units and years of data collection for its internal records to be credible. For example, if a retail store has five employees with no workers compensation losses for the last two years, then that does not mean there is no risk of workers compensation injuries. The retail store has insufficient loss experience and therefore quantity of data to meaningfully estimate loss probability for the coming period. However, if the retail store has several hundred employees and collected data on its workers compensation losses for the last five years, then there would likely be enough loss exposure units (employees) over a long enough period of time (five years) to have a sufficiently robust amount of internal loss data. Such data would more accurately estimate the probability of future workers compensation losses. For those organizations that use the internal records of their own past losses to estimate future losses, the **law of large numbers** makes such estimates more accurate the larger the organization is.

Law of large numbers
A mathematical principle stating that as the number of similar but independent exposure units increases, the relative accuracy of predictions about future outcomes (losses) also increases.

An organization's lack of operational diversification can make it sensitive to a loss in one location. Also, an organization with only one location may have enough internal loss data to accurately estimate losses with high frequency and low severity but not losses with low frequency and high severity.

In addition to using objective data to estimate future losses quantitatively, a risk management professional can also use subjective data to estimate losses qualitatively. Estimating losses qualitatively draws upon the education, training, and expertise of practitioners in relevant fields to estimate, in their judgment, the probabilities that certain losses will occur. Such qualitative estimates can be used alone (such as when sufficient objective loss data are unavailable) or in conjunction with quantitative estimates.

Examples of techniques used in qualitative analysis include these:

- Scenario analysis
- Failure mode and effects analysis

Scenario analysis is a process of analyzing possible future losses by considering alternative possible outcomes. It does not show one exact picture of the future; instead, it presents several alternative pictures. A range of possible future losses is proposed and the development paths leading to that range are provided. In contrast to quantitative analysis, scenario analysis does not extrapolate past loss data. It does not assume that what occurred in the past will occur in the future. Instead, it tries to consider possible developments and turning points, which may only be connected to the past. In short, several scenarios are proposed to show possible future losses. It is typically useful to generate three scenarios:

- Optimistic
- Pessimistic
- Most likely

Failure modes and effects analysis (FMEA) is another technique used in qualitative analysis. It analyzes the severity and frequency of potential losses. A successful FMEA activity helps a team to identify potential losses (or failure modes) based on past experience with similar products or processes. This can enable the team to design those failures out of the system with minimal effort and resource expenditure. Effects analysis refers to studying the frequency and severity of those failures.

Hazard Risk Evaluation

The International Organization for Standardization (ISO) defines an organization's level of risk as the magnitude of a risk or combination of risks, expressed in terms of the combination of consequences and their likelihood.[1] The level of risk is used to determine the amount of hazard risk to retain based on the organization's risk criteria.

The level of hazard risk can also be used in budgeting. An organization will usually want to include in its budget a sufficient amount to pay the portion of expected losses that it plans to retain. That budgeted amount also depends on the organization's degree of financial conservatism.

The decision as to the amount of an organization's retained hazard risk must be made in the context of the organization's other types of risk levels, such as operational, financial, and strategic risks. For example, if a pharmaceutical company expects to have a high level of operational and strategic risk by introducing a new drug in the coming period, then it may want to retain a lower amount of hazard risk or budget a higher amount for the same.

However, hazard risk is generally not correlated with the organization's other types of risks, providing a diversification benefit. When a hazard risk loss occurs, it does not usually increase the likelihood or negative consequences of events from other types of risk.

The amount of hazard risk to retain also depends on the level of insurance premiums. When insurance premiums are inexpensive, such as in a soft market, an organization may not want to retain risk that it could cost effectively transfer away to an insurer. Conversely, when insurance premiums are expensive, such as in a hard market, it may not be reasonable to purchase first-dollar insurance.

Apply Your Knowledge

Ruth is a risk management professional for a dot-com company. The company just started its operations last month and wants Ruth to do a quantitative risk analysis of its hazard risks. What will Ruth likely use as a source of data on past losses?

Feedback: Ruth would prefer to use the company's internal records of its own past losses. However, the company has not operated long enough to generate a sufficient amount of data to use when calculating future loss estimates. Alternatively, Ruth can use insurance industry data. However, there are several concerns from using this source, such as only insured losses are included and classifications of losses may vary between insurers. These concerns may negatively influence the creditability of Ruth's estimate, but insurance industry data may be the only source available until the company has been in operation longer.

STEPS IN ESTIMATING HAZARD LOSSES

Estimating hazard losses is fundamental to the quantitative evaluation and comparison of risk financing plans and to the determination of related cash flow needs. The accidental loss forecasting process is especially important to the assessment of risk financing plans that involve some loss retention.

Overview of the Procedure

An organization's management typically asks its risk management professional to determine how much it should budget in the coming year for retained losses, such as for general liability. A basic loss forecast provides the amount, on average, that an organization must pay for retained losses, but actual losses in any one year may be considerably higher or lower.

Estimating hazard losses (dollar amounts) entails calculating an estimate of the expected (or average) losses for the coming year based on past data, which requires an organization's risk management professional to complete these four steps:

1. Collect and organize past data
2. Limit individual losses
3. Apply trend and loss development factors to the data
4. Forecast losses

Step 1: Collect and Organize Past Data

The organization's risk management professional first must collect past loss and exposure data and organize them for further analysis. Ideally, a minimum of five years of past loss and exposure data are needed to make an accurate forecast; many organizations collect as much as ten years of data.

Loss Data

Paid losses, loss reserves, loss adjustment expense reserves, and **incurred losses** usually are accumulated on an accident-year basis; that is, they are related to all accidents that occur in a twelve-month period.

As loss payments are made during the accident year, paid losses increase and reserves decrease equally. Therefore, incurred losses are unchanged. However, incurred losses do change when a reserve is amended because of additional information about a claim or because a new claim is reported. An accident year's accounts can be kept open for many years until all of that year's losses are paid.

The formula for calculating incurred losses is:

Incurred losses = Paid losses + Loss reserves + Loss adjustment expense reserves

The organization's risk management professional collects the past loss data, often in a spreadsheet. For each year of loss data, the spreadsheet will list the paid loss and loss reserves (which normally include loss adjustment expense reserves) per loss. The past loss, loss reserves, and loss adjustment reserves are added to determine the incurred loss. All the individual losses are then added to determine yearly totals.

These are factors to consider when evaluating an organization's loss data:

- Timeframe—It is necessary to collect loss data from previous accident years because an organization's paid losses and loss reserves change over time.
- Loss development and payout pattern—An analysis of the previous evaluations allows an organization to track past **loss development** and **loss payout patterns**.
- Large claims—For large claims, such as those over $100,000, an organization's risk management professional should obtain specific information on the cause and circumstances of loss so that loss control techniques can help mitigate similar future losses and to determine whether it is an anomaly that can be discounted or part of a pattern that needs to be incorporated in the forecast.

Loss adjustment expense reserves

Estimates of the future cost of defending and settling claims for losses that have already occurred.

Incurred losses

The sum of the paid losses and loss reserves and loss adjustment expense reserves.

Loss reserve

In financial statements, a liability on an insurer's balance sheet that shows the estimated amount that will be required to settle claims that have occurred but have not yet been paid.

Paid losses

Losses that have been paid to, or on behalf of, insureds during a given period.

Loss payout pattern

A listing of incurred loss payments over time.

Loss development

The increase or decrease of incurred losses over time.

Exposure Data

Exposure data must be collected by type of coverage for each past year and projected for the coming year. To be useful, an organization's exposure data

Exposure unit
A fundamental measure of the loss exposure assumed by an insurer.

must be broken down into measurable units. An **exposure unit** for general liability insurance can be annual sales (in thousands of dollars), building square footage, units (apartments), admissions (theaters), or another measure of public liability.

For a manufacturer, the exposure unit often used is sales. Similarly, number of vehicles or miles driven is a common exposure unit for commercial automobile liability insurance, and payroll or the number of employees is commonly used for workers compensation insurance.

An organization's risk management professional can obtain the organization's historical sales data (usually for the previous five years) and projected sales data (for the next two years) from its records and internal forecasts.

Step 2: Limit Individual Losses

Once past data have been collected and organized, individual loss size must be limited, as necessary. Limiting losses involves capping them at a specific dollar amount. For example, constructing a loss payout pattern that limits losses to $50,000 means losses of $50,000 or less are listed at their actual amount and individual losses of more than $50,000 are reduced to a value of $50,000. Forecasting and financing of losses above this layer can be considered separately.

Risk management professionals limit losses to match the range of losses or layers being forecast. Limiting losses stabilizes them. That is, an organization's losses do not vary significantly from year to year when losses that exceed $50,000 are capped. This allows a risk management professional to focus on the layer of losses that have sufficient frequency to be predictable and, therefore, retainable.

A risk management professional may be able to use industry-wide loss data, if available, to supplement the organization's loss data in the $50,001 to $1 million layer. However, a risk management professional is more likely to use **increased limit factor tables** developed by insurance advisory organizations.

Increased limit factor table
A table used by insurers to price layers of coverage in excess of the insurer's base limit.

For example, a primary insurer's base limit for general liability policies may be $100,000 per occurrence and $200,000 aggregate (denoted as $100/$200), but those base limits can be increased in increments (for example, $200/$200, $100/$300, $1,000/$3,000, and so forth) by applying an increased limit factor to the premium developed for the base limit. Increased limit factor tables are actuarially developed and based on considerable industry-wide loss data, making them a sound foundation for forecasting losses.

Step 3: Apply Trend and Loss Development Factors to the Data

Trend factors reflect changes that occur over time, such as inflation, regulatory changes, and legal rulings. Applying trend factors to data allows the risk management professional to make all the data comparable by nullifying external factors and more accurately use past loss data to project future loss amounts.

Trend factor
An adjustment to loss data for a change in general economic conditions, such as inflation.

Loss development factors ordinarily are used to forecast liability losses, which tend to exhibit patterns of late claim reporting and underreserving. Because property losses ordinarily are reported and paid quickly, loss development factors typically are not used for a property loss forecast.

Loss development factor
An actuarial means for adjusting losses to reflect future growth in claims due to both increases in the incurred amount for reported losses and incurred but not reported (IBNR) losses.

Loss Development

Loss development presents an obstacle to accurately forecasting losses. Unlike other historical data, such as an organization's historical sales data for 20X1 through 20X5, past loss data are subject to change long after the end of the accident year. Earlier accident years, such as 20X1, are probably less subject to development than more recent accident years, such as 20X5. Risk management professionals may reasonably conclude that the total incurred loss amount for 20X1 as of 20X5 is the ultimate loss for that year.

To estimate ultimate losses (final actual losses) for an accident year, an **ultimate loss development factor** is applied to past incurred losses for each year. The factors applied bear an inverse relationship to the age of each accident year because most loss development occurs early in the life of a claim.

Ultimate loss development factor
A factor that is applied to the most recent estimate of incurred losses for a specific accident year to estimate the ultimate incurred loss for that year.

Loss Development Factors

Loss development factors can help estimate the ultimate value (final actual losses) of a group of claims, as opposed to an individual claim. For example, the loss development factor of 3.75 for bodily injury liability claims evaluated eighteen months after the beginning of an accident year means that the ultimate value of those claims will, on average, be 3.75 times their incurred value at eighteen months. Therefore, the projected ultimate value for bodily injury liability claims for which $100,000 has been paid during the first eighteen months after the beginning of the accident year and for which the reserve for future payments at the eighteen-month evaluation is $250,000 (a total incurred amount of $350,000) is $350,000 times 3.75, or $1,312,500. See the exhibit "Typical Loss Development Factors—General Liability."

Loss development factors reflect the average development for an entire group of losses, including an amount for unreported losses, and therefore should be applied only to total aggregate losses for each past year. Some loss development factors apply only to open claims, and others to open and closed claims together.

Typical Loss Development Factors—General Liability

Evaluation Date (Months After Beginning of Policy Year)	Bodily Injury Liability	Products Liability
18	3.75	4.52
30	2.10	2.27
42	1.48	1.49
54	1.30	1.34
66	1.20	1.21
78	1.12	1.14
90	1.07	1.08

Loss development, and consequently loss development factors, vary by type of loss exposure. Some categories of losses settle more quickly than others.

[DA01773]

Calculating Loss Development Factors

Loss development factors are available from several insurance advisory organizations and trade organizations. They must relate to the body of past data to which they will be applied. For example, when forecasting losses for a manufacturer, typical loss development factors for general liability can be used. However, the manufacturer's loss exposure should be similar to other manufacturers whose data were used to generate the general liability loss development factors. Even then, the loss reserves may not have been similarly set.

If an organization has a sufficiently large number of past losses, the risk management professional may decide that loss development factors can be calculated from the organization's own past loss data and applied to the most recent evaluation of prior loss years. This approach is preferable to using industry-wide factors because it calculates loss development factors from the same data to which those factors are applied. See the exhibit "General Liability (Losses Limited to $50,000 for All Evaluation Dates)."

The exhibit shows an organization's past losses from a perspective of a June 6, 20X6, evaluation. The $139,000 represents the June 20X6 evaluation of the 20X1 accident year, which takes place sixty-six months after the beginning of that year. The June 20X6 evaluation of the 20X2 accident year is $158,000, which occurs fifty-four months after the beginning of that accident year. The other numbers in the diagonal are the June 20X6 evaluation of their respective accident years. Such tables of dollar amounts or development factors for losses often are called **loss triangles** because, when tabulated, the projected dollar amounts fall on the diagonal, or the hypotenuse, of a triangle.

Loss triangle

A table of successive years of loss data.

General Liability (Losses Limited to $50,000 for All Evaluation Dates)

Months From the Beginning of the Accident Year

Accident Year	18	30	42	54	66
20X1	$63,551	$100,410	$120,492	$134,951	$139,000
20X2	72,238	119,915	146,296	$158,000	
20X3	71,069	113,710	$141,000		
20X4	73,780	$121,000			
20X5	$70,750				

Total Incurred Losses

Loss triangles show past losses from the perspective of a particular evaluation date.

[DA01775]

The organization's total losses are assumed to be fully developed for each year after sixty-six months. This assumption probably would not be true for many liability loss exposures, such as general liability, workers compensation, and medical malpractice. These claims generate periodic payments that extend over long periods. Nevertheless, for 20X1, because no further development is expected beyond sixty-six months, $139,000 is the estimated ultimate amount of losses to be paid. To estimate the ultimate amount of losses for every other year, a risk management professional should calculate twelve-month loss development factors for each past year. See the exhibit "Calculation of General Liability Period-to-Period Loss Development Factors."

The top part of the "Calculation of General Liability Period-to-Period Loss Development Factors" exhibit shows the calculation of twelve-month period-to-period loss development factors. For example, the eighteen-to-thirty-month factor of 1.58 for year 20X1 is the thirty-month evaluation ($100,410) divided by the eighteen-month evaluation ($63,551) for year 20X1. The other twelve-month period-to-period loss development factors are similarly calculated. The individual twelve-month loss development factors for each past year are then averaged to forecast twelve-month loss development factors. For example, the twelve-month loss development factors for eighteen to thirty months for the 20X1 through 20X4 past accident years are averaged to determine a forecast period-to-period factor of 1.62 for that period.

The bottom part of the "Calculation of General Liability Period-to-Period Loss Development Factors" exhibit shows the period-to-period factors used to estimate ultimate losses at each evaluation date. For example, if total incurred losses are evaluated as of thirty months after the beginning of the policy year,

Calculation of General Liability Period-to-Period Loss Development Factors

Accident Year	Months From the Beginning of the Accident Year 18–30	31–42	43–54	55–66
20X1	1.58	1.20	1.12	1.03
20X2	1.66	1.22	1.08	
20X3	1.60	1.24		
20X4	1.64			
Average	1.62	1.22	1.10	1.03

54 months to ultimate	1.03 =	1.03*
42 months to ultimate	1.10 × 1.03 =	1.13
30 months to ultimate	1.22 × 1.10 × 1.03 =	1.38
18 months to ultimate	1.62 × 1.22 × 1.10 × 1.03 =	2.24

* Rounded

Changes in periodic loss evaluations can be converted to loss development factors, which can be used to estimate ultimate loss amounts.

[DA01776]

the factor used to estimate ultimate losses is 1.38. Each factor at the bottom of the exhibit is calculated by multiplying the forecasted or average factors for each interim period. For example, the factor for thirty months to ultimate (or sixty-six months) is estimated by multiplying the average twelve-month loss development factor for thirty to forty-two months (1.22) by the average factor for forty-three to fifty-four months (1.10) and multiplying the total (1.342) by the average factor for fifty-five to sixty-six months (1.03). That is, 1.22 × 1.10 × 1.03 = 1.38226, which rounds to 1.38, as shown on the second line from the bottom of the exhibit.

The period-to-period factors are used to estimate the organization's ultimate incurred losses for each of the past accident years. To estimate the ultimate incurred losses for each year, total incurred losses for each past accident year are taken from the "General Liability (Losses Limited to $50,000 for All Evaluation Dates)" exhibit, and the calculated loss development factors at the bottom of the "Calculation of General Liability Period-to-Period Loss Development Factors" exhibit are applied to the total incurred losses. See the exhibit "Ultimate Incurred General Liability Losses (Limited to $50,000)."

Adjustments must be made to the organization's past loss figures when changes to loss exposures, insurers, or claim administrators occur. If the loss development pattern for a particular year is highly unusual, data from that year should not be analyzed. Estimating future loss development based on past

Ultimate Incurred General Liability Losses (Limited to $50,000)

Evaluation Accident Year	Total Date (Months)	Loss Incurred Losses	Development Factor	Estimated Ultimate Incurred Losses
20X1	66	$139,000	1.00	$139,000
20X2	54	158,000	1.03	162,740
20X3	42	141,000	1.13	159,330
20X4	30	121,000	1.38	166,980
20X5	18	70,750	2.24	158,480

Estimated ultimate incurred losses are determined by multiplying the appropriate loss development factor by the amount of total incurred losses.

[DA01779]

loss development is an acquired skill. Experience and good judgment should be used when calculating and applying loss development factors.

Trend Factors

To make data comparable, the organization's estimated ultimate incurred losses and exposure base data must be adjusted for inflation to the year 20X7. Economic news reports on inflation can provide the trend factors to make this adjustment. Different trend factors are used for losses and for exposure bases. See the exhibit "Estimated Ultimate Incurred General Liability Losses (Limited to $50,000 and Adjusted for Inflation to the Year 20X7)."

Estimated Ultimate Incurred General Liability Losses (Limited to $50,000 and Adjusted for Inflation to the Year 20X7)

Accident Year	Estimated Ultimate Incurred Losses	Trend Factor to 20X7	Adjusted Total Incurred Losses
20X1	$139,000	1.66	$230,740
20X2	162,740	1.60	260,384
20X3	159,330	1.55	246,962
20X4	166,980	1.50	250,470
20X5	158,480	1.44	228,211

Adjusted total incurred losses are estimated ultimate losses multiplied by an appropriate trend factor.

[DA01780]

The organization's estimated exposure base data must also be adjusted for inflation to the year 20X7. See the exhibit "Past Exposure Information Adjusted for Inflation to the Year 20X7."

Past Exposure Information Adjusted for Inflation to the Year 20X7

Accident Year	Actual Sales (000)	Trend Factor to 20X7	Adjusted Sales (000)
20X1	$47,421	1.59	$75,399
20X2	50,020	1.47	73,529
20X3	55,169	1.36	75,030
20X4	58,921	1.26	74,240
20X5	64,282	1.17	75,210

Projected exposure (sales for year 20X7) is $75,000,000.

Adjusted sales are calculated by multiplying actual sales by the appropriate trend factor to reflect inflation.

[DA01782]

Step 4: Forecast Losses

Forecasting the organization's losses for the next accident year entails comparing both the adjusted total loss and the adjusted exposure base data for each past year and forecasting the organization's losses per unit of sales. Then, by using the forecasted exposure base amount, the organization's total losses may be estimated for 20X7. See the exhibit "Calculation of General Liability Losses per $1,000 of Sales (All Losses in 20X7 Constant Dollars and Limited to $50,000)."

The organization's projected sales for year 20X7 total $75 million, or 75,000 units of sales at $1,000 each. Based on the average losses of $3.26 per $1,000 that the risk management professional calculated in the "Calculation of General Liability Losses per $1,000 of Sales" exhibit and total sales of $75 million, the forecasted losses are $245,000 ($3.26 × 75,000, rounded). The forecasted losses are for losses limited to $50,000, which could apply to the deductible layer for an organization. The forecasted losses represent the long-run average expected losses and do not indicate the variability around the average in any one year.

Calculation of General Liability Losses per $1,000 of Sales (All Losses in 20X7 Constant Dollars and Limited to $50,000)

Accident Year	Adjusted Total Incurred Losses	Adjusted Sales	Losses per $1,000 of Sales
20X1	$230,740	$75,399	$3.06
20X2	260,384	73,529	3.54
20X3	246,962	75,030	3.29
20X4	250,470	74,240	3.37
20X5	228,211	75,210	3.03
		Average	$3.26

[DA01785]

APPLYING INCREASED LIMIT FACTORS

A risk management professional should know how increased limit factors can supplement an organization's past loss data because using these factors may be the only feasible method to estimate total large hazard losses.

The first step in estimating expected losses arising from hazard risk is to collect and organize past loss data. When collecting past loss data, an organization typically has many small losses and fewer larger losses to draw on. Credible estimates must be based on a substantial number of losses. The larger losses, though fewer in number, are a significant portion of the total cost of loss and therefore should be accounted for when a risk management professional is forecasting an organization's hazard losses.

Tarnton Company is a denim clothing manufacturer. It has enough of its own past general liability losses, when they are limited to $50,000, to estimate such losses in the future. It has estimated such losses will total $245,000 next year.

It would prefer to again use its own losses to estimate its future large losses, such as those between $50,001 and $1 million; however, that source of loss data does not have enough losses to be statistically credible by itself. Therefore, Tarnton's risk management professional must use another source of loss data to supplement its own loss data when estimating Tarnton's future large losses.

Industry-wide loss data are not available, so Tarnton's risk management professional has decided to use increased limit factor tables developed by an insurance advisory organization.

Overview of the Procedure

Increased limit factor

A factor applied to the rates for basic limits to arrive at an appropriate rate for higher limits.

When applying **increased limit factors** to hazard loss estimates, three steps are involved:

1. Developing increased limit factors
2. Calculating the increased limit factor for a specific layer of losses
3. Forecasting losses at various loss limits

Step One—Developing Increased Limit Factors

Insurance advisory organizations develop increased limit factors from aggregated insurer data, because few insurers would have sufficient claims in high-limit layers to make conclusive loss forecasts. The increased limit factors shown in the "General Liability Increased Limit Factor Table" exhibit were developed to increase liability limit from the basic liability limit ($25,000) to higher liability limit. Consequently, the increased limit factor for $25,000 is 1.00. If Tarnton wanted liability coverage limit of $100,000, the premium developed for the basic coverage limit, such as $5,000, would be increased by a factor of 1.55, or $7,750. The implication is that a premium surcharge of 55 percent (a factor of 1.55) is sufficient to pay for those losses that lie between the basic coverage limit of $25,000 and the increased limit of $100,000.

Step Two—Calculating the Increased Limit Factor for a Specific Layer of Losses

Tarnton's risk management professional can use the increased limit factor table shown in the exhibit to determine the increased limit factor for a specific layer of losses. See the exhibit "General Liability Increased Limit Factor Table."

General Liability Increased Limit Factor Table

Loss Limit	Increased Limit Factor
$25,000	1.00
50,000	1.20
100,000	1.55
200,000	1.80
500,000	2.20
1,000,000	2.50

[DA01786]

The increased limit factor from $50,000 to $1 million can be calculated from the data in the "General Liability Increased Limit Factor Table" exhibit. That calculation uses the increased limit factors at each limit, as shown here:

$50,000 to $1,000,000 = 2.50 ÷ 1.20 = 2.08

Step Three—Forecasting Losses at Various Loss Limits

Tarnton can now estimate the total losses under the $1 million limit. See the exhibit "Tarnton's Forecasted Losses at Various Loss Limits Using Increased Limit Factors."

Tarnton's Forecasted Losses at Various Loss Limits Using Increased Limit Factors

Limit	Increased Limit Factor	Forecasted Losses (rounded to the nearest $1,000)
$50,000	N/A	$245,000
$1,000,000	2.08	$510,000

[DA08680]

The average expected losses for the layer from $50,000 to $1 million are calculated by determining the difference in the forecasted losses at the $50,000 and $1 million limits:

$510,000 – $245,000 = $265,000

Based on the results of the three steps, the average general liability losses are expected to be $245,000 for losses in the $0 to $50,000 range and $265,000 for losses in the $50,001 to $1 million range. Total losses in the $0 to $1 million range are expected to average $510,000. However, in any one year, actual losses may be much higher or lower.

If Tarnton can comfortably afford to retain losses up to $510,000, it may consider a $1 million deductible. Alternatively, the company should assess whether the premium charged by its insurer for $1 million in coverage is reasonable when considering the total average expected losses is $510,000.

Apply Your Knowledge

The management of Tarnton wants to know the average expected general liability losses in the $50,000 to $100,000 layer. What should their risk management professional tell them?

Feedback: The increased limit factor from $50,000 to $100,000 can be calculated from the data in the "General Liability Increased Limit Factor Table" exhibit. That calculation uses the increased limit factors at each limit in this manner:

$$\$50{,}000 \text{ to } \$100{,}000 = 1.55 \div 1.20 = 1.29$$

These are Tarnton's forecasted losses at the $100,000 limit:

$$\$245{,}000 \times 1.29 = \$316{,}050$$

These are Tarnton's average expected general liability losses in the $50,000 to $100,000 layer:

$$\$316{,}000 - \$245{,}000 = \$71{,}000$$

ESTIMATING HAZARD LOSS VOLATILITY

Forecasting accidental losses is fundamental to the quantitative evaluation of risk financing plans and loss control techniques. One step in forecasting accidental losses is to forecast the probable variation from expected losses.

This section illustrates the use of probability distributions and probability intervals to estimate the probable variation from expected losses. The loss forecasts used in this section provide information on the probability of alternative loss outcomes around a long-term average or expected amount for the Tarnton Company.

The Tarnton Company manufactures denim clothes. Its operations include dyeing, cutting, and sewing cloth to create finished goods.

Tarnton has a broad range of loss exposures, but its risk management professional focuses on the organization's general liability loss exposures. If the company's sales total $75 million in 20X7, the expected general liability losses are $245,000. But it is unlikely that Tarnton's retained losses for 20X7 will equal $245,000, and they may be considerably higher or lower.

Forecasting Probable Variation From Expected Loss

To estimate the probability of alternative total loss outcomes, Tarnton separately analyzes its loss frequency, which is a quantitative measure of likelihood, and loss severity, which is a quantitative measure of consequences. These analyses yield three types of probability distributions:

- **Frequency probability distribution**
- **Severity probability distribution**
- **Total loss probability distribution**

Frequency probability distribution

A representation that shows the probability of various numbers of losses over a certain period, such as a calendar year.

Severity probability distribution

A representation that shows the probability of various sizes of each individual loss.

Total loss probability distribution

A representation that shows the probability of total loss outcomes for a given period, such as a calendar year, and is constructed by combining the frequency and severity probability distributions.

To measure the effectiveness of various loss control techniques, it is important to understand all three types of probability distributions. Loss control can reduce the frequency of loss (loss prevention), the severity of loss (loss reduction), or both. For example, increasing the size of a liability insurance deductible will not affect the frequency distribution of retained losses but will change both the severity and total loss distributions of retained losses.

Frequency Probability Distribution

Tarnton experienced a total of twenty-six losses in years 20X1 through 20X5. The frequency distribution of these losses needs to be analyzed. See the exhibit "Frequency Distribution of Losses for Tarnton."

Frequency Distribution of Losses for Tarnton

Year	Frequency
20X1	5
20X2	7
20X3	6
20X4	4
20X5	4
Total	26

[DA01709]

Because losses are evaluated as of 6/30/X6, it is likely that some claims have yet to be reported, especially for more recent years. Based on the past patterns of claim reporting, Tarnton can assume that two more claims will be reported for each of the 20X4 and 20X5 years, making the frequency for years 20X4 and 20X5 six. The total frequency over the five-year period becomes thirty, for an average claim frequency of six losses per year.

The past frequency observations can be grouped together to develop a frequency probability distribution in which the sum of the probabilities of the various outcomes shown would be 100 percent, or 1.00. See the exhibit "Frequency Probability Distribution for Tarnton."

The bar chart in the exhibit shows the relative probability of various outcomes. The horizontal axis represents the frequency amounts, and the vertical axis represents the probabilities of each individual frequency amount. Some frequency outcomes, such as three and nine, were not observed but probably would occur if the sample were based on a large number of past years. The frequency distribution can be used to determine the average claim frequency, which is the **expected value** of that distribution.

Expected value
The weighted average of all of the possible outcomes of a probability distribution.

Frequency Probability Distribution for Tarnton

Frequency	Number of Outcomes	Probability
5	1	.20
6	3	.60
7	1	.20

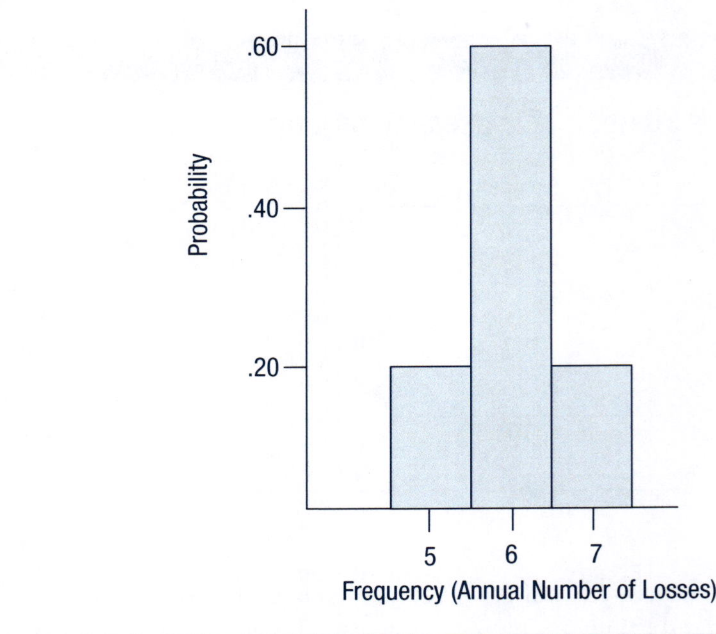

[DA01710]

The expected value is determined by multiplying each possible outcome by its probability and summing the results. See the exhibit "Calculation of Mean Frequency for Tarnton."

Calculation of Mean Frequency for Tarnton

Frequency	Probability	Frequency × Probability
5	.20	1.0
6	.60	3.6
7	.20	1.4
Mean Frequency		6.0

[DA01711]

Superimposing a curve over the frequency probability distribution for Tarnton suggests the shape of a curve. This curve indicates that loss frequency is positively skewed—that is, loss frequencies are concentrated at low-frequency levels to the left of the curve. Further, as severity increases, frequency decreases. So, after peaking at six losses, the curve slopes down as it goes to the right. The area beneath the curve shows the probability of all possible frequency outcomes, which should equal 1.00. See the exhibit "Frequency Probability Distribution Showing All Possible Outcomes for Tarnton."

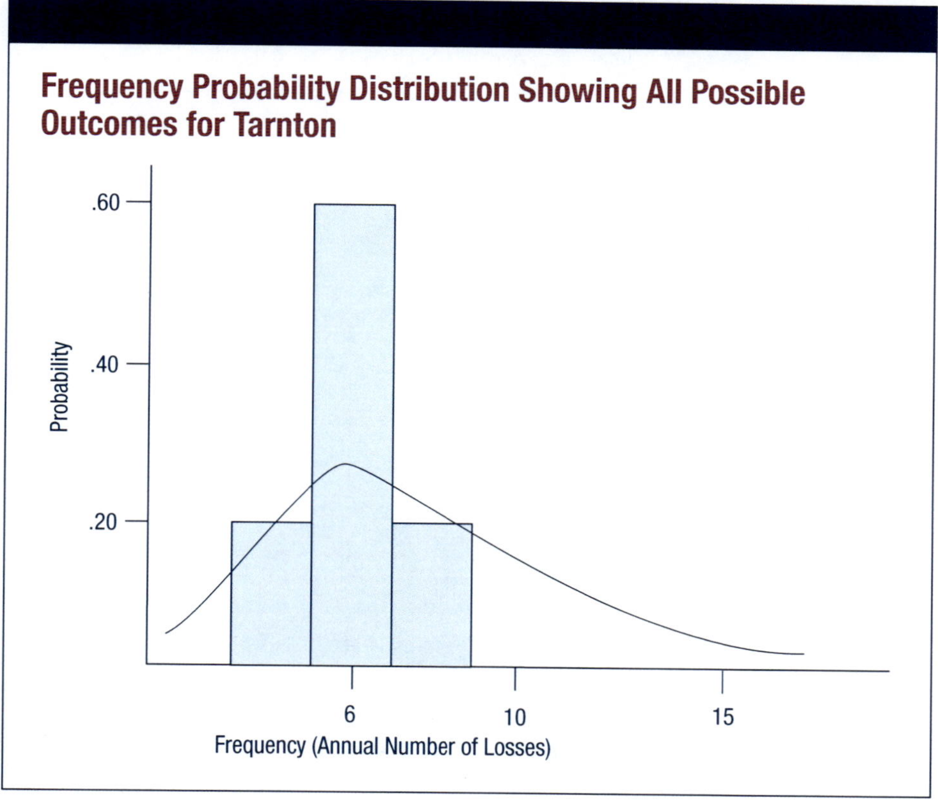

[DA01712]

Severity Probability Distribution

A severity probability distribution is determined similarly to a frequency probability distribution but is based on the size of individual losses rather than on annual frequency figures. The severity probability distribution is a quantitative representation of a range of consequences resulting from an event. To stabilize loss severity, Tarnton's individual losses are capped at or limited to $50,000. Tarnton's total incurred losses, after being adjusted for inflation, can be sorted into ranges of severity and listed in a table or represented in a bar chart. See the exhibit "Severity Ranges and Loss Severity Probability Distribution for Tarnton."

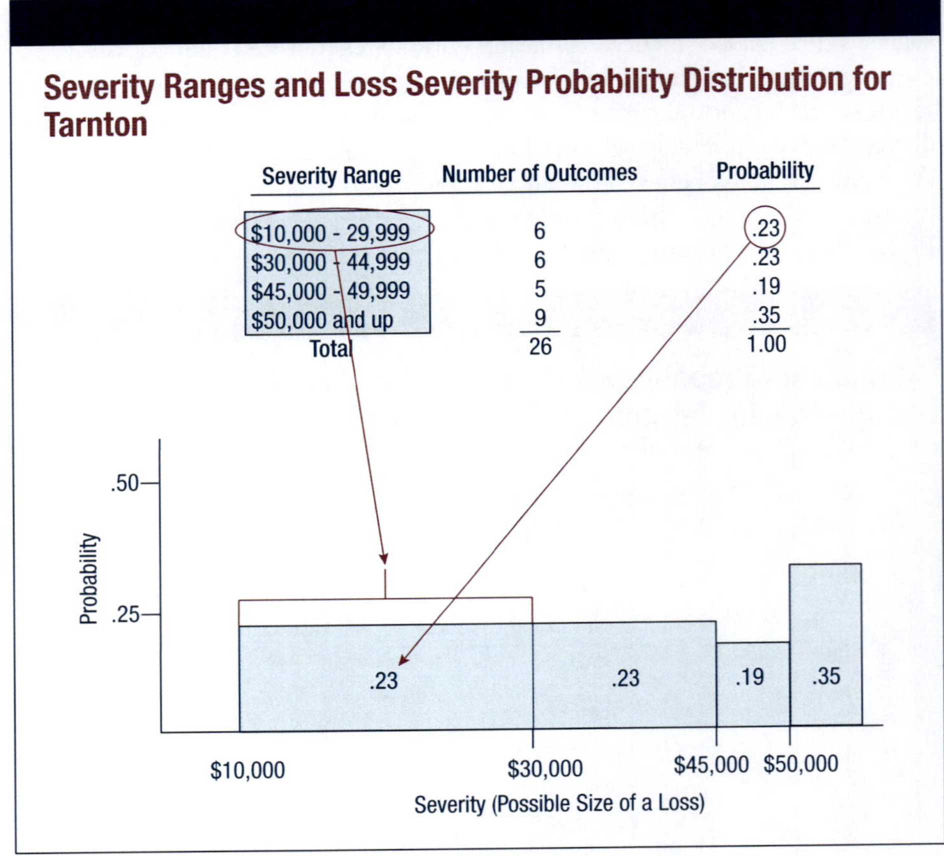

[DA01714]

As with the previously constructed frequency distribution, past losses are insufficient to accurately represent the probability of loss at all of the different loss outcomes. The bar chart in the "Severity Ranges and Loss Severity Probability Distribution for Tarnton" exhibit suggests the shape of a curve that shows the probability of various loss severities that could be derived with additional observations. The "Loss Severity Probability Distribution Showing All Possible Outcomes for Tarnton" exhibit shows that curve superimposed on the bar chart. Note that the bar chart indicates the nine losses of $50,000 and above are all close to the $50,000 amount. However, those losses are normally spread out in much higher amounts, as indicated by the curve. See the exhibit "Loss Severity Probability Distribution Showing All Possible Outcome Consequences for Tarnton."

Just as with the frequency distribution, the mean or average severity can be determined by multiplying the average severity outcome in each range by the probability of the losses falling within that range. The "Calculation of Mean Severity for Tarnton" exhibit shows how Tarnton's mean or average severity is determined. (All losses greater than $50,000 are limited to $50,000.) See the exhibit "Calculation of Mean Severity for Tarnton."

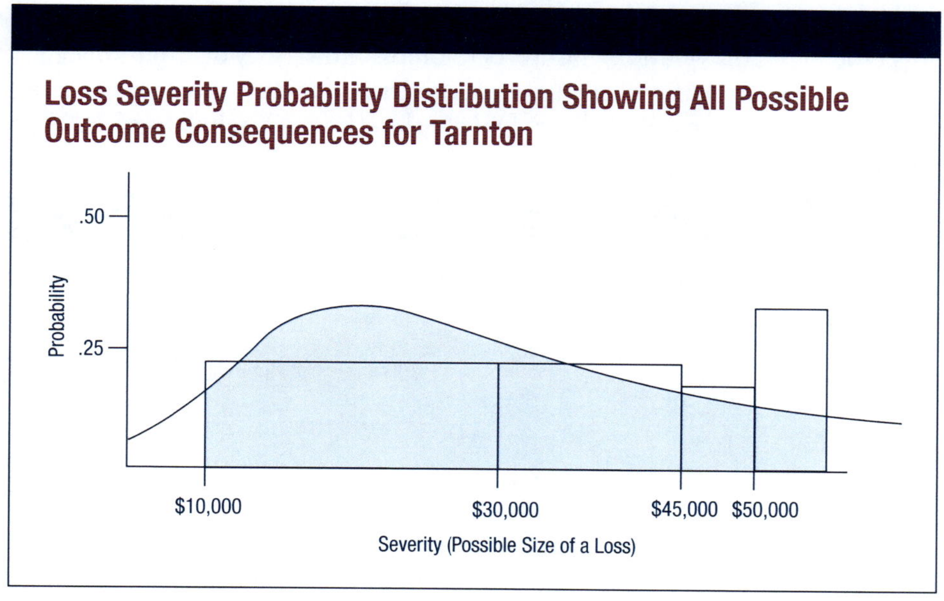

[DA01715]

Calculation of Mean Severity for Tarnton

Severity Range	Mean Severity	Probability	Mean Severity × Probability
$10,000 – 29,999	$20,000	.23	$ 4,600
30,000 – 44,999	37,500	.23	8,625
45,000 – 49,999	47,500	.19	9,025
50,000 and over	50,000	.35	17,500
Total		1.00	$39,750

[DA01716]

Total Loss Probability Distribution

The total loss probability distribution is the probability distribution for total losses over a given period, generally a calendar year. It is a quantitative measure of the organization's level of risk. The mean of the total loss probability distribution can be calculated by multiplying the mean of the frequency distribution by the mean of the severity distribution. For Tarnton, the mean frequency is six, and the mean severity is $39,750, resulting in the mean or average of total losses of $239,000 (rounded to the nearest $1,000) for an average year. It is important to note that, for any given year, Tarnton's frequency may vary from six and its average severity may vary from $39,750, which could result in higher or lower total losses.

The range of possible total losses for a given period is represented by the total loss probability distribution. Tarnton's total loss probability distribution can be constructed from the frequency and severity probability distributions. See the exhibit "Total Loss Probability Distribution (Losses Limited to $50,000) for Tarnton."

Total Loss Probability Distribution (Losses Limited to $50,000) for Tarnton

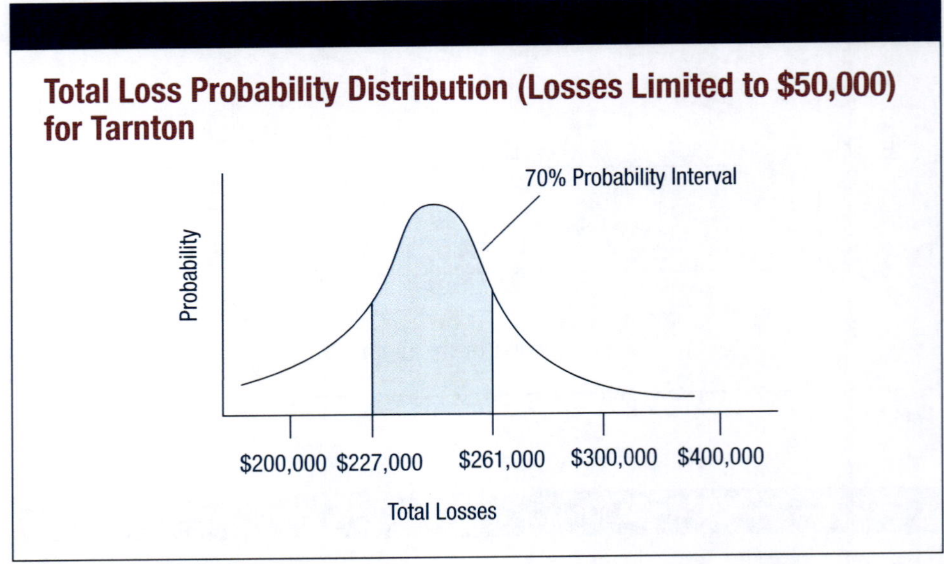

[DA01717]

Probability Intervals

To determine the extent to which actual losses are likely to vary from the long-term average total losses, actuaries use the total loss probability distribution to calculate probability intervals. A probability interval is a representation that shows the probability of outcomes falling within certain ranges of a probability distribution. The probability interval is determined by the area underneath a probability distribution curve.

For example, assume that Tarnton's total losses will fall between $227,000 and $261,000 in seven out of ten years. The seven years would constitute a 70 percent probability interval.

SUMMARY

An organization can use risk analysis, either quantitatively or qualitatively, on its hazard risks to estimate its future losses. If an organization is able to obtain a creditable source of data, it can rely on the results from its quantitative analysis. Otherwise, qualitative analysis may be the best alternative. Once future losses are estimated, risk evaluation is appropriate to determine the amount to retain in light of the organization's level of risk, risk criteria, and other risks.

Forecasting losses is a four-step process that requires the risk management professional to collect and organize past data, limit individual losses, apply trend and loss development factors to the data, and forecast losses.

Applying increased limit factors to hazard loss estimates requires three steps: developing increased limit factors, calculating the increased limit factor for a specific layer of losses, and forecasting losses at various loss limits.

Forecasts of probable variation from expected loss help organizations anticipate variations from forecasted expected losses. Loss frequency and loss severity distributions can be used to determine the total loss probability distribution, which shows the range of possible total losses.

To determine the extent to which actual losses are likely to vary from the long-term average total losses, probability intervals are calculated by actuaries using the total loss probability distribution. A probability interval shows the probability of outcomes falling within certain ranges.

ASSIGNMENT NOTE

1. ISO Guide 73, "Risk management—Vocabulary," section 3.6.1.8 (Geneva, Switzerland: ISO, 2009), p. 8.

Direct Your Learning

3

Transferring Hazard Risk Through Insurance

Educational Objectives

After learning the content of this assignment, you should be able to:

- Describe the purpose and operation of insurance, including risk reduction through pooling and services provided by insurers.
- Explain how insurance benefits individuals, organizations, and society.
- Describe the characteristics of an ideally insurable loss exposure.
- Describe the types of property and liability deductibles.
- Describe the purpose, operation, advantages, and disadvantages of large deductible plans.
- Explain why organizations need excess and/or umbrella liability insurance.
- Describe the basic differences between excess liability insurance and umbrella liability insurance.
- Describe the different types of excess liability insurance and how each operates.
- Explain how excess and umbrella liability insurance can be used in a layered liability insurance program, and describe the problems that may occur.
- Describe the options for structuring an international insurance program.

Outline

Risk treatment
Transfer
Insurance
Non insurance
Retention
Formal
Informal

Transferring Hazard Risk Through Insurance

3

PURPOSE AND OPERATION OF INSURANCE

Insurance is a component of most risk financing plans. Organizations that want the security and certainty of insurance can purchase an insurance policy that transfers hazard risk to an insurer.

The purpose of insurance is to facilitate the spread of hazard risk among those that have similar loss exposures. Not only do insurers accept an organization's risk of loss, but they also provide services in areas such as risk control, claim processing, and legal advice. To some organizations, these specialized services may be as important as the risk transfer aspect of insurance.

Because its meaning depends on context, the term "insurance" can be confusing when used in relation to risk financing. Often, "insurance" is used to describe a risk financing plan in which the premium is a fixed amount; that is, the premium is not adjusted based on actual losses that occur during the policy period. In this context, an insurance plan transfers to the insurer the risk that an insured organization's losses will exceed the premium, which is based on average expected losses.

These types of insurance plans are often referred to as guaranteed-cost insurance plans, because they guarantee, or fix, the amount of premium the insured organization will pay for the policy, regardless of the value of the actual losses the policy covers. Guaranteed-cost can be a misnomer, however, because various insurance pricing plans contain a loss-sensitive element that adjusts the price of insurance based on the amount of actual losses.

Pooling

Risk management professionals must understand why insurance works in order to adequately evaluate its effectiveness relative to other risk financing techniques that rely on risk pooling. Pooling is a fundamental risk management concept that is essential to the operation of insurance. Consequently, pooling should be understood on its own and in context with insurance.[1]

Unlike insurance, pooling reduces risk without transferring it. Generally, a **pool** is an association of persons or organizations that combine their resources to economically finance recovery from accidental losses. Pools reduce risk when the pooled losses are independent (or uncorrelated). Losses are independent when each loss occurs independently and they are not subject to a common cause of loss.

Pool

A group of organizations that band together to insure each other's loss exposures.

For example, windstorm-related losses sustained by a building in California and by a building in Minnesota are uncorrelated because each building was damaged by a different windstorm. However, the windstorm exposures of two adjacent buildings are positively correlated, because both could be damaged by the same windstorm. The following examples demonstrate how pooling serves to reduce risk without actually transferring it.

How Pooling Reduces Risk

Suppose that two organizations—Galston and Atwell—are each exposed to the possibility of an accident in the coming year. Assume that both Galston and Atwell have a 20 percent chance of an accident that will cause a \$2,500 loss and that each has an 80 percent chance of not experiencing an accident. Also assume that Galston's and Atwell's accidental losses are uncorrelated. Finally, assume that neither organization will have more than one accident during the year. A probability distribution—which presents probability estimates of a particular set of circumstances and the probability of each outcome—can indicate each organization's accidental losses without pooling. See the exhibit "Probability Distribution of Accidental Losses for Each Organization (Galston and Atwell) Without Pooling."

Probability Distribution of Accidental Losses for Each Organization (Galston and Atwell) Without Pooling

Outcomes	Probability
\$ 0	.80
\$2,500	.20

[DA05490]

Because Galston and Atwell each face a 20 percent chance of having an accident that causes \$2,500 in losses, the expected loss (the average cost per year over the long term) for each organization without pooling is \$500.

Expected loss = (.80 × \$0) + (.20 × \$2,500) = \$500

Four years out of every five—that is, 80 percent (or .80) of the time—expected loss is \$0 for both Galston and Atwell. Over the long term, one year out of every five—that is, 20 percent (or .20) of the time—it is \$2,500.

The variability in losses can be measured using standard deviation. Standard deviation is the average of the differences (deviation) between possible outcomes and the expected value of those outcomes. In this example, the standard deviation is \$1,000.

$$\text{Standard deviation} = \sqrt{.8(\$0 - \$500)^2 + .2(\$2,500 - \$500)^2} = \$1,000$$

Suppose Galston and Atwell agree to evenly split any losses that the two may incur. That is, they agree to share losses equally, each paying half their combined average loss. This constitutes a pool, because Galston and Atwell are pooling their resources to collectively pay for losses that may occur. Four possible outcomes can result from this arrangement, each with its own probability. See the exhibit "Probability Distribution of Losses Paid by Each Organization (Galston and Atwell) With Pooling."

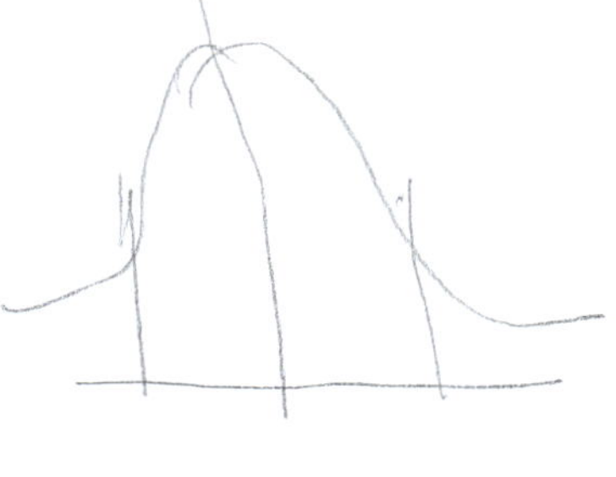

Probability Distribution of Losses Paid by Each Organization (Galston and Atwell) With Pooling

	Possible Outcomes	Probability	Total Losses	Losses Paid by Each Organization (Average Loss)
1.	Neither Atwell nor Galston has an accident.	(.8)(.8) = .64	$ 0	$ 0
2.	Atwell has an accident, but Galston does not.	(.2)(.8) = .16	$2,500	$1,250
3.	Galston has an accident, but Atwell does not.	(.2)(.8) = .16	$2,500	$1,250
4.	Both Atwell and Galston have an accident.	(.2)(.2) = .04	$5,000	$2,500

[DA01355]

Because Galston's losses are independent of Atwell's, the probability that neither organization will have an accident is simply the probability that Galston will not have an accident multiplied by the probability that Atwell will not have an accident. Therefore, the probability of the first listed in the exhibit is .8 × .8 = 0.64. The greater the probability, the more likely an outcome will occur. The probability that Atwell will have an accident but Galston will not equals .2 × .8 = .16. The probability that Galston will have an accident but Atwell will not is also .16. Therefore, the probability that only one of the organizations will have an accident equals .16 + .16 = .32. The probability of the fourth outcome (both have an accident) is .2 × .2 = .04.

This example demonstrates that pooling does not change accident frequency or severity but does change the probability distribution of losses facing each

organization. The probability that Galston will pay losses equal to \$2,500 is reduced from .20 to .04. This is because Galston will not need to pay \$2,500 unless both Galston and Atwell experience an accident.

Given that their accidents are independent, or uncorrelated, the probability that both Galston and Atwell will have an accident is lower than the probability that only Galston, or only Atwell, will have an accident.

Although the probability that either Galston or Atwell will face a \$2,500 loss is reduced, the probability that neither organization will have a loss is also reduced from .80 to .64. Even if Galston does not have an accident, Atwell might have one, and vice versa.

Although both Atwell's risk and Galston's risk are reduced by pooling, each organization's expected loss is unchanged. It still equals \$500. See the exhibit "Expected Losses Paid by Each Organization (Galston and Atwell) With Pooling."

Expected Losses Paid by Each Organization (Galston and Atwell) With Pooling

(a)	(b)	(a) × (b)
Losses by Each Organization (Average Loss)	Probability	
\$ 0	.64	\$ 0
\$1,250	.16	\$200
\$1,250	.16	\$200
\$2,500	.04	\$100
Total	**1.00**	**\$500**

[DA01358]

Because the pooling arrangement reduces the probabilities of the extreme outcomes, the standard deviation of expected losses paid by both Galston and Atwell is reduced. Recall that, without pooling, the standard deviation of losses in this example is \$1,000. With pooling, the standard deviation of losses declines to \$707.

$$\text{Standard deviation} = \sqrt{.64 \times (\$0 - \$500)^2 + .32 \times (\$1{,}250 - \$500)^2 + .04 \times (\$2{,}500 - \$500)^2} = \$707$$

In summary, pooling does not change either organization's expected loss but makes both of their actual losses more consistent and less variable. Pooling, therefore, ultimately reduces each organization's risk.

Adding organizations to the pool further reduces risk for each participant. To illustrate, suppose that Calloway, who has the same probability distribution for losses as Atwell and Galston, joins the pool. At year's end, each organization will pay one-third of their collective total losses (the average loss).

The addition of a third organization whose losses are independent of the other two further reduces the probability of extreme outcomes ($0 or $2,500). For example, for Atwell to pay $2,500 in accident costs, all three organizations must have a $2,500 loss. The probability of this occurring is .2 × .2 × .2 = .008 As a consequence, the standard deviation for each organization decreases with the addition of another participant. While risk (standard deviation) decreases, each organization's expected loss remains constant at $500.

The probability distribution of each organization's accident cost will continue to change as more participants are added to the pool. See the exhibit "Distribution of Average Losses."

Note that as the number of pool participants increases, the probability of extreme outcomes (very high average losses and very low average losses) decreases. Stated differently, the probability that average losses (the amounts paid by each participant) will be close to $500 (the expected loss) increases. Also, as the number of participants increases, the probability distribution of each organization's loss (the average loss) becomes more bell-shaped. A bell-shaped (or symmetrical) distribution is characteristic of a normal distribution, which has known characteristics that can be used to develop reliable forecasts.

In summary, pooling increases the predictability of each of its participants' losses by reducing the variability of their average loss. Therefore, pooling reduces each participant's risk. As even more participants are added, the loss probability distribution becomes increasingly bell-shaped.

Although pooling does not prevent losses or transfer risk, it does reduce the amount of risk borne by each participant. The law of large numbers provides a mathematical explanation of the risk reduction that results from pooling.

How the Law of Large Numbers Explains Pooling

When the number of participants in a pool becomes very large, the standard deviation of each participant's loss approaches zero, rendering the risk negligible for each participant. This result reflects what is known as the law of large numbers. Although the law of large numbers can be expressed mathematically, it essentially postulates that the mean of a random sample of a population approaches the mean (expected value) of the population as a whole as the sample size increases.

Distribution of Average Losses

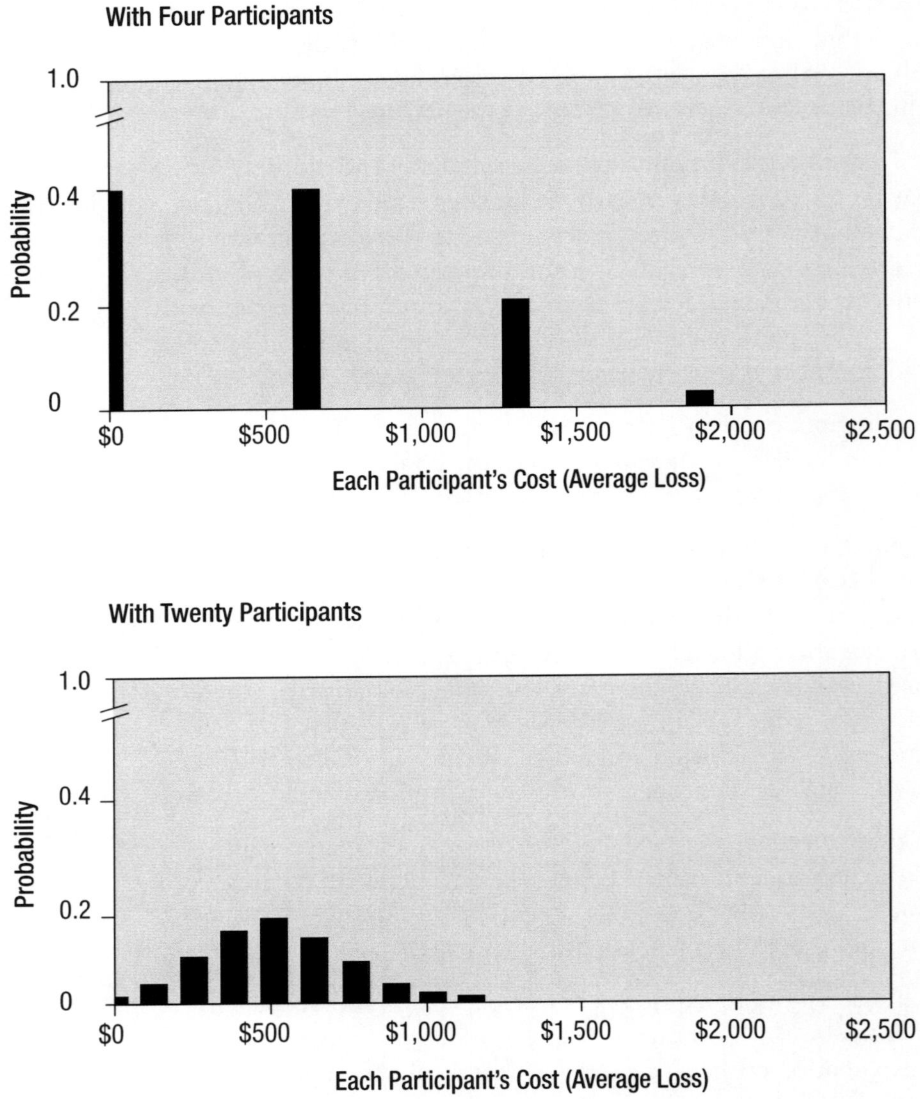

[DA08617]

When applied to a pool, the law of large numbers relies on independent (uncorrelated) losses to accurately predict expected losses. However, hazard risks are often positively correlated.

How Positively Correlated Losses Affect a Pool

Positively correlated losses increase the probability that multiple pool participants will suffer simultaneous losses. For example, a natural disaster may affect only one pool participant but probably will inflict losses on many other

pool participants. Conversely, positively correlated losses imply that when one pool participant incurs losses below expectations or suffers no loss, then so will other pool participants. Therefore, when losses are positively correlated, their distribution has a greater variability (higher standard deviation), and average losses are more difficult to predict. This effect can be demonstrated with a hypothetical involving two cases in which 1,000 participants are in the pool and each participant has an expected loss of $500. See the exhibit "Distribution of Average Losses With and Without Positive Correlation."

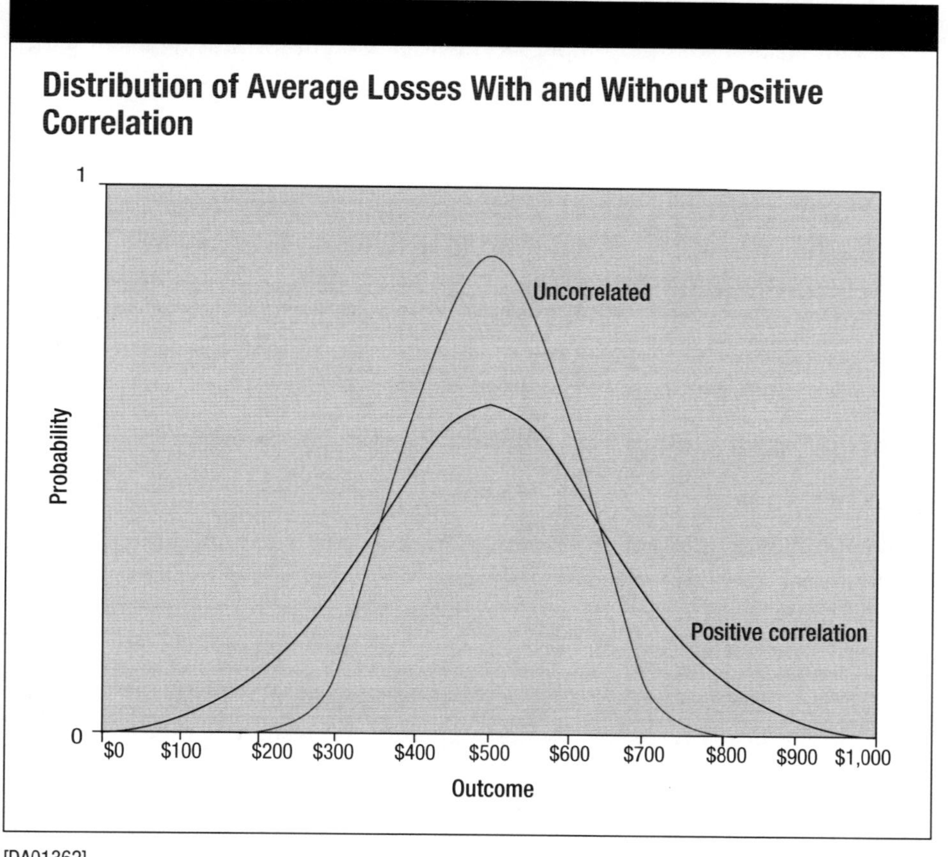

[DA01362]

In one case, each participant's losses are uncorrelated; in the other, they are positively correlated. As illustrated, when losses are positively correlated, their distribution has a greater variability (higher standard deviation), which means that losses are less predictable.

Loss correlation has important implications for risk management and insurance. Positively correlated losses have the potential of causing simultaneous loss to large numbers of pool participants, thereby undermining the risk sharing principles on which pooling is based.

How Insurance Differs From Pooling

Pooling is a mechanism for sharing losses, but not for transferring risks. Insurance, although it is based on loss-sharing principles, is a risk-transfer technique that provides stronger guarantees that sufficient funds will be available in the event of a loss than does pooling alone.

Although an insurer fundamentally resembles a formal pooling mechanism, the two are distinct in these two important ways:

- Insurance transfers risk from the insured to the insurer in exchange for premiums, rather than simply serving as a conduit for sharing losses with others.
- The insurer has additional financial resources from which it can fund losses, enabling it to provide a stronger guarantee that sufficient funds will be available in the event of a loss, further reducing risk.

Risk charge
An amount over and above the expected loss component of the premium to compensate the insurer for taking the risk that losses may be higher than expected.

Counterparty risk
The risk that the other party to an agreement will default.

The premiums an insurer receives should be sufficient to pay for losses, expenses, profits, and contingencies. Contingencies are often addressed by including a **risk charge** (or risk loading) in the premium. The premium amount compensates the insurer for assuming the insured's risk. Insurer collection of premium eliminates the **counterparty risk** that is present in pooling.

Insurers have net worth (called policyholders' surplus) available to satisfy losses that exceed premiums paid by insureds. Net worth is the excess of assets over liabilities. Excess assets may be the result of retained earnings or contributed capital. Regardless of its source, an insurer's net worth provides it with the financial strength it needs to financially endure unexpected losses that would otherwise bankrupt a pool, which has no surplus from which to draw.

Risk transfer, and the resulting financial stability, is not the only aspect of insurance that organizations seek. Many organizations also value the risk management services provided by insurers as part of the insurance product.

Insurer-Provided Risk Management Services

Many organizations rely on their insurers to provide risk management services. These same services are needed by organizations that choose to retain their hazard risk. Insurers provide risk management services because they derive an immediate benefit when their insureds' losses are prevented or reduced. Likewise, organizations benefit from these services.

When organizations consider risk financing techniques other than insurance, they should consider the cost of insurer-provided risk management services as well as the expense the organization would incur to replace them. Services that can be purchased independently of the insurance product from many insurers or third-party administrators include risk control services and claim and legal services.

Risk Control Services

Because they handle the losses of many different insureds, insurers develop expertise in assessing and controlling risk. This expertise is especially important when dealing with hazards that may result in employee injury as well as for high-severity losses. Insurers provide assistance both in identifying loss exposures and in recommending ways to control the associated risk of loss.

With insurance, insurers bear the cost of losses, which provides a strong financial incentive for them to identify and implement measures that control their insureds' losses. Insurers provide risk control services to organizations both to complement insurance coverage and as a separate fee-based service. Insured organizations strive to control their losses because the premium for the next coverage period may be based, in part, on current loss experience.

Claim and Legal Services

Because they handle claims made by many different policyholders, insurers are adept at claim handling. Settling claims, administering claim payments, and preventing fraud are among the specialized areas of expertise necessary to handle claims.

Under guaranteed-cost insurance, an insurer has a financial incentive to control claim costs because of its contractual obligation to pay for losses regardless of their severity. Insurers have other specialized areas of claim expertise, such as the management of medical and disability claims. In addition, insurers have knowledge of systems to report, track, and pay for claims.

Many claims, especially liability claims, require attorneys with special expertise. Insurers not only employ staff attorneys with such expertise, but they also develop a network of legal resources over a large geographic area, benefiting policyholders that have widespread operations.

With liability insurance, insurers are often viewed as a third party by the claimant and the insured. Sometimes this is advantageous in that it reduces stress on other relationships between two parties that may need to cooperate in other matters. For example, workers compensation claims potentially create conflict between worker and employer. The conflict is usually mitigated when an insurer, rather than the employer, negotiates issues involving the claim.

BENEFITS OF INSURANCE

Insurance is a prominent risk management technique, and several risk financing measures involve the use of insurance to some degree. It is therefore important for risk management and insurance professionals to consider the benefits of insurance when selecting the most appropriate techniques for meeting risk management goals.

When used as a risk financing measure, insurance can help an individual or organization achieve risk financing goals such as paying for losses, manag-

ing cash flow uncertainty, and complying with legal requirements. Insurance also provides benefits to individuals, organizations, and society as a whole by promoting insureds' loss control activities, enabling insureds to use resources efficiently, providing support for insureds' credit, providing insurers with a source of investment funds, and reducing social burdens.

Paying for Losses

The primary role of insurance is to indemnify individuals and organizations for covered losses. This benefit is consistent with the risk financing goal of paying for losses. Provided that the loss is to a covered loss exposure and a covered cause of loss, insurance will indemnify the insured, subject to any applicable deductibles and policy limits.

Managing Cash Flow Uncertainty

Insurance also enables an individual or organization to meet the risk financing goal of managing cash flow uncertainty. Insurance provides the insured with some degree of financial security and stability. The insured can be confident that as long as a loss is covered, the financial effect on the insured's cash flow is reduced to any deductible payments and any loss amounts that exceed the policy limits. The remainder of the loss will be paid by the insurer, reducing the variation in the insured's cash flows.

Meeting Legal Requirements

The final risk financing goal that insurance meets is the goal of meeting legal requirements. Insurance is often used or required to satisfy both statutory requirements and contractual requirements that arise from business relationships.

For example, all states have laws that require employers to pay for the job-related injuries or illnesses of their employees. Employers generally purchase workers compensation insurance to meet this financial obligation. In addition, certain business relationships require proof of insurance. For example, building contractors are usually required to provide evidence of liability insurance before a construction contract is granted.

Promoting Risk Control

A major benefit of insurance is the promotion of risk control. Insurance often provides the insured with the incentive to undertake cost-effective risk control measures. Insurers provide this incentive through risk-sharing mechanisms such as deductibles, premium credit incentives, and contractual requirements.

Because these incentives can lead to a reduction in losses paid by the insurer and therefore lower premiums, they benefit not only the individual insured but also all other insureds. Furthermore, risk control measures can save not only financial resources but also the lives of individuals or employees. Therefore, society as a whole benefits.

Enabling Efficient Use of Resources

People and businesses that face an uncertain future often set aside funds to pay for future losses. However, insurance makes it unnecessary to set aside a large amount of money to pay for the financial consequences of loss exposures that can be insured. In exchange for a relatively small premium, individuals and organizations can free up additional funds. As a result, the money that would otherwise be set aside to pay for possible losses can be used to improve an individual's quality of life or to contribute to the growth of an organization.

Providing Support for Insured's Credit

Insurance can also provide support for an insured's credit. Before making a loan, a lender wants assurance that the money will be repaid. For example, when loaning money to a borrower to purchase property, the lender usually acquires a legal interest in that property. This legal interest enables the lender to take actions such as repossessing a car or foreclosing a home mortgage if the loan is not repaid. Without this ability to recover the loan amount, the lender would be less likely to make the loan. Insurance facilitates loans to individuals and organizations by guaranteeing that the lender will be paid if the collateral for the loan (such as a house or a commercial building) is destroyed or damaged by an insured event, thereby reducing the lender's uncertainty.

Providing Source of Investment Funds

Insurance provides a source of investment funds for both insureds and insurers:

- Insureds are not required to set aside large retention funds to pay for losses that are covered by insurance.
- The premiums collected by insurers are invested until needed to pay claims. Such investments can provide money for projects such as new construction, research, and technology advancements.

Insurers also invest in social projects, such as cultural events, education, and economic development projects. Investment funds promote economic growth and job creation that, in turn, benefit individuals, organizations, and society. Also, because investment brings additional funding to insurers in the form of interest, this additional income helps keep insurance premiums at a reasonable level.

Reducing Social Burdens

Finally, insurance can help reduce social burdens. For example, the social costs of natural disasters, such as Hurricanes Katrina and Rita in 2005, are increased by uninsured losses suffered by individuals and organizations that can amount to billions of dollars. Without other assistance, the victims of natural disasters would rely on the state or federal government. Insurance helps to reduce this burden by providing compensation to the affected parties.

Compulsory auto insurance is another example, because it provides compensation to auto accident victims who might otherwise be unable to afford proper medical care or who might be unable to work because of the accident. Without insurance, victims of job-related or auto accidents might become a burden to society and need some form of state welfare. See the exhibit "Benefits of Insurance."

Benefits of Insurance

Benefit	Explanation
Pay for losses	The primary role of insurance is to indemnify (restore to pre-loss status) individuals and organizations for covered losses.
Manage cash flow uncertainty	Insurance provides financial compensation when covered losses occur. Therefore, insurance greatly reduces the uncertainty created by many loss exposures.
Comply with legal requirements	Insurance can be used both to meet the statutory and contractual requirements of insurance coverage and to provide evidence of financial resources.
Promote risk control activity	Insurance policies may provide insureds with incentives to undertake risk control activities as a result of policy requirements or premium savings incentives.
Efficient use of insured's resources	Insurance makes it unnecessary to set aside a large amount of money to pay for the financial consequences of loss exposures that can be insured. This allows that money to be used more efficiently.
Support for insured's credit	Insurance facilitates loans to individuals and organizations by guaranteeing that the lender will be paid if the collateral for the loan (such as a house or a commercial building) is destroyed or damaged by an insured event, thereby reducing the lender's uncertainty.
Source of investment funds	The timing of insurer's cash flows, premiums collected up front, and claims paid at a later date enable insurers to invest funds in a variety of investment vehicles.
Reduce social burden	Insurance helps to reduce the burden to society of uncompensated accident victims.

[DA02722]

IDEALLY INSURABLE LOSS EXPOSURES

Insurance covers events that may or may not happen. When covered events do occur, a financial loss usually results. By transferring the potential costs of the uncertain event to an insurer, the insured reduces or eliminates the possibility of suffering a large financial loss.

By charging a premium in return, the insurer can make a profit if it handles a volume of similar transactions efficiently. Therefore, each party to the contract receives some benefit from the transaction.

The transaction is not likely to be advantageous to the insurer unless the loss exposure has certain characteristics that make it ideally insurable from the insurer's standpoint.

Insurers generally prefer to provide insurance for the potential financial consequences of loss exposures that have these characteristics:

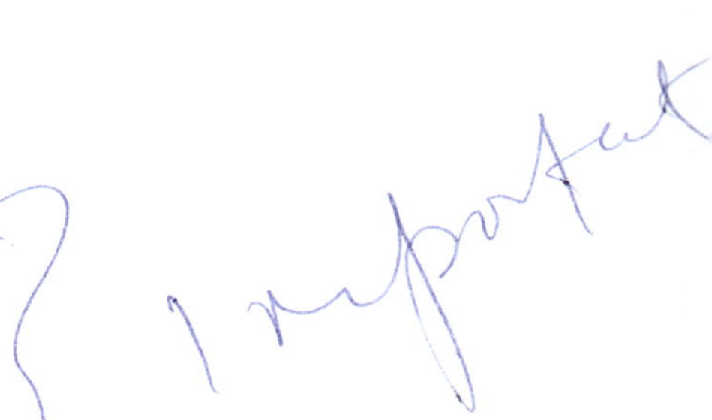

- Loss exposure involves pure, not speculative, risk.
- Loss exposure is subject to accidental loss from the insured's standpoint.
- Loss exposure is subject to losses that are definite in time and that are measurable.
- Loss exposure is one of a large number of similar, but independent, exposures.
- Loss exposure is not subject to a loss that would simultaneously affect many other similar loss exposures; loss would not be catastrophic.
- Loss exposure is economically feasible to insure.

Pure Risk

One purpose of insurance is to make the insured financially whole after a loss, that is, to restore the insured to the same financial position the insured had before the loss. A speculative risk offers the possibility of gain as well as loss. Therefore, if a loss exposure involved a speculative risk and the insured gained as a result of that risk, this purpose of insurance would be defeated.

Accidental Loss

An ideally insurable loss exposure also involves a potential loss that is accidental from the insured's standpoint. If the insured has some control over whether a loss will occur, the insurer is at a disadvantage because the insured may have an incentive to cause a loss.

If losses are not accidental, the insurer cannot calculate an appropriate premium because the chance of a loss could increase as soon as a policy is issued. If the loss exposure involves only accidental losses the insurer can better estimate future losses and calculate an adequate premium for the exposure.

A loss that is not accidental may be a case of insurance fraud—as when an insured intentionally deceives an agent or an insurer to collect money. Controlling insurance fraud is considered one way to keep insurance rates reasonable. For such reasons, it is contrary to public policy for insurers to cover intentional losses.

Definite in Time and Measurable

To be insurable, a loss should have a definite time and place of occurrence, and the amount of the loss must be measurable in monetary terms. If the time and location of a loss cannot be precisely determined and the amount of the loss cannot be measured, writing (that is, issuing) an insurance policy that defines what claims to pay and how much to pay for them becomes difficult.

Losses are impossible to predict if they cannot be measured. The sudden bursting of a water pipe that causes water damage in the insured's bathroom is an occurrence that has a definite time and place. It can therefore be measured and insured. If a slow leak in a pipe causes decay and rotting of the insured's bathroom floor over several years, the resulting loss does not have a definite time of occurrence and is generally not insurable.

Large Number of Similar, Independent Exposures

An ideally insurable loss exposure must be common enough that the insurer can pool a large number of homogeneous, or similar, exposure units. This characteristic is important because it enables the insurer to predict losses accurately and to determine appropriate premiums.

Loss exposures that satisfy this requirement, such as the possibility of damage to homes, offices, trucks, or automobiles, allow the insurer to take advantage of the law of large numbers. The insurer can determine appropriate premiums based on the experience of thousands of similar exposure units and make reasonably accurate predictions about losses.

The inability of insurers to predict losses, and thus to determine adequate premiums, makes most insurers reluctant to insure unusual loss exposures. Predicting the number of losses each year to space stations in outer space would be difficult, because there are very few exposure units. Moreover, each loss could drastically affect the profitability of an insurer and the insurance business as a whole.

Not Simultaneous and Not Catastrophic

Insurers generally prefer to provide insurance for loss exposure that is not subject to a loss that would simultaneously affect many other similar loss exposures; loss would not be catastrophic. Effective pooling of exposure units assumes that the exposure units are independent. Independence means that a loss suffered by one insured does not affect any other insured or group of insureds. If exposure units are not independent, a single catastrophe could cause losses to a sizable proportion of insureds at the same time.

For example, if all of the homes and businesses in a particular city were insured by the same insurer, the insurer would probably suffer a financial disaster if a hurricane leveled the city. The insurer would be unlikely to have the financial resources to pay all claims of all the insureds affected by the hurricane.

The tendency of insurers to avoid insuring catastrophic losses does not mean that hurricane damage to property is not insurable. Coverage for windstorm damage, including hurricane and tornado damage, is readily available throughout most of the United States. However, an insurer avoids possible financial disaster by managing its pool of insureds in such a way that it does not have a large proportion of its insureds exposed to loss in any single event.

For windstorm coverage, the insurer must diversify the homes and businesses it insures so that it does not have a large concentration of insureds in any one geographic area. Consequently, the insurer maintains as much independence as possible among its insureds.

If each of many insurers issued a relatively small number of policies in the city devastated by the hurricane, no one insurer would face financial ruin. Some insurers failed to maintain such independence among loss exposures in 1992 when Hurricane Andrew swept across Florida, resulting in several insurer insolvencies.

Economically Feasible to Insure

Insurers seek to cover only loss exposures that are economically feasible to insure. Because of this constraint, loss exposures involving only small losses as well as those involving a high probability of loss are generally considered uninsurable. Writing insurance to cover small losses does not make sense when the expense of providing the insurance probably exceeds the amount of potential losses.

Insurance to cover the disappearance of office supplies from a company, for example, could require the insurer to spend more to issue claim checks than it would to pay for the claims. It does not make sense to write insurance to cover losses that are almost certain to occur. In such a situation, the premium would probably be as high as or higher than the potential amount of the loss. For example, insurers generally do not cover damage due to wear and tear of an automobile because autos are certain to incur such damage over time.

DEDUCTIBLES

Although it generally represents only a dollar figure entry on the declarations page of an insurance policy, the deductible directly affects the amount of the insured organization's recovery, if any, from an insurer.

Deductible
A portion of a covered loss that is not paid by the insurer.

Deductibles support the economical operation of insurance. Insurance is generally used to transfer only those financial consequences that the insured cannot afford to retain. Deductibles allow the insured organization to obtain the risk transfer it needs while retaining those losses it can safely absorb.

Insurance can be purchased with no or small deductibles, but the insured organization pays a higher premium as a consequence. The cost of insurer-paid claims, regardless of their size, is an expense that insurers pass along to insureds as part of the insurance premium.

Consequently, no or small deductible insurance policies are costly from both the insured's and the insurer's perspective. The insured organization with no or low deductible would be better off financially in the long run by directly paying those losses it can afford to retain.

Insurers charge a lower premium when the insured accepts a higher deductible. Insured organizations evaluate deductibles relative to the amount of premium savings that the deductible provides, as well as the likelihood of loss under the deductible. Additionally, the insured organization must be able to fund those losses that occur within the deductible.

For example, an insured organization with a $1,000 property deductible that is considering a $10,000 property deductible would need a substantial premium savings and confidence in its estimate of the losses that may occur during the policy term. Consequently, choosing a deductible is a subjective decision, despite the abundance of past loss data that may be at the organization's disposal.

Deductibles are usually found in property insurance policies, but organizations can purchase liability insurance policies with deductibles as well. Deductibles are usually specified dollar amounts, but not always. Various types of property and liability deductibles may be included in an insurance plan.

Property Deductibles

Insurance policies usually do not specify the type of deductible, but rather describe the operation of the deductible that applies to the particular policy. Property deductibles, however, generally fall into these categories:

Flat deductible
A deductible stated in a specified dollar amount.

- **Flat, or straight, deductible**—Deductibles usually apply per occurrence regardless of the number of items of covered property that are damaged. For example, if the insured organization suffers a wind loss to three buildings, then the deductible amount would be subtracted from the total amount of loss. The insurer, in this instance, would net the deductible from the amount payable to the insured organization. The insurance coverage specified in the policy is diminished by the amount of the deductible. For example, coverage for a structure insured for $500,000 with a $5,000 deductible would provide only $495,000 in indemnification

should a total loss occur. Losses that do not exceed the deductible are not paid by the insurer.

- **Disappearing, or franchise, deductible**—For example, the insured organization may choose a $5,000 disappearing deductible that is reduced for losses that exceed $5,000 and that does not apply for losses that surpass $25,000. Disappearing deductibles disappear when the insured organization incurs a significant loss, thereby allowing the policy to pay the entire amount.
- **Percentage deductible**—Some percentage deductibles are a specified percentage of the loss, while other percentage deductibles are a specified percentage of the amount of insurance on the affected property or a specified percentage of the value of the affected property. For example, Insurance Services Office, Inc. (ISO), offers two earthquake endorsements. Among the differences in these endorsements, one has a deductible that applies as a percentage of the amount of insurance, while the other has a deductible that applies as a percentage of the property's value.
- **Aggregate annual deductible**—After the aggregate annual deductible has been met, the insurer provides first-dollar coverage on all subsequent losses. Aggregate annual deductibles are also used in liability policies that contain deductibles.

Disappearing deductible
A deductible that decreases in amount as the amount of loss increases, and disappears entirely to provide full coverage after a loss surpasses a specified amount.

Percentage deductible
A deductible expressed as a percentage of some other amount, such as the amount of insurance, the covered property's value, or the amount of the loss.

Aggregate annual deductible
A deductible that limits the total amount of losses retained during a year.

Liability Deductibles

Risk management professionals are accustomed to property insurance deductibles, but the use of liability insurance deductibles is not as routine. As mentioned, selecting a deductible amount and weighing the premium savings provided by the insurer relative to the possible retained losses is subjective.

However, risk management professionals are more likely to retain a share of property losses than liability losses because a liability loss has more intangible elements. Unlike property claims, one occurrence under a liability insurance policy may result in multiple liability claims, and those claims, and their deductibles, can aggregate to substantial amounts.

Unlike property deductible provisions that must be read to be categorized, most liability deductibles are clearly specified. The most frequently used liability deductibles include these:

- Per claim deductible
- Per accident or occurrence deductible
- Waiting period deductible

A **per claim deductible** applies if, for example, five people make claims against the insured organization for bodily injury or property damage incurred in one occurrence. The deductible applies separately to each person's claim.

Per claim deductible
A deductible that applies to all damages sustained by any one person or organization as a result of one occurrence.

Per accident or per occurrence deductible
A deductible that applies only once to the total of all claims paid arising out of one accident or occurrence.

If, instead, a **per accident/occurrence deductible** applied in the same accident, only one deductible would apply instead of a deductible applying to each claim.

The operation of a liability deductible differs from that of a property deductible. Under the terms of a typical liability deductible endorsement, the insurer pays the entire amount of the liability claim and is then reimbursed by the insured organization for the deductible amount. The amount of liability coverage is in excess of the liability deductible. That is, unlike a property deductible, a liability deductible does not diminish the amount of coverage provided by the insurer.

For example, an insurer that provides a $300,000 liability coverage limit with a $50,000 liability deductible would respond to claims up to $350,000 but expect reimbursement from the insured organization for $50,000. Given the same deductible amount, a claim for $100,000 would also require a $50,000 reimbursement by the insured, whereas claims below the $50,000 deductible would be paid for by the insurer but reimbursed in their entirety by the insured organization.

Waiting period
A statutory time period in which the injured worker must wait after an injury before benefits can begin.

A **waiting period deductible** takes another approach. Workers compensation disability benefits are payable to disabled employees only after a waiting period that usually ranges from three to seven days after the injury. In most states, disability benefits are retroactive to the date of the injury if the injured employee is unable to work for a specified period, which can be as short as five days or as long as six weeks, depending on the applicable statute.

LARGE DEDUCTIBLE PLANS

Some organizations want to lower their cost of risk by assuming significant retention amounts within an insurance plan. These large deductible plans are treated separately from insurance plans with typical deductible amounts that are used for both property and liability insurance coverages.

Large deductible plan
An insurance policy with a per occurrence or per accident deductible of $100,000 or more.

A **large deductible plan** is an insurance policy with a per occurrence or per accident deductible of $100,000 or more. Such plans are typically used for workers compensation, automobile liability, or general liability.

Technically, any insurance deductible plan constitutes a hybrid plan because it combines elements of both loss retention and loss transfer. However, large deductible plans involve considerably more retention than do ordinary deductibles, and therefore truly constitute a risk financing plan that has many of the characteristics of **self-insurance**.

Self-insurance
A form of retention under which an organization records its losses and maintains a formal system to pay for them.

Purpose and Operation of Large Deductible Plans

Organizations use large deductible plans to lower their cost of risk. Large deductible plans enable the organization to pay a reduced insurance premium while retaining losses below the deductible level. The organization transfers

the financial consequences for losses that are above the deductible to the insurer.

As losses occur, the insurer settles each claim and then periodically bills the insured organization for the amount of the loss and claim-handling expense up to the deductible level. Consequently, large deductible plans enable organizations to defer cash outflows for accidental losses.

Large deductible plans are a form of risk retention; that is, the assumption of hazard risk that could be otherwise transferred to an insurer. Organizations that choose large deductible plans usually make a commitment to controlling losses they would otherwise retain. The exhibit shows the operation of a large deductible plan. See the exhibit "Operation of a Large Deductible Plan."

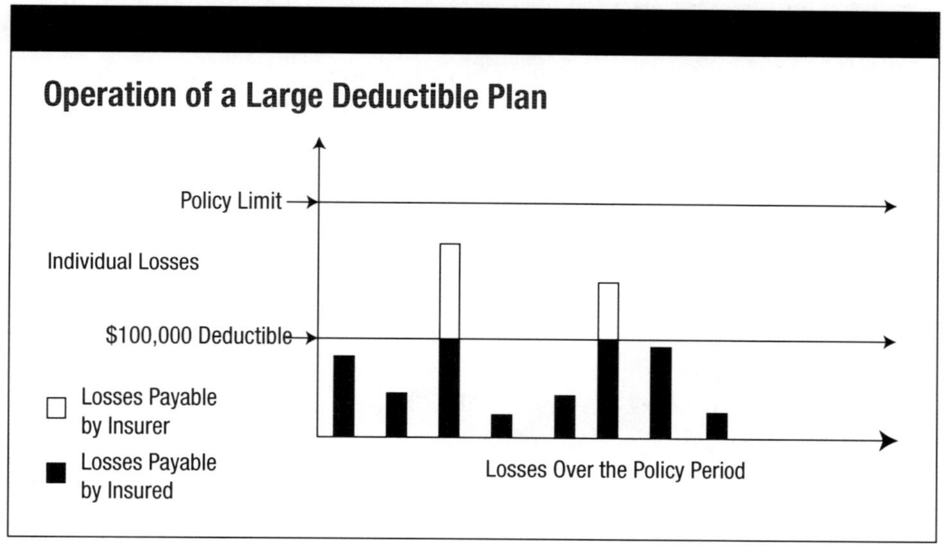

[DA01498]

The insured organization usually must provide the insurer with a form of financial security, or collateral, such as a letter of credit, to guarantee payment of covered losses up to the deductible level. Frequently, at the request of the insurer, the insured will also set up a trust fund into which an initial loss fund is deposited with monthly reimbursement of the fund based on claims paid from the fund by the insurer.

Large Deductible Versus Self-Insured Retention (SIR)

A large deductible is similar to a self-insured retention (SIR). Both a large deductible and a SIR require the insured organization to retain a relatively large amount of loss. A key difference is that, with a SIR, the insured organization is responsible for adjusting and paying its own losses up to the SIR amount. Organizations with SIRs frequently outsource these tasks to an independent claim adjusting organization and pay a fee for that service.

To compensate for a lack of control over individual self-insured claims, a policy with a SIR usually requires strict reporting to the insurer of any claims that have the potential to exceed the amount of the SIR.

Under a large deductible plan, the insurer adjusts and pays all claims for loss, even those below the deductible level, and seeks reimbursement from the insured. In effect, the insurer is guaranteeing the payment of all claims. Therefore, a large deductible plan gives the insurer direct control over individual claims that start out small but have the potential to exceed the deductible level.

Uses of Large Deductible Plans

Large deductible plans are used for workers compensation, auto liability, and general liability policies. In a large deductible plan applicable to these coverages, the workers compensation deductible can apply on a per person and/or a per accident basis, whereas the auto liability deductible usually applies on a per accident basis and the general liability deductible on a per occurrence basis.

The plan can also include an aggregate deductible, which caps total deductible payments over a period of time (usually one year). The exhibit shows an example of a large deductible plan for an organization's workers compensation loss exposure. The example illustrates how large deductible plans can be tailored to meet the insured organization's loss expectations and financial ability to retain accidental losses. See the exhibit "Example of a Large Deductible Plan for an Organization's Workers Compensation Loss Exposure."

Under a large deductible plan, the amount that the insurer incurs to adjust losses, including legal defense costs, can be inside or outside the deductible. If it is inside, or included, the insurer adds it to the amount of the loss for the purpose of determining the total amount that is subject to the deductible.

If it is outside, it is not added to the amount of the loss for the purpose of determining the amount subject to the deductible and is usually prorated between the insured and the insurer based on the size of the loss.

Example of a Large Deductible Plan for an Organization's Workers Compensation Loss Exposure

Assume that a large deductible plan applied to workers compensation incorporates the following:

- A deductible of $100,000 for each injured person
- A deductible of $250,000 per accident, regardless of the number of persons injured
- An annual aggregate deductible of $350,000

Assume six employees are injured in a single year, with four employees injured in a single accident. The table below shows the cost of the losses for each employee.

Accident No.	Employee No.	Amount of Loss	Amount Payable Under Deductible
1	1	$150,000	$100,000
1	2	85,000	85,000
1	3	70,000	65,000
1	4	10,000	0
2	5	50,000	50,000
3	6	60,000	50,000
		$425,000	**$350,000**

Under this large deductible plan, the insured organization would reimburse the insurer $100,000 for Employee 1 (subject to the per person deductible) and a total of $250,000 for Employee 1 through Employee 4 because they were involved in a single accident. In addition, the insured organization would reimburse the insurer for an additional $100,000 for Employee 5 and Employee 6 together, with the annual aggregate deductible capped at $350,000.

[DA01499]

Advantages and Disadvantages of Large Deductible Plans

An organization's motive for adopting a large deductible plan is to reduce its cost of risk. Even though most of the premium reduction is offset because the organization must pay for its losses under the deductible, reducing the premium reduces costs for two main reasons:

- States impose various charges, such as premium taxes and residual market loadings. A **residual market loading** is an amount charged to make up for losses in a state-sponsored plan to insure high-risk exposures, such as an assigned risk plan for auto insurance. A residual market loading is calculated based on a percentage of premium.

Residual market loading
An amount charged to make up for losses in a state-sponsored plan to insure high-risk exposures, such as an assigned risk plan for auto insurance.

- An insurance premium includes charges for the insurer's overhead costs and profit.

A large deductible plan dramatically reduces the cost of risk compared with other insurance plans by avoiding a substantial amount of premium taxes, residual market loadings, and insurer overhead and profit charges.[2]

Another advantage of a large deductible plan is that it allows the insured organization to benefit from the cash flow available on the reserves (funds set aside) for retained losses. The insured organization reimburses the insurer as it pays losses under the deductible.

Workers compensation, auto liability, and general liability losses are usually paid over several years after they are incurred so the insured organization can retain its funds until claims are actually paid, thereby enhancing the insured organization's cash flow.

As with any risk financing plan with a retention component, losses under a large deductible plan may be higher than expected, lowering an organization's net income and cash flow. By keeping its per occurrence (or accident) and annual aggregate deductibles at a prudent level, an organization can manage its uncertainty about the cost of its retained losses.

NEED FOR EXCESS OR UMBRELLA LIABILITY COVERAGE

Excess liability insurance and umbrella liability insurance are similar types of coverage that organizations buy for a variety of reasons, including the need to increase the limits of their commercial general liability, commercial auto, employers liability, and other primary liability policies.

The need for excess or umbrella liability insurance is closely related to three basic issues involved in the use of liability insurance:

- Difficulty in estimating maximum possible loss (MPL) for liability loss exposures
- Layering of liability coverages
- Effect of aggregate limits

Difficulty in Estimating Maximum Possible Loss

Most property loss exposures have a reasonably clear MPL. For example, the MPL for a building that would cost $2 million to rebuild is $2 million; no loss to the building could exceed the amount of money necessary to rebuild it. There is no comparable way to estimate the MPL for most liability loss exposures.

Awards to injured persons can reach large totals. These are examples of amounts of damages juries in the United States have awarded for types of claims that are commonly covered under commercial liability policies:[3]

- $1.672 billion—Intellectual Property Liability
- $300 million—Products Liability
- $178 million—Breach of Fiduciary Liability

Although these verdicts are extreme examples, and may have subsequently been appealed or reduced, multimillion-dollar verdicts have become increasingly common. No million-dollar verdicts occurred in the U.S. before 1962, but, according to the 2007 edition of *Current Award Trends in Personal Injury*, in 2004 and 2005 in the U.S., 64 percent of products liability awards, 55 percent of medical professional awards, 13 percent of premises liability awards, and 5 percent of vehicular liability awards were for $1 million or more.[4] The possibility of a liability loss in excess of $1 million exists for virtually every organization, regardless of its size or the type of product or service that it offers.

Layering of Liability Coverages

Insurers that provide primary liability insurance are often unwilling to provide a limit greater than $1 million per occurrence. An insured that wants higher limits than are available from its primary insurers can do so only by obtaining additional policies. To achieve its desired limits, a business may need to purchase one or more excess or umbrella liability policies.

A primary liability policy and corresponding excess or umbrella liability policies are referred to as "layers" of insurance. The various layers of insurance applicable to a particular set of liability loss exposures can be depicted with the primary layer on the bottom and subsequent layers stacked above. The widely used term "underlying insurance" corresponds to this depiction. With reference to a particular excess or umbrella liability policy, **underlying insurance** is the insurance in a lower layer. See the exhibit "Layers of Liability Insurance."

Underlying insurance
Insurance that applies below an excess or umbrella liability policy.

Ordinarily, the coverage provided by the primary insurer must be exhausted before the next layer of insurance makes any payment. For example, assume that an insured has a commercial general liability (CGL) policy with a $1 million each occurrence limit (this is the primary coverage, or first layer) and an umbrella liability policy with a $5 million each occurrence limit (this is the second layer). If the insured became legally obligated to pay $1.8 million in damages for bodily injury to a third party, the primary insurer would pay its $1 million limit, and the umbrella insurer would pay the remaining $800,000.

The primary layer in an insurance program is not always financed through insurance. Some organizations that are financially able to pay sizable losses out of their own funds prefer to retain (self-insure) the first layer. For example, a large business might decide to retain the first $500,000 of its liability losses and buy excess liability insurance to pay for losses exceeding $500,000.

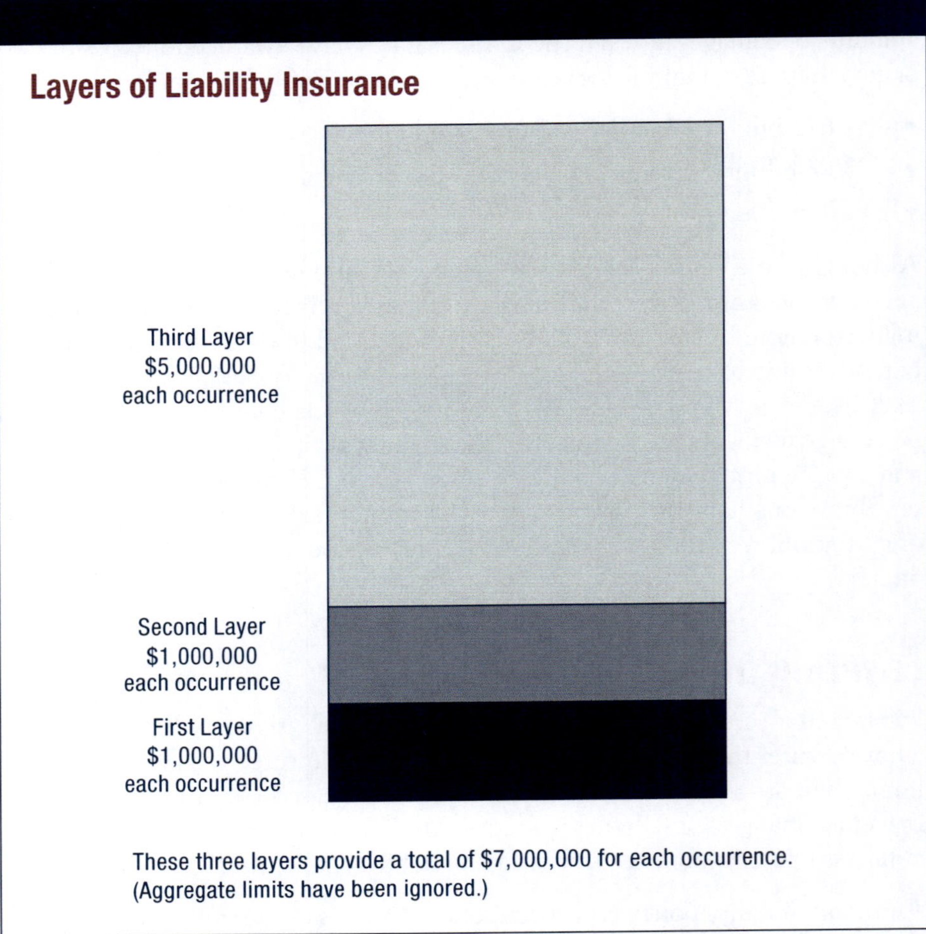

[DA05032]

Effect of Aggregate Limits

In addition to an each occurrence limit, one or more aggregate limits for the policy period often apply to a liability insurance policy. Even if an insured never sustains a loss that exceeds the each occurrence limit of one of its primary policies, the insured could have several liability losses during one policy year that could exhaust an aggregate limit, leaving a subsequent claim uninsured or underinsured.

For example, assume that an insured has a CGL policy with a $1 million each occurrence limit, a $2 million general aggregate limit, and a $2 million products-completed operations aggregate limit. If the insured has four products liability losses for $500,000 each during the policy period, the policy will pay nothing for other products liability losses that occur during the same policy period, even if no subsequent claim exceeds the each occurrence limit (because $500,000 × 4 = $2 million, the products-completed operations aggregate limit).

BASIC DIFFERENCES: EXCESS AND UMBRELLA LIABILITY POLICIES

Excess liability policies and umbrella liability policies can be used to insure liability loss exposures that are too severe to be adequately covered under primary liability policies.

This is the basic distinction between excess liability insurance and umbrella liability insurance:

- An **excess liability policy** is designed to provide excess limits of coverage above the limits of the underlying coverage. An excess liability policy therefore offers no broader protection than that provided by the underlying coverage. In fact, the excess liability coverage may be even more restrictive than the underlying coverage. An excess liability policy, for example, may not provide defense coverage.
- An **umbrella liability policy** is a type of excess liability policy that not only provides additional limits (as excess liability policies do), but also provides coverage not available in the underlying coverages, subject to the insured's assumption of a self-insured retention, or retained limit. Most umbrella liability policies also provide defense coverage.

Excess liability policy
A policy that covers liability claims in excess of the limits of an underlying policy or a stated retention amount.

Umbrella liability policy
A liability policy that provides excess coverage above underlying policies and may also provide coverage not available in the underlying policies, subject to a self-insured retention.

In the example in the exhibit, both the excess liability policy and the umbrella policy provide $1 million of additional liability coverage for the same losses covered by the underlying policies. In addition, the umbrella policy covers some losses not covered by the underlying insurance, subject to a self-insured retention of $25,000. See the exhibit "Excess Liability Policy Versus Umbrella Liability Policy."

In actual practice, the distinction between excess and umbrella liability coverage is often unclear, especially because the courts and many in the insurance profession use the terms interchangeably. Moreover, many insurers providing excess and umbrella liability insurance do not use standardized policies. Rather, they develop their own policies, which vary considerably in the coverage that they offer and the format in which they are presented. What one insurer calls an excess liability policy may in reality be an umbrella policy, and what another insurer calls an umbrella policy may actually be an excess liability policy.

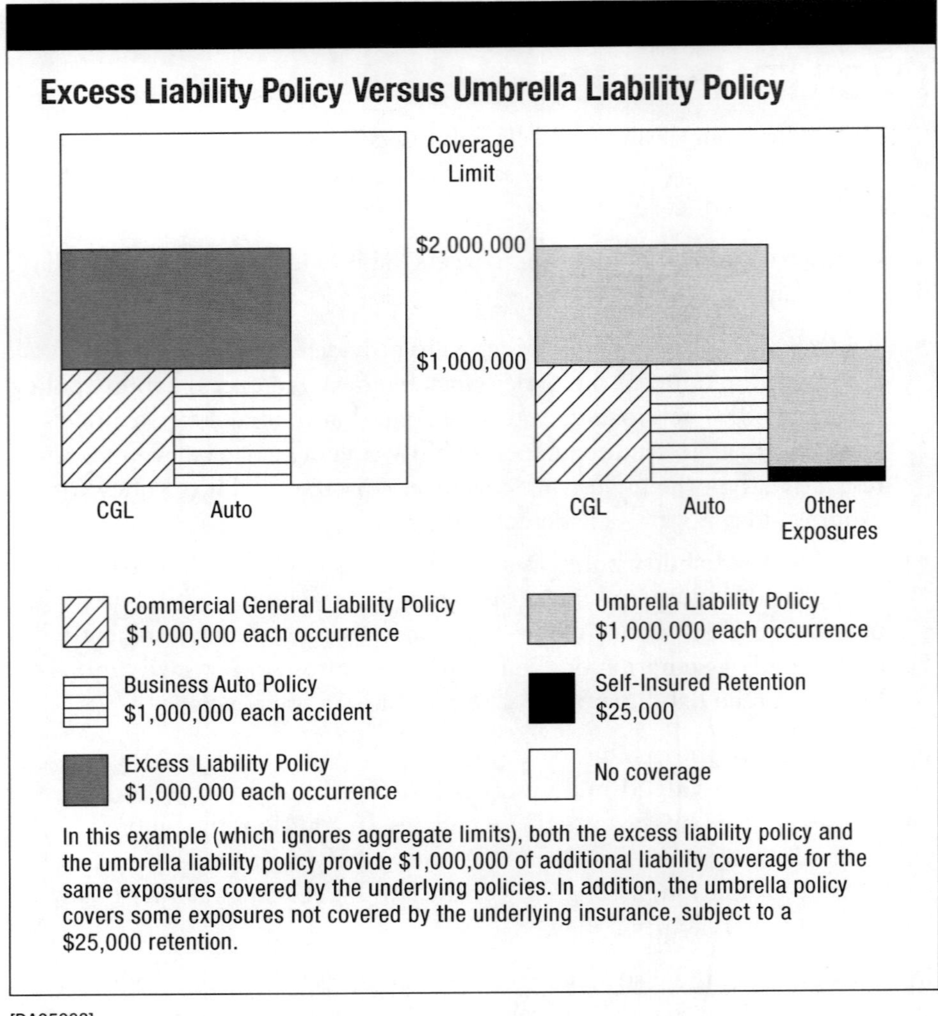

[DA05033]

EXCESS LIABILITY INSURANCE

Organizations that need liability coverage beyond that provided by their commercial general liability policy may purchase excess liability insurance.

An excess liability insurance policy may take any of three basic forms:

- A following-form policy subject to the same provisions as the underlying policy
- A self-contained policy subject to its own provisions only
- A combination of these two types

In addition, when excess liability insurance applies above a retained primary layer instead of underlying insurance, two additional types of excess liability insurance—specific excess and aggregate excess—are often used, particularly in connection with self-insured workers compensation obligations.

Following-Form Excess Liability Policies

As illustrated in the exhibit, a following-form excess liability policy is an excess liability policy that covers a claim in excess of the underlying limits only if the loss is covered by the underlying insurance. A "true" following-form excess liability policy would state that, except for the policy limits, all of the provisions and conditions of the designated underlying policy are incorporated into and adopted by the excess liability policy, and it would contain no provisions conflicting with the underlying policy. See the exhibit "Application of Primary and Excess Liability Policies."

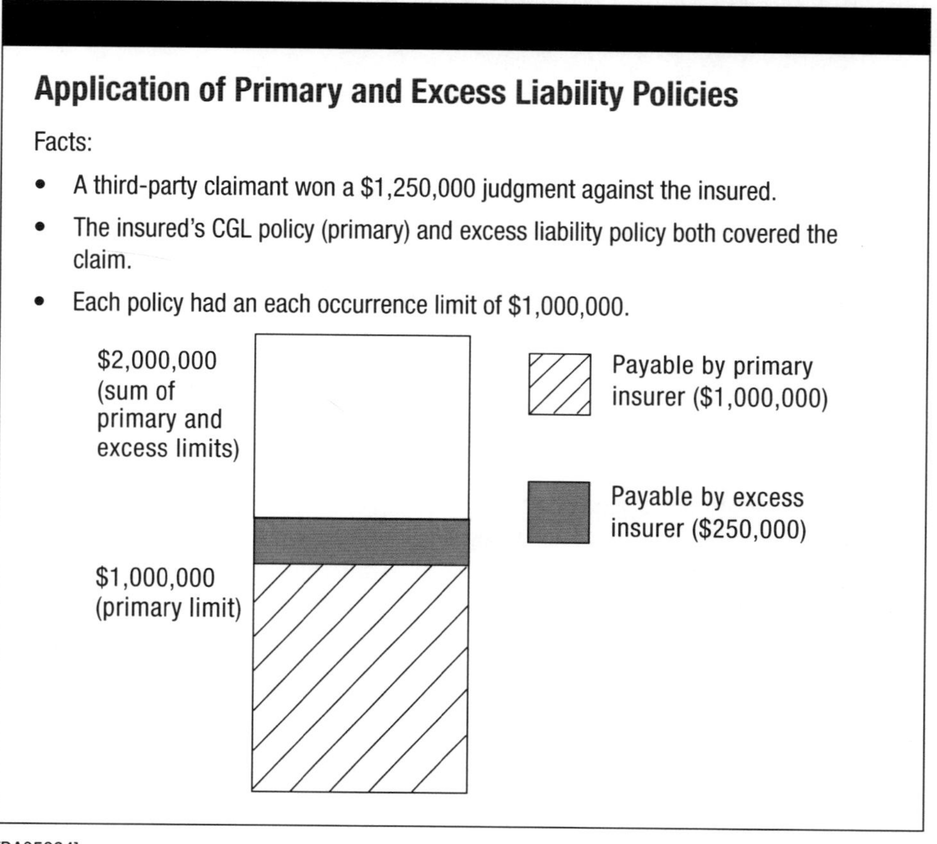

[DA05034]

Although many excess liability policies are called following-form policies, most follow the provisions of the underlying policy only to the extent that the provisions of the underlying policy do not conflict with those of the excess liability policy. The result is that the coverage provided by an underlying policy and the coverage provided by a following-form excess liability policy are likely to differ. If the underlying policy would provide coverage for a loss that the excess liability policy would not cover, the provisions of the excess liability policy may take precedence when the loss reaches this layer, thus covering a narrower scope of events than the primary policy.

Self-Contained Excess Liability Policies

Self-contained excess liability policy

An excess liability policy that is subject to its own provisions only and does not depend on the provisions of the underlying policies for determining the scope of its coverage.

A **self-contained excess liability policy** does not depend on the provisions of the underlying policies for determining the scope of the coverage (with one exception). Therefore, coverage gaps between the excess and underlying layer can occur. A self-contained excess liability policy applies to a loss that exceeds the limits of the underlying policy only if the loss is also covered under the provisions of the self-contained excess liability policy. For example, a self-contained excess liability policy may not cover injury within the products-completed operations hazard, even though the underlying policy does. In that case, the excess liability policy would not pay for a products liability claim, even though the claim was covered by the underlying policy and exceeded the each occurrence limit of the underlying policy.

One exception to the usual approach of a self-contained excess liability policy occurs when the excess liability policy provides coverage in excess of a reduced or an exhausted underlying aggregate limit. Some excess liability policies provide this coverage subject to their own provisions, but others specifically state that they will provide this coverage subject to the provisions of the underlying coverage. This approach can work to the insured's benefit when the excess liability policy contains exclusions or other restrictions that are not present in the underlying policy.

Combination Excess Liability Policies

An excess liability policy may combine the following-form and self-contained approaches by incorporating the provisions of the underlying policy and then modifying those provisions with additional conditions or exclusions in the excess liability policy.

One type of combination form is an excess liability policy that provides the broader coverages typically found in an umbrella liability policy, but without any obligation to "drop down" (provide primary coverage) when a claim is excluded by the primary policy but covered by the excess liability policy. A loss excluded under the primary policy may be covered under the excess policy to the extent it exceeds the primary policy limits. Because some insurers use the terms "excess liability" and "umbrella liability" interchangeably, insureds may not be aware that combination excess liability policies do not drop down (except to replace depleted aggregate limits).

One distinguishing feature of a true umbrella liability policy is a provision stating that the policy applies over a self-insured retention if the underlying policy does not cover a loss covered by the umbrella. In the absence of this provision, the policy is probably not a true umbrella liability policy.

Specific and Aggregate Excess Liability Insurance

Specific excess liability insurance and aggregate excess liability insurance are commonly used in connection with self-insured workers compensation plans. These types of policies are designed to apply over a self-insured layer instead of a primary layer of commercial insurance.

A specific excess liability policy requires the insured to retain a stipulated amount of loss from the first dollar for all losses resulting from each single occurrence. The insurer then pays losses from that occurrence in excess of the retention, up to the policy limit. For example, if the policy required a retention of $100,000, the insurer would pay all loss resulting from a single occurrence in excess of $100,000 up to the policy limit of $1 million.

Aggregate, or stop loss, excess liability insurance policy
An excess liability policy that requires the insured to retain a specified amount of loss from the first dollar during a specified period of time, usually one year; the insurer then pays all loss for that period that exceeds the retention, up to the policy limit.

An **aggregate excess liability policy** (also called a stop loss excess liability policy) requires the insured to retain a specified amount of loss from the first dollar during a specified period of time, usually one year. The insurer then pays, up to the policy limit, all losses for that period that exceed the retention. See the exhibit "Aggregate Excess Versus Specific Excess."

Aggregate Excess Versus Specific Excess

Aggregate Excess Liability Policy

$100,000 aggregate retention	$1,000,000 maximum limit
Losses from separate occurrences	$ 25,000
	75,000
	90,000
	35,000
Total losses	$225,000
Aggregate retention	100,000
Excess insurance will pay	$125,000

Specific Excess Liability Policy

$100,000 per occurrence retention	$1,000,000 maximum limit
Losses from separate occurrences	$ 25,000
	75,000
	90,000
	35,000
	$225,000

Because none of the losses exceeds the $100,000 per occurrence retention, the insured must retain all losses.

[DA05035]

Some policies combine the specific and aggregate excess approaches. Such policies provide the insured with the benefits of both approaches. For example, an insured may incur several moderate losses during a policy period, none of which exceeds the each occurrence retention. Under a specific excess liability policy, the insured would not be able to collect any insurance proceeds. With the combination aggregate excess and specific excess policy, if the total of losses for the policy period exceeded the aggregate retention, the insured could collect insurance proceeds for the amount of loss in excess of the aggregate retention. See the exhibit "Combination Aggregate Excess and Specific Excess Policy."

Combination Aggregate Excess and Specific Excess Policy

Aggregate Excess	Specific Excess
$200,000 aggregate retention	$100,000 per occurrence retention
$1,000,000 maximum limit	$1,000,000 maximum limit

Losses from separate occurrences:	$ 25,000
	75,000
	90,000
	35,000
	$225,000

None of the losses exceeds the per occurrence retention. Therefore, the specific excess part of the policy would pay nothing. However, since total losses exceed the $200,000 aggregate retention, the aggregate excess part of the policy would pay $25,000.

[DA05036]

STRUCTURING A LIABILITY INSURANCE PROGRAM

Liability insurance is often arranged in layers. The primary (first) layer consists of one or more primary coverages (such as commercial general liability [CGL], business auto, and employers liability), with each occurrence limits typically ranging between $500,000 and $2 million. In some cases, principally with large organizations, the primary layer is self-insured (retained).

Working Layer and Buffer Layer

Many organizations have only one layer in excess of the primary. Typically, an organization in this category has an umbrella liability policy above its primary CGL, commercial auto, and employers liability coverages. It may also have one or more separate excess liability policies providing a second layer of coverage above other primary policies that are not covered by the umbrella policy. The primary and umbrella layers are generally referred to as the **working layers**, because they are the layers most often called on to pay claims.

Working layers
The layers of coverage in an organization's insurance program that are most often called on to pay claims.

Buffer layer
A level of excess insurance coverage between a primary layer and an umbrella policy.

In some cases, an insured must purchase a **buffer layer** of excess insurance between the primary layer and the umbrella policy. This approach is used when the umbrella insurer will not provide coverage unless the insured has underlying coverage limits higher than those that the primary insurer is willing to provide.

For example, an umbrella liability insurer may require minimum limits of $2 million per occurrence for the underlying CGL and auto liability coverages. One of the primary insurers, however, may be willing to provide limits of only $1 million. To qualify for the umbrella policy, the insured must obtain additional limits of $1 million.

This can be accomplished by purchasing an excess liability policy with its own limits of $1 million, which, when combined with the primary policy limits of $1 million, would provide the $2 million of underlying coverage required by the umbrella insurer. Insureds that must purchase buffer layer coverage should try to obtain a policy that follows the provisions of the underlying policy as closely as possible, and the policy periods should be concurrent.

Insureds that want higher limits of liability above the working layers usually do so through one or more additional layers of excess liability coverage. The number of layers varies, depending on the limits desired by the insured and the limits available from the prospective insurers. It is unusual to find a true umbrella policy in the higher layers of excess liability coverage. A multi-layered liability insurance program that includes a buffer layer policy is shown in the exhibit. See the exhibit "Layered Liability Insurance Program."

Problems in Layering Coverage

Problems can occur when coverage is layered. The aggregate limits may vary with the umbrella and excess layers. The umbrella policy, for example, may be subject to a general aggregate limit and a products-completed operations aggregate limit, whereas some of the excess layers may be subject to a so-called basket aggregate limit, which applies to all coverages. Moreover, the excess liability policies may differ as to the insurer's obligations concerning defense. Some excess liability policies may include coverage for defense costs (usually within policy limits), whereas others may not recognize such costs in determining whether underlying policy limits have been exhausted.

In addition, whenever excess liability layers are to apply over the first umbrella layer, the excess layers should follow the provisions of the umbrella policy exactly. However, excess liability policies are seldom true following-form policies in every aspect of coverage.

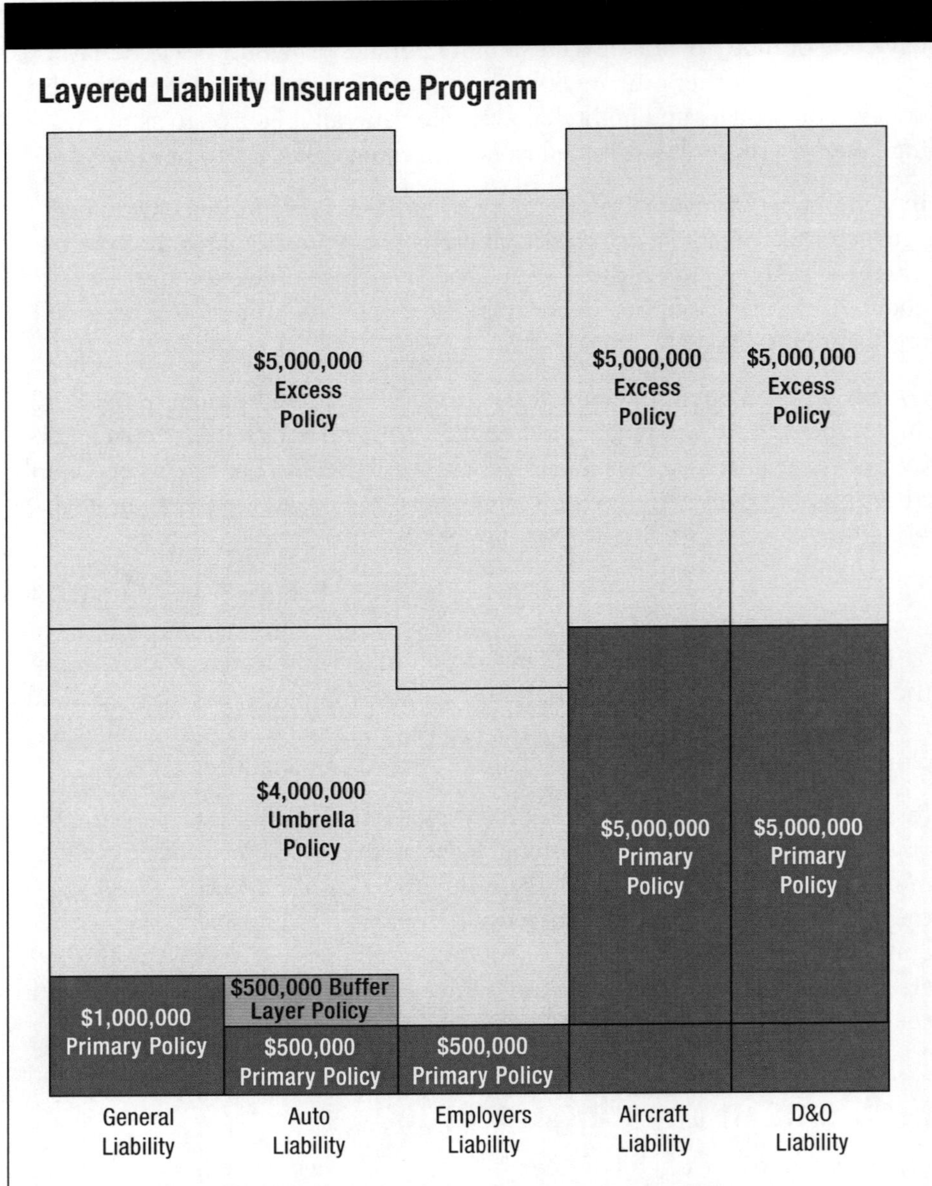

[DA05043]

Even when an excess liability policy states that it is a following-form policy, it must be compared with the umbrella (or other underlying) policy to discover ways in which coverage under the excess liability policy is more restrictive than that provided by the underlying policy. Many excess liability policies contain wording similar to this:

> Except as otherwise provided by this policy, the insurance shall follow all of the terms, conditions, definitions, and exclusions of the underlying designated policies.

Adequacy of Excess Liability Limits

The layering of coverage allows many insureds the opportunity to secure high levels of protection. However, whether those limits are adequate is another matter. Consider a corporation with $1 million in assets. If it carries $1 million in liability insurance, a $2 million court judgment could cause bankruptcy. If it carries $2 million of liability insurance, a $3 million judgment could cause bankruptcy. Moreover, even a smaller uninsured verdict of, for example, $500,000 could bankrupt the firm or seriously impair its financial condition, particularly when the possibility of several such losses in a single year is acknowledged.

How should a risk manager determine the adequacy of liability insurance limits? Unfortunately, that question has no uniformly satisfactory answer. There is no monetary limit on the amount a jury might award.

Accordingly, risk managers of large corporations commonly buy the highest limits they can obtain and hope that those limits will be adequate. This approach neither guarantees that the available limits will be sufficient nor addresses the issue of whether the protection obtained was secured at reasonable prices. Even organizations that are willing and able to pay for high limits often do not believe that their limits are adequate. Some organizations feel the need for higher limits but are not willing or able to pay for them, and some find that higher limits are unavailable.

Given the problems of growing loss severity, insurance availability, and price, organizations must coordinate their insurance-buying decisions with careful consideration of all available alternatives. If an organization retains the small losses that are so costly to insure and instead spends its premium dollars to buy the high limits needed, and if it implements effective risk control, it should be in a much better position to obtain protection against catastrophic liability losses at feasible costs. In short, an organization can get the most risk management value from insurance only when it is properly combined with noninsurance techniques.

STRUCTURING AN INTERNATIONAL INSURANCE PROGRAM

Businesses cannot ignore the opportunities in the global market and typically must expand internationally to achieve their highest growth potential. Yet as a company expands internationally, so does its risk. In response, its risk management professional must know how to best structure its international insurance program to address that risk.

When structuring an international insurance program, an insured's risk management professional must decide whether to buy admitted insurance (for a decentralized structure) or nonadmitted insurance (for a centralized structure). This decision should be based on the advantages and disadvantages of

both types of insurance. It is also possible that the best structure is a package policy, such as for exporters who have no foreign, permanent place of business to insure. For those multinational companies with permanent foreign locations, the preferred structure often includes a collection of admitted and nonadmitted insurance called a controlled master program. Such a program has advantages and disadvantages to consider before selecting it as a structure.

Admitted Versus Nonadmitted Insurance

Admitted insurer
An insurer to which a state insurance department has granted a license to do business within that state.

An **admitted insurer** is authorized to do business in the country in which it sells polices. If a multinational company relies heavily on admitted insurance for its coverage, then it is likely following a decentralized approach to cover its international exposures. Relying on locally written coverage has several consequences, such as the policy being written in the language of the country in which it was sold and in compliance with local laws.

Purchasing admitted coverage locally offers several advantages:

- The policy will be serviced locally, and local management is more likely accustomed to local practices.
- Premiums paid to admitted insurers are tax-deductible as a business expense, while those paid to an insurer that is not admitted may not be tax-deductible.
- Premiums and claims are paid in the local currency, which eliminates foreign exchange rate risks unless purchases must be on imported equipment or materials.
- Local agents and brokers may be able to understand local coverage nuances and advise coverage better.
- Complying with local laws and doing business locally helps integrate the company into the local economy and community.

Purchasing admitted coverage locally has several disadvantages as well:

- The risk manager for a multinational company may have difficulty interpreting a policy written in a foreign language, which could lead to multiple problems, such as nonuniform conditions, coverage gaps, and underinsurance.
- If competition among insurers locally is not robust or if tariffs are high, the local policy may be more expensive. It can be more difficult to assess the financial strength of the local insurer as well.
- Effective solvency regulation, financial statements, and rating agencies of insurers may be lacking locally.
- Purchasing locally also lessens a company's purchasing power and decentralizes risk management strategy, which can weaken the implementation of enterprise risk management (ERM).

A **nonadmitted insurer** is unauthorized to do business in the country in which it sells policies. For example, when an insurer in the country of a parent company sells insurance to the parent company's subsidiary in a foreign country (where the insurer is not an authorized insurer by the foreign country's government), it has sold nonadmitted insurance.

Nonadmitted insurer
An insurer not authorized by the state insurance department to do business within that state.

Purchasing nonadmitted coverage locally offers several advantages:

- Administrative control can be centralized, which can be more efficient.
- The financial strength of the insurer is more easily determined.
- The policy is written in the language of the country where the parent company is domiciled, making it easier to understand and administer.
- The insurance coverage may also be cheaper because of lower tariffs, rate regulation, or consolidation of purchasing power.
- The premium and claim payments will be made in the domestic country's currency, thereby eliminating foreign exchange rate risk if only a single currency is used.

Purchasing nonadmitted coverage locally has these disadvantages as well:

- Claim adjusting can be substantially more complicated without local coverage and local insurer representatives; this can be especially prominent with liability claims.
- Local management may not have confidence in the nonadmitted coverage provided by the parent company's insurer and may decide to buy its own coverage locally.

Exporters Package Policy

The **exporters package policy** is intended for those insureds without a permanent office or place of business in the foreign country where they operate. Insureds that are expanding their business on a global basis often find themselves in this situation and discover they have several new loss exposures that can be covered by this package policy. The policy covers foreign general liability, nonowned and hired automobile insurance, and foreign voluntary workers compensation. The policy also offers coverage for personal property (such as laptops, projector equipment, and sales samples), kidnap and ransom, and travel accident losses. For an insured with a permanent place of operations in a foreign country, its coverage needs may be better addressed by a controlled master program.

Exporters package policy
Nonadmitted package policy tailored to organizations with incidental exposures in countries other than their home country.

Controlled Master Program

A **controlled master program** is a collection of admitted and nonadmitted insurance policies. The admitted policies cover the foreign subsidiaries of a multinational business and are purchased in the local insurance market of the foreign countries. The nonadmitted policy covers all of the insured's inter-

Controlled master program
Nonadmitted master policy issued in the country in which the insured is domiciled paired with locally admitted policies issued in the foreign countries in which the insured operates.

national operations on a blanket basis and is often purchased in the country where the parent company is domiciled. The nonadmitted policy is a master policy that can include difference-in-conditions or difference-in-limits coverage that would prevent a gap in protection if the admitted policies purchased locally provide lower limits or less coverage than the parent company requires.

United States multinational companies usually have separate policies for their U.S. domestic exposures. These policies help prevent potential difficulties in foreign or domestic insurance from affecting each other. Non-U.S. multinational companies also often purchase separate policies for their U.S. exposures. This can prevent their global program from being exposed to an unfavorable U.S. liability environment.

The exhibit illustrates an insurer providing admitted insurance to a multinational company's subsidiaries located in foreign countries. The local subsidiaries purchase property and liability insurance that provides local compulsory coverage as well as other coverage placed locally. Risks that are not covered locally because of limit of coverage or restriction on perils covered may be covered under the master policy. The master policy insurer also covers the company's domestic exposures in the country where it is domiciled with separate property and liability policies. Toward the top of the exhibit, two excess polices are shown. One is the umbrella policy, which protects the company from excess liability losses in selected lines of coverage. The other is the whole account insurance, which protects the company from excess losses in the entire portfolio of coverage. See the exhibit "Illustration of an Integrated Controlled Master Program."

Illustration of an Integrated Controlled Master Program

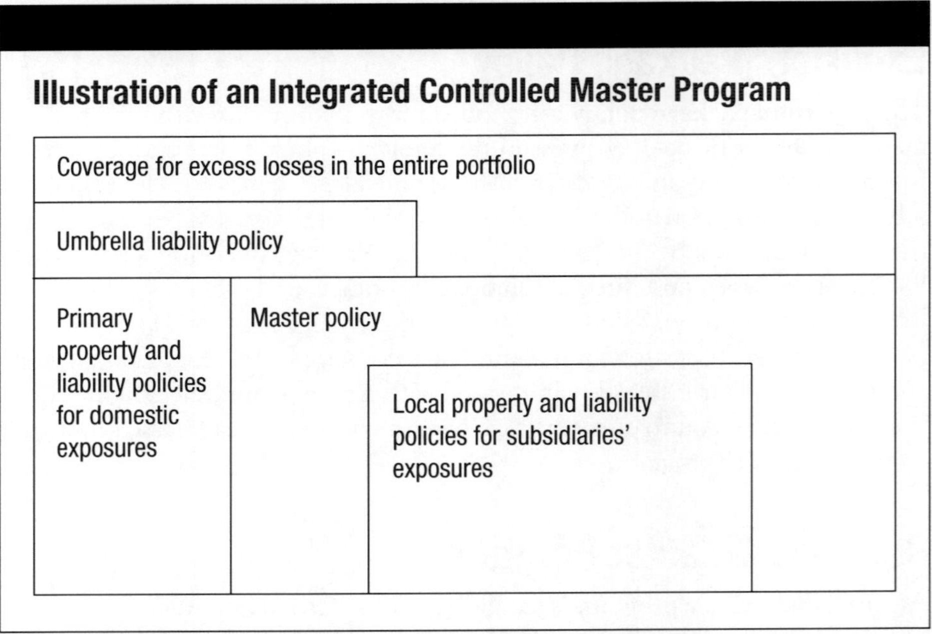

Based on: Harold D. Skipper and W. Jean Kwon, Risk Management and Insurance: Perspectives in a Global Economy (Malden, Mass.: Blackwell Publishers, 2007), p. 366. [DA08697]

All policies are coordinated from one central location. This collection of policies has several advantages and disadvantages.

Advantages of Controlled Master Programs

Controlled master programs provide numerous advantages, including a uniformly consistent insurance program that is centralized yet captures the benefits of local policies. The benefits of local policies include compliance with individual countries' regulations on contracts, nonadmitted insurance, premium allocation, and tariffs.[5]

By combining the policies under one program, the company's purchasing power is consolidated, and duplicate coverage is eliminated. Both of these factors reduce premiums and other costs. Further, the global nature of the program allows a company to negotiate worldwide rates, terms, and conditions that reflect its global size and experience. So the company gains greater **economy of scale** and scope in external risk financing through insurance.[6]

Economy of scale
A reduction in the average cost of a product or a process as the size of a company increases.

The centralized global approach of the program makes a company's risk management goals more likely to be realized and gives a risk manager more opportunities to implement a consistent global ERM strategy.

The multinational reach of the program also reduces the accumulation of risk and diversifies the risk across a company's subsidiaries. The program generates a large volume of useful risk management information from countries around the world. This allows risk managers to determine best practices and form an intra-company risk management community.

The primary advantage is the prevention of gaps in coverage. What the local policy doesn't cover, the master policy may cover. In addition to difference-in-conditions or difference-in-limits coverage, master policies can also cover currency devaluation, coinsurance deficiency, tax liability, or neighbors and tenants liability. These coverages are usually not available in U.S. policies but are frequently needed by multinational companies.

Disadvantages of Controlled Master Programs

Controlled master programs create disadvantages as well. The program generates a large amount of information that must be reviewed and analyzed. This consumes considerable resources to stay current.

Another disadvantage is that local risk managers may resist relinquishing their responsibility of purchasing all the coverage for a foreign subsidiary. It may be difficult for the local risk manager to instead focus on coordinating coverage with a master policy.

Also, if the same insurer and its foreign local subsidiaries are used to provide the master policy and the local policies to further aid in coordinating coverage between policies, a counterparty risk may be a concern.

Apply Your Knowledge

Julie exports leather goods in a dozen foreign countries. She sells her goods exclusively through vendors and has no stores or warehouse storage facilities in any foreign country. However, she frequently goes to vendors' offices to make sales presentations to convince them to sell her goods. She brings her laptop and samples of her goods on the sales calls. She also rents a car to travel to and from the sales calls. She has heard that some of the countries to which she goes on sales calls have problems with kidnapping and ransom. What coverage should she consider?

Feedback: Julie should consider an exporters package policy. It covers foreign general liability, nonowned and hired automobile insurance, and foreign voluntary workers compensation. She particularly needs the nonowned and hired automobile insurance coverage as she drives to and from the sales calls. Optional coverage is available for her personal property, which would include her laptop and sales samples. Another optional coverage she may want to consider is for her kidnap and ransom exposure.

SUMMARY

Insurance is an effective risk financing technique because it offers the financial certainty of risk transfer while including services that address the insured organization's need to control risks and mitigate losses. Insurance's effectiveness increases when loss exposures have certain characteristics. Organizations that want to incorporate security and certainty in their risk financing plan usually choose insurance as its primary feature. The operation of insurance relies on pooling. Pooling arrangements reduce risk without transferring it.

The benefits of insurance include paying for losses, managing cash flow uncertainty, complying with the law, promoting risk control, allowing efficient use of the insured's resources, providing support for the insured's credit, providing a source of investment funds, and reducing social burdens.

Insurance covers events that may or may not happen. By charging the insured a premium in return for assuming the potential costs for the uncertain event, the insurer can make a profit if it handles a volume of similar transactions efficiently. The transaction is not likely to be advantageous to the insurer unless the loss exposure has characteristics that make it ideally insurable from the insurer's standpoint.

An insurance deductible directly affects the amount that the insured organization recovers, if any, from an insurer. Insurance can be purchased with no or small deductibles, but the insured organization pays a more expensive premium as a consequence. Deductibles are usually found in property insurance, but organizations can purchase liability insurance policies with deductibles as well.

Large deductible plans enable the organization to pay a reduced insurance premium while retaining losses below the deductible level. As losses occur, the insurer settles each claim, then periodically bills the insured organization for the amount of the loss and the claim handling expense up to the deductible level.

The maximum possible loss for liability loss exposures is difficult to estimate accurately. Organizations therefore generally want high limits of liability insurance. However, primary insurers typically offer limits of $1 million per occurrence. To obtain higher limits, organizations usually must obtain additional policies, which come in two basic types: excess liability policies and umbrella liability policies.

Excess and umbrella liability policies can be used to insure liability loss exposures that are too severe to be adequately covered under primary liability policies.

A true following-form excess liability policy covers excess losses subject to the same provisions in the referenced underlying policy. A self-contained excess liability policy is subject only to its own provisions. Some excess liability policies combine these two approaches. Specific excess liability policies and aggregate excess liability policies apply over a self-insured layer instead of a primary layer of commercial insurance. Policies that combine the specific and aggregate excess approaches provide the insured with the benefits of both approaches.

Liability insurance is often arranged in layers. The primary (first) layer consists of one or more primary coverages (such as CGL, business auto, employers liability), with each occurrence limits typically ranging between $500,000 and $2 million.

Organizations may also have one or more separate excess liability policies providing a second layer of coverage above other primary policies that are not covered by the umbrella policy.

When structuring an international insurance program, an insured's risk management professional should consider whether to buy admitted insurance (for a decentralized structure) or nonadmitted insurance (for a centralized structure). This decision should be based on the advantages and disadvantages of both types of insurance. The best structure may be a package policy, such as for exporters who have no foreign, permanent place of business to insure. However, for many established multinational companies with permanent foreign locations, the preferred structure includes a collection of admitted and nonadmitted insurance called a controlled master program. That program has advantages and disadvantages to consider as well.

ASSIGNMENT NOTES

1. Discussion here is drawn from Scott E. Harrington and Gregory R. Neihaus, Risk Management and Insurance, 2nd ed. (New York: McGraw-Hill, 2003), pp. 54–63.
2. Several states have taken steps to impose premium taxes and residual market loadings on the retained-loss portion of large deductible plans.
3. Verdictsearch Web site, "Top 100 of 2009," www.verdictsearch.com/index.jsp?do=top100 (accessed November 19, 2010).
4. Catherine Thomas, ed., *Current Award Trends in Personal Injury*, 46th ed. (Horsham, Pa.: LRP Publications, 2007), p. 44.
5. Zack Phillips, "Master Program Packs Advantages, Risk Manager Says," Business Insurance, April 4, 2010, www.businessinsurance.com/article/20100404/ISSUE03/304049993 (accessed February 1, 2012).
6. Harold D. Skipper and W. Jean Kwon, Risk Management and Insurance: Perspectives in a Global Economy (Malden, Mass.: Blackwell Publishers, 2007), p. 367.

Direct Your Learning

4

Self-Insurance Plans

Educational Objectives

After learning the content of this assignment, you should be able to:

- Describe the purpose and operation of self-insurance plans.
- Describe the two types of self-insurance plans.
- Describe the administration of individual self-insurance plans.
- Describe the advantages and disadvantages of self-insurance plans.
- Given a case, justify a self-insurance plan that can meet an organization's risk financing needs.

Outline

Self-Insurance Plans

4

PURPOSE AND OPERATION OF SELF-INSURANCE PLANS

Some organizations are able to forecast their accidental losses with enough accuracy to determine whether they can be retained through a formalized plan to fund possible losses in lieu of insurance. This practice is known as self-insurance.

The term "self-insurance" is often used informally to include any loss amount an organization retains, such as the retained portion of losses under deductible plans, retrospective rating plans, captive insurance plans, pools, and finite risk plans, as well as retentions for unanticipated losses (also called retention by default, or simply "going bare"). However, self-insurance is actually a distinct risk financing plan.

Formal self-insurance plans require organizations to have sufficient financial resources and risk tolerance to retain potentially significant losses. Therefore, organizations with self-insurance plans have usually embraced risk control as part of their corporate culture.

Purpose of Self-Insurance Plans

The purpose of a self-insurance plan is to enable an organization to lower its long-term cost of risk by allowing it to pay for its own losses without incurring the transaction costs associated with insurance.

Self-insurance is a form of retention under which an organization records its losses and maintains a formal system to pay for them. Self-insurance can be contrasted with **informal retention**, which is a form of retention by which an organization pays for its losses with its cash flow and/or current (liquid) assets but does not anticipate losses and, consequently, does not involve formal payment procedures or methods for recording losses.

Informal retention
A type of retention in which an organization pays for losses with its cash flow and/or current assets and generally keeps no record of losses.

Self-insurance is best applied to losses that are of both high frequency and low severity. Such losses are somewhat predictable in total over a defined time period, such as one year. (Losses that are both low frequency and low severity are easily self-insured; however, they are usually retained informally, thus eliminating the associated administrative costs.)

High-severity losses are unsuitable for self-insurance because they are typically low frequency and therefore are relatively unpredictable, as well as too large to retain. Some organizations also self-insure medium-severity losses, although the resulting financial effect can be unpredictable, depending on their frequency.

Operation of Self-Insurance Plans

A self-insurance plan is usually coupled with the purchase of excess liability insurance to cover severe losses. Excess liability insurance limits the organization's exposure to loss to an acceptable level and limits the accumulation of losses. Low-frequency and high-severity losses are often addressed by insurance or other risk transfer plans. The exhibit shows how a self-insurance plan and excess liability insurance may address an organization's loss exposures relative to the frequency and severity of potential losses. See the exhibit "Self-Insurance Combined With Other Excess Liability Insurance."

Self-Insurance Combined With Other Excess Liability Insurance

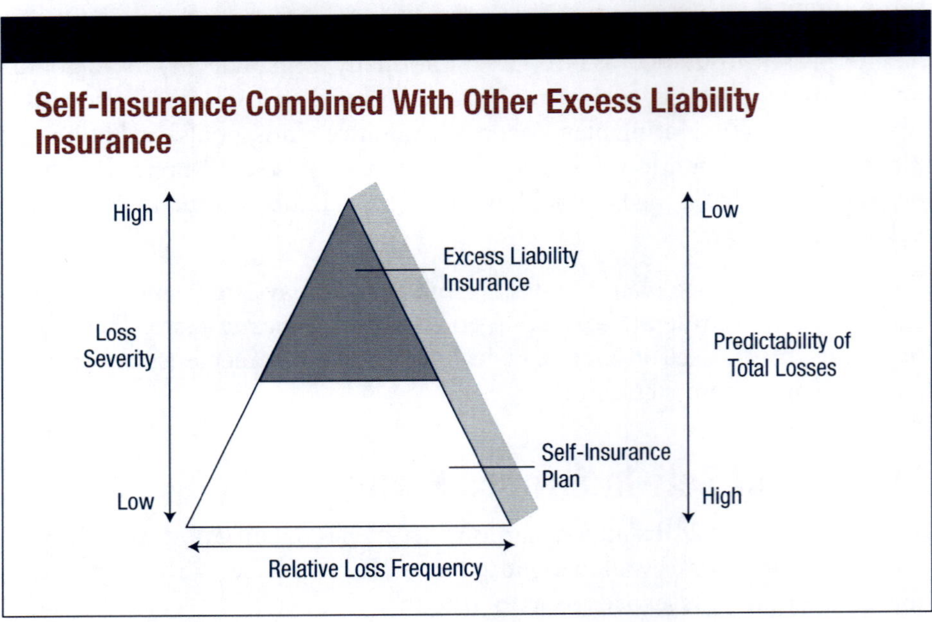

[DA01670]

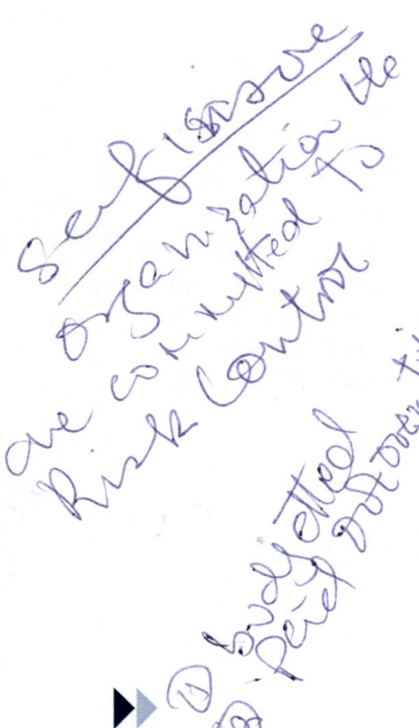

Self-insurance is most appropriate for organizations that are committed to risk control, are able to tolerate risk retention, and are willing to devote capital and resources to the program's financing and administration.

Many organizations begin to consider self-insurance when their annual minimum insurance premium exceeds $500,000 for any one type of insurance coverage. More specific guidelines exist to help organizations determine whether their annual minimum premium is sufficient to make self-insurance an economically feasible alternative.

Self-insurance is particularly well-suited for financing losses that can be budgeted and paid out over time, because the self-insured organization saves money that it would otherwise pay toward premiums in the meantime. For this reason, workers compensation, general liability, and automobile liability loss exposures are often self-insured. One source estimates that 6,000 U.S. organizations use self-insurance plans for their workers compensation loss exposures.[1]

Other loss exposures that are often self-insured include auto physical damage and professional liability, as well as flood and earthquake, for which there is a limited insurance market. Organizations can also use self-insurance to administer healthcare benefits.

Self-Insured Healthcare Benefits

Since the passage of the Employee Retirement Income Security Act (ERISA), organizations have been allowed to self-insure healthcare benefits instead of purchasing healthcare insurance. Self-insured health plans (also called employer-based health plans) are the means through which over 50 million U.S. employees receive healthcare benefits.[2]

As with self-insurance plans for property-casualty loss exposures, self-insured healthcare plans are formal retention plans designed to fund and administer healthcare benefits. Most self-insured healthcare benefit plans require employees to contribute funds to offset the plan's cost. These plans also involve using a third-party administrator and purchasing excess insurance.

Organizations considering self-insurance must weigh its cash flow benefits against its tax ramifications. Self-insured organizations must recognize losses when they are incurred and establish a liability for them. Self-insured losses are not a tax-deductible expense until they are actually paid. Organizations that purchase insurance from an insurer, however, may treat the insurance premium as a tax-deductible expense regardless of when, or if, losses are incurred.

TYPES OF SELF-INSURANCE PLANS

Self-insurance plans can be implemented for one organization (individual self-insurance plans) or for more than one organization (group self-insurance plans).

Individual self-insurance plans can be used to address a number of loss exposures, whereas group self-insurance plans can be used only to address workers compensation loss exposures and healthcare benefits. See the exhibit "Types of Self-Insurance Plans and Applicable Loss Exposures."

Individual Self-Insurance Plans

Individual self-insurance plan
A retention plan that involves only one organization.

An **individual self-insurance plan** is a retention plan that involves only one organization. Any organization can self-insure its loss exposures, provided that the state (or states) in which it operates permits self-insurance plans and

Types of Self-Insurance Plans and Applicable Loss Exposures

Individual Self-Insurance Plans	Group Self-Insurance Plans
• Workers compensation	• Workers compensation
• Auto liability	• Healthcare benefits
• General liability	
• Auto physical damage	
• Professional liability	
• Earthquake	
• Flood	
• Healthcare benefits	

[DA01525]

that it satisfies any applicable regulatory requirements. Generally, only workers compensation, auto liability, and general liability self-insurance plans are subject to state regulatory control.

Group Self-Insurance Plans

Group self-insurance plan

A group of employers in the same industry that jointly (as a whole) and severally (individually) guarantee payment of workers compensation benefits to the employees of the group's members. A not-for-profit association or corporation is typically formed to which they pay premiums for self-insurance purposes.

A **group self-insurance plan** is an organization of several similar employers that have formed a not-for-profit association or corporation to which they pay premiums to manage self-insurance of their workers compensation and healthcare benefits loss exposures.

Unlike individual self-insurance plans, which can be used with several types of loss exposures, group self-insurance plans can be used only for workers compensation loss exposures and healthcare benefits. See the exhibit "States Allowing Individual and/or Group Workers Compensation Self-Insurance Plans."

A group self-insurance plan operates like an insurer in that it pools the loss exposures of its members. The plan's administrator issues member agreements, collects premiums, and manages claims. The administrator also purchases excess liability insurance (or excess of loss reinsurance) and makes required state regulatory filings.

A group self-insurance plan can benefit an organization that is too small to self-insure its loss exposures on its own. Savings are achieved through economies of scale in administration, claim handling, and the purchase of excess liability insurance (or reinsurance).

States Allowing Individual and/or Group Workers Compensation Self-Insurance Plans

State	Individual Allowed	Group Allowed	State	Individual Allowed	Group Allowed
Alabama	X	X	Missouri	X	X
Alaska	X		Montana	X	X
Arizona	X	X	Nebraska	X	
Arkansas	X	X	Nevada	X	X
California	X	X	New Hampshire	X	X
Colorado	X	X	New Jersey	X	X[1]
Connecticut	X	X	New Mexico	X	X
Delaware	X	X	New York	X	X
District of Columbia	X		North Carolina	X	X
Florida	X	X	North Dakota[2]		
Georgia	X	X	Ohio	X	
Hawaii	X	X	Oklahoma	X	X
Idaho	X		Oregon	X	X
Illinois	X	X	Pennsylvania	X	X
Indiana	X		Rhode Island	X	X
Iowa	X	X	South Carolina	X	X
Kansas	X	X	South Dakota	X	
Kentucky	X	X	Tennessee	X	X
Louisiana	X	X	Texas	X	
Maine	X	X	Utah	X	
Maryland	X	X	Vermont	X	X
Massachusetts	X	X	Virginia	X	X
Michigan	X	X	Washington	X	X[3]
Minnesota	X	X	West Virginia	X	
Mississippi	X	X	Wisconsin	X	
			Wyoming[2]		

[1] Municipalities, school boards, hospitals, and community colleges only.
[2] Self-insurance not permitted.
[3] School districts and public or not-for-profit hospitals only.

Source: www.irmi.com/Expert/Articles/2001Fuge08.aspx (accessed March 18, 2006). [DA01526]

ADMINISTRATION OF INDIVIDUAL SELF-INSURANCE PLANS

Administration activities for self-insured plans can be time consuming, especially for an organization that is self-insured in several states.

A self-insurance plan requires funding, keeping records of claims, adjusting claims, and reserving losses. It also entails managing litigation; making regulatory filings; paying taxes, assessments, and fees; and maintaining excess liability insurance.

The self-insured organization can perform these activities itself or hire another organization to perform them on its behalf.

Funding

The reserves for self-insured loss payments can be funded or unfunded. If they are unfunded, the self-insured organization pays for losses out of its cash flow or available current (liquid) assets. If they are funded, the reserves are backed by an internal fund that is recorded as an asset on the organization's balance sheet. This fund is used by the organization to pay for its retained losses as they become due.

An organization that maintains an internal fund incurs an opportunity cost, because the cash is tied up in relatively liquid assets and, therefore, probably earns a lower return than it could if it were invested in illiquid assets. Investment earnings from the internal funds may be sufficient to offset the cost of administering the self-insurance plan.

Recordkeeping

A self-insured organization must track its self-insured claims with a recordkeeping system that produces information that would be found in an insurer's loss report. The information contained in this system should include claims identified by number and type, as well as the amount paid and reserved for each claim. The system also can contribute to the organization's risk control program by compiling information on the cause of each loss.

Claim Settlement

A self-insured organization must devote considerable resources to claim settlement. As with insurance, claims must be investigated, evaluated, negotiated, and paid. Also, the self-insured organization may wish to pursue legal action against parties responsible for a loss. These claim settlement activities require a staff with specialized knowledge and skills. Some self-insured organizations create an in-house department to settle claims. This can require a significant commitment of organizational resources, depending on the organization's

work and its geographic diversity. Others hire a **third-party administrator (TPA)**. TPAs usually settle claims, keep claim records, and perform statistical analyses. An arrangement in which a TPA is hired to settle claims is sometimes called an administrative services only (ASO) plan.

Third-party administrator (TPA)
An organization that provides administrative services associated with risk financing and insurance.

Whether in-house or from a TPA, a claim representative must determine which property is damaged, who is liable for the loss, and how much money should be paid. While investigating and evaluating a claim, a claim representative must obtain and verify information, then compare it with other sources. For example, a claim representative may do any of these:

- Investigate an accident scene
- Verify a claimant's statement of salary with the claimant's employer
- Compare a claimant's statement of the circumstances surrounding an accident with a police report's description

When new information contradicts previously known information, a claim representative reexamines all of the information and investigates further to resolve the conflict or to determine which information is most credible. To determine the value of a loss, a claim representative usually consults numerous sources of information, such as valuation guides and records of prior claims with similar characteristics. To negotiate a claim settlement, the claim representative must have a thorough grasp of all the associated facts and communicate effectively.

Loss Reserves

Claim reporting does not always result in the immediate payment or denial of a claim. Like insurers, self-insurers must recognize potential claim payments as a liability on their financial statements in the form of loss reserves. Loss reserves are estimates of the amounts to be paid in the future for losses that occurred in the past.

Claim representatives play a vital role in establishing a self-insurer's loss reserves. After the claim representative receives a claim notice, obtains initial information, and verifies that the self-insurance plan covers the loss, the claim representative establishes a reserve for the loss. Loss reserving is straightforward for most property claims in which the claim representative can readily establish that loss has occurred and can estimate its amount. However, liability claims involve the estimation of bodily injury and property damage loss, and consequently are more difficult to accurately estimate.

The accuracy of a loss reserve's estimate has significant implications for the self-insured organization. An overestimation of loss reserves results in an understatement of net income. Conversely, an understatement of loss reserves results in an overstatement of net income. Therefore, an unethical organization could manipulate its loss reserve amounts in order to minimize the volatility of its financial results over time (a practice known as earnings smoothing). Generally accepted accounting principles (GAAP) state that

a loss reserve must be established if these two conditions are met: The loss occurred before the date of the financial statements, and the amount that will be paid on the loss can be reasonably estimated.

Incurred but not reported (IBNR) losses
Losses that have occurred but have not yet been reported to the insurer.

Sometimes losses have occurred so recently that the self-insurer is not informed of them yet. In other instances, the bodily injury or property damage is latent and, consequently, the injured party has yet to discover it or pursue a claim. These losses are called **incurred but not reported (IBNR) losses**. A self-insured organization should include reserves for its retained IBNR losses if they can be reasonably estimated. A self-insured organization with a large volume of losses per year usually can reasonably estimate its retained IBNR loss liability.

The preceding financial accounting rules help to prevent a self-insured organization from using self-insured loss reserves to "smooth" its earnings. For example, under GAAP, a self-insured organization cannot post loss reserves as a liability on its balance sheet and as an expense on its income statement if the losses have not yet occurred. If the organization were able to do this, it could later use those reserves and prematurely charged expenses to offset a year of higher-than-normal self-insured losses.

Loss reserving requires a great deal of careful analysis. Reserving for an individual claim is not a one-time activity. The loss reserve must be constantly evaluated and reevaluated as new information about the claim becomes available until the claim is settled.

Litigation Management

Litigation management involves controlling the cost of legal expenses for claims that are litigated. Activities involved in litigation management include evaluating and selecting defense lawyers, supervising them during litigation, and keeping records of their costs. It also involves auditing legal bills and evaluating alternative fee-billing strategies.

Another important aspect of litigation management involves the cost-effective resolution of claim disputes. A self-insured organization should set guidelines for the conditions under which it settles claims in order to avoid continuing litigation. The organization should also set guidelines for using alternative dispute resolution (ADR) techniques, such as mediation and arbitration. Insurers, TPAs, and large self-insured organizations often employ litigation managers who oversee the litigation management process.

Regulatory Filings

To self-insure workers compensation and/or auto liability loss exposures, an organization must qualify as a self-insurer separately in, and make periodic filings with, each state in which it seeks to self-insure such loss exposures. Because each state has its own unique set of requirements for organizations to qualify as self-insurers, organizations that operate in several states can

face complex challenges. These requirements specify items such as financial security filing fees, taxes, assessments, excess liability insurance, and periodic reports.

As a result of these varying regulatory requirements, an organization may self-insure its workers compensation and/or auto liability loss exposures only in some of the states in which it operates. Consequently, self-insurance may be practical for certain loss exposures in certain states and not in others. See the exhibit "States Allowing Individual and/or Group Workers Compensation Self-Insurance Plans."

States Allowing Individual and/or Group Workers Compensation Self-Insurance Plans

	South Carolina	Pennsylvania
Security	Determined individually subject to a minimum of $250,000. A surety bond or letter of credit is acceptable.	Surety bond, letter of credit, or government securities held in trust are acceptable. Amount determined individually, based on the applicant's total greatest annual incurred losses in Pennsylvania during the latest three policy years and its credit or debt rating.
Filing Fee	$250 per self-insurer plus $100 per subsidiary.	$500 initially, $100 at renewal.
Taxes, Assessments, and Fees	2.5% of total cost. Second injury fund contribution also required.	Annual assessments for various funds, including second injury fund.
Excess Insurance Requirements	Specific excess required—minimum self-insured; amount determined by the commission.	Specific and aggregate excess may be required.

South Carolina Workers' Compensation Commission, www.sc.gov/ (accessed February 3, 2012); Pennsylvania Department of Labor and Industry, www. portal. state.pa.us (accessed February 3, 2012). [DA01472]

Taxes, Assessments, and Fees

Most states require self-insurance plans to pay taxes, assessments, and fees, but each state has its own approach to determine the amounts owed. For example, some states require self-insured organizations to pay a percentage of their workers compensation losses. Other states impose a tax based on a percentage of what the organization would have paid to an insurer in premium.

This cost component of a self-insurance plan is generally lower than that of insurance, because the state's charges are not levied against the self-insured organization's administrative and risk control expenses. An insurance plan includes these expenses in its premium. The premium for insurance also includes a residual market loading that is passed along to the insured organi-

zation. Self-insured organizations do, however, pay a residual market loading as part of the premium for excess liability insurance. Some states require self-insured organizations to pay a percentage of their workers compensation losses. Other states impose a tax based on a percentage of what the organization would have paid to an insurer in premium.

Excess Liability Insurance

Many states require a self-insurer to purchase excess liability insurance. Some states specify the conditions under which such a purchase must be made. In other states, the agency responsible for self-insurance reviews each applicant and decides whether to require excess liability insurance. If excess liability insurance is required, specifications must be determined and bids obtained from various insurers. Finally, the excess liability insurance program must be reviewed periodically to ensure that it continues to meet the organization's needs.

ADVANTAGES AND DISADVANTAGES OF SELF-INSURANCE PLANS

To recommend self-insurance as a viable risk financing alternative, the risk management professional must understand its advantages and disadvantages relative to insurance, as well as the associated administrative tasks it requires.

As with any risk financing plan, using a self-insurance plan involves advantages and disadvantages. Some advantages and disadvantages mirror those associated with other retention plans, while others are unique to self-insurance plans.

Advantages of Self-Insurance Plans

Self-insurance provides several advantages to an organization when compared with insurance. The major advantages of self-insurance plans are these:

- Control over claims
- Loss control
- Long-term cost savings
- Cash flow benefits

One major advantage of self-insurance is that it allows an organization to exercise direct control over claim settlement. (This advantage also exists with other retention plans.) The self-insured organization can select its own panel of defense attorneys and set specific guidelines for settling its claims. For example, the organization can determine the amount of effort it will invest in defending, rather than settling, a claim. The ability to set guidelines for settlement offers could be particularly important to an organization whose claims could affect its reputation, such as those involving allegations that it negligently manufactured a product, for instance.

Claims can be minimized or eliminated through loss control. Self-insurance's emphasis on loss control is another of its advantages. When an organization directly pays the cost of its own losses, it has an incentive to prevent and reduce them because, by doing so, it saves the associated loss payments and the expense of settling the claims. Also, the organization avoids having to devote resources in the aftermath of a loss, such as spending time to tend to workers' injuries or repairing damage. Furthermore, loss prevention efforts help the organization avoid possible major disruptions in its operations, such as those caused by a plant's total shutdown after an explosion.

Self-insurance's long-run costs tend to be lower than the cost of risk transfer. This advantage of self-insurance allows an organization to save money because it does not have to contribute to an insurer's overhead costs and profits, which are included in the expense component of an insurance premium. A self-insured organization also does not have to pay an insurer's risk charge and is not subject to premium taxes and residual market loadings. However, self-insurance is subject to various other taxes, assessments, and fees.

An organization that self-insures can gain an advantage from the cash flow generated by retained losses that are paid over a time period. Present value analysis can be used to measure this advantage of self-insurance and should be applied to all the costs of a self-insurance plan, not just paid losses. This analysis allows the present value cost of a self-insurance plan to be compared with the present value cost of other plans that involve retaining low- to medium-severity losses, such as a large deductible plan, a retrospective rating plan, or a captive insurance plan. Present value analysis can also be used to compare the cost of self-insurance and insurance.

Disadvantages of Self-Insurance Plans

Self-insurance also has disadvantages when compared with insurance. The major disadvantages of self-insurance include these:

- Uncertainty of retained loss outcomes
- Administrative requirements
- Deferral of tax deductions
- Contractual requirements

One major disadvantage of self-insurance is the associated uncertainty of retained loss outcomes, which can negatively affect an organization's earnings, net worth, and cash flow. (The organization can benefit if retained loss outcomes are better than expected.) When an organization decides to finance losses by self-insuring rather than transferring them using insurance, it faces the possibility that self-insured losses will be much more frequent or severe than initially expected. Therefore, an organization should limit its self-insured loss retention to a level that, combined with its other risks, fits within its risk criteria.

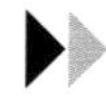

A self-insured loss retention can apply on a per occurrence or per accident basis, an aggregate stop-loss basis, or a combination of the two. With a per occurrence or per accident basis, a limit applies to the amount that the self-insured organization will pay for each loss occurrence or accident, regardless of the number of claims that arise from a single occurrence or accident. On an aggregate stop-loss basis, a limit applies to the amount that the self-insured organization will pay in total for all loss occurrences or accidents that take place during a specified period.

The administrative requirements that self-insurance imposes on an organization constitute another of its disadvantages. Claims must be recorded, adjusted, and reserved; litigation must be managed; regulatory filings must be made with the states (depending on the type of loss exposure); and taxes, assessments, and fees must be paid (depending on the type of loss exposure). These services are normally provided by an insurer under an insured plan.

All risk retention and transfer expenses are tax deductible. However, the value of the tax-deductible expense varies depending on when it is paid. Because of the time value of money, organizations derive a greater economic benefit by taking tax benefits sooner rather than later. Under a self-insurance plan, an organization is allowed a tax deduction only as losses are paid out rather than as they are incurred. Depending on the type of loss exposure involved, losses may not be paid out until several years after they are incurred. Therefore, tax deductions are delayed under a self-insurance plan when compared with the timing of tax deductions under many other types of risk financing plans. An organization is not allowed to deduct its self-insured loss reserves, which are estimates of loss amounts that have occurred but will not be paid until future years.

This deferral of tax deductions is another disadvantage of self-insurance. By contrast, insurance allows an organization to take a tax deduction in the year in which the premium is paid. This disadvantage of self-insurance is more significant for liability losses than for property losses, which tend to be paid soon after they occur.

General business contracts often require one party to purchase insurance for another party's benefit. Sometimes an organization finds it difficult to use its self-insurance plan for this purpose, which is another disadvantage of self-insurance.

For example, if an organization leases a building, it may be required to name the landlord as an additional insured under a general liability insurance policy that covers liability arising from the building's occupancy. The landlord may not accept the tenant's self-insurance plan and, instead, may insist that the tenant purchase a general liability insurance policy for this purpose.

SELECTING A SELF-INSURANCE PLAN

Self-insurance plans enable an organization to lower its long-term cost of risk by allowing it to pay for its own losses without incurring many of the transaction costs associated with insurance. However, these plans are not appropriate for all organizations or all types of losses for an organization. Knowing which factors to consider when deciding whether to self-insure losses is an essential skill for a risk management professional.

Case Facts

Utmost Good Foods (UGF) processes food products that it sells around the country. It ships its products to customers using its own fleet of trucks. UGF management wants Lucy, its risk management professional, to study whether the company should self-insure the physical damage that its trucks sustain throughout the year. Management thinks it is currently paying too much for this coverage and is convinced that this is because its insurer does not completely recognize UGF's superior loss control efforts in relation to the hazards of trucking.

Physical damage losses to UGF's trucks generally have high frequency and low severity. Despite the low severity, its insurer charges an average of $500,000 a year in premium to cover these losses. The coverage includes a deductible for each occurrence, but it is a negligible amount.

The chief financial officer (CFO) assures Lucy that UGF is willing to set aside the amount it normally would pay its insurer in premium to pay for next year's losses and the cost to administer the self-insurance plan. Lucy predicts the losses will be $380,000 and that the cost to administer the plan will be $80,000 next year. Currently, there are no liens on the trucks by a lender.

Overview of Steps

The first step in deciding whether to select a self-insurance plan is to determine whether the organization can meet requirements to implement such a plan. If these requirements can be met, an organization can move to the next step: to analyze the advantages and disadvantages of a self-insurance plan.

Step 1: Meeting the Requirements of a Self-Insurance Plan

These are requirements of a self-insurance plan:

- Self-insuring a type of loss that is predictable
- Having sufficient financial resources and risk tolerance to retain potentially significant losses

- Having the organization willing to commit capital and resources to administer a self-insured plan
- Having the organization embrace loss control as part of its corporate culture

Because physical damage losses to UGF's trucks generally have high frequency and low severity, Lucy can predict that future losses will be $380,000 with higher credibility than if these losses had a low frequency of occurring. Being able to accurately predict future losses reduces the uncertainty for UGF and makes these losses more suitable for retention.

The CFO's strong financial commitment to Lucy indicates that the management of UGF has more than sufficient assets to retain these losses and that it also has sufficient risk tolerance to be self-insured.

In addition to the amount needed to pay expected losses, the CFO assured Lucy that UGF will set aside the costs to administer the self-insurance plan. This demonstrates that UGF is willing to commit capital and resources to administering such a plan.

UGF management's belief that its insurer will never completely recognize UGF's superior loss control effort because of the hazards of trucking indicates that UGF believes in loss control. It is also evidence that loss control has become an essential part of UGF's corporate culture.

It appears UGF can meet all the requirements to implement a self-insured plan if it chooses to do so. Because UGF is self-insuring physical damage to its trucks, it does not need to qualify as a self-insurer in jurisdictions in which it operates. The next step is to determine whether it should implement such a plan.

Step 2: Analyzing the Advantages and Disadvantages of a Self-Insured Plan

To determine whether UGF should implement a self-insurance plan, the company must carefully consider the advantages and disadvantages of such a plan when compared with insurance.

Advantages

These are the major advantages for UGF to use a self-insurance plan instead of insurance:

- Control over claims
- Loss control
- Long-term cost savings
- Cash flow benefits

Control over claims allows UGF to set specific guidelines for adjusting losses. Physical damage to its own trucks does not require hiring a defense attorney, but it can mean selection of UGF-approved repair shops. To be approved, these shops may not only have demonstrated the ability to properly repair UGF's trucks but also to do so at a reasonable price and in a timely fashion. Repairing UGF's trucks quickly can help the company preserve its reputation as a reliable supplier of food products to its customers.

Claims can be minimized or eliminated through loss control. A self-insurance plan for UGF allows it to directly pay the costs of its own losses, which creates a financial incentive for it to prevent or reduce them. By minimizing losses, UGF would also avoid having to devote resources in the aftermath of a loss, such as having to send another truck off its most efficient route to make the deliveries a damaged truck is unable to make.

Long-term costs of a self-insurance plan tend to be lower than the cost of risk transfer. The lower costs of the plan are a result of not having to contribute to an insurer's overhead costs and profits, which, for UGF, are included in the expense component of its insurance premium of $500,000. UGF's expected costs of its retained losses plus the cost to administer the plan is $380,000 plus $80,000, respectively, for a total of $460,000. Therefore, the cost of the plan is expected to be $40,000 lower each year, compared with insurance.

Many self-insured organizations cite cash flow benefits as a major advantage of self-insurance plans when compared with insurance. Insurance premiums are typically due at the beginning of the covered time period. In comparison, retained losses are not payable until they occur and are adjusted, which may result in payment many months after an insurance premium is due. Accordingly, under a self-insurance plan, UGF would retain use of the $500,000 insurance premium until it is needed to pay losses and administrative costs as they are incurred throughout the coverage period. The time value of money and present value analysis suggest that the later UGF can make payments, the greater its present cash flow will be—a benefit of a self-insurance plan. However, this benefit is not as prominent with property claims as it is with liability claims. Property claims are typically adjusted and paid soon after they occur, while liability claims can take years to be reported and years more to settle.

Overall, there appear to be several significant advantages to UGF if it chooses to self-insure the physical damage losses to its trucks.

Disadvantages

These are the major disadvantages for UGF to use a self-insurance plan instead of insurance:

- Uncertainty of retained loss outcomes
- Administrative requirements

- Deferral of tax deductions
- Contractual requirements

Generally, one of the most important disadvantages of self-insuring is the uncertainty of retained losses. If UGF's retained losses are more frequent or severe than Lucy initially expected, its earnings, net worth, and cash flow can be negatively affected. However, uncertainty will be much more of a concern with losses that have a lower frequency and higher severity than with physical damage losses to UGF's own trucks. The high frequency of these losses allows Lucy to predict with much more certainty what the future claims will be. The low severity provides assurance that if the losses do occur more frequently than expected, they will not threaten the survival of UGF.

Most property claims do not have the same potential for high severity as liability claims. Therefore, the disadvantage of uncertainty is minimized if UGF selects physical damage losses to its own trucks to self-insure.

The administrative requirements of self-insurance are another disadvantage, although there are fewer requirements for physical damage claims to an organization's own property. UGF's claims would still need to be recorded, adjusted, and reserved, but these actions will be less burdensome with UGF's own property claims. In fact, Lucy can set up a recording system to compile information on the cause of each loss. This information will help her control future losses.

Reserving losses are also much simpler with UGF's own property claims, as a claim representative can readily establish that a property loss has occurred and can accurately estimate its amount. Liability claims are more difficult to reserve because they involve estimating the bodily injury and property damage losses of an adverse party. Further, reserving for a liability loss is often not a onetime event. For example, as new medical information comes in, the reserve for bodily injury liability must be reevaluated. This occurs much less frequently with an organization's own property claims.

Another consideration is that UGF's need to manage litigation would occur less frequently, and maybe only when it wished to pursue legal action against a party responsible for causing physical damage to one of its trucks. Also, with physical damage claims, there are likely no regulatory filing requirements with government entities because these claims do not involve workers compensation, auto liability, or general liability. As a result, while administrative requirements would still exist for UGF if it self-insured, by choosing to self-insure only its own property claims, the company would simplify or eliminate many of those requirements.

Under a self-insurance plan, UGF is allowed a tax deduction only as losses are paid out, rather than as they are incurred. In contrast, tax deduction for paying an insurance premium is allowed in the same year it is paid. This is normally more of a concern when liability losses are covered by self-insurance, rather than property losses, which tend to be paid soon after they occur; therefore, this disadvantage will likely have a minimal effect on UGF.

Contractual requirements can also be a disadvantage of self-insurance. UGF may have to take out a loan from a lender and use some of its trucks as collateral for the loan. The lender will want to protect that collateral and may require in its loan agreement that UGF purchase physical damage coverage on its trucks. As a result, UGF may not have the option to self-insure these losses, or it may forfeit that option if it must take out a loan and use its trucks as collateral. Because there are no liens on the trucks by a lender, this disadvantage will not prevent UGF from selecting a self-insurance plan; however, it may be a concern if UGF needs to borrow money in the future. Lucy can consult with UGF's CFO to determine the likelihood of this event.

Overall, there appear to be relatively few disadvantages to UGF if it chooses to self-insure the physical damage losses to its trucks.

SUMMARY

Self-insurance lowers the long-term cost of risk by allowing an organization to pay for its own losses without the transaction costs associated with insurance. Self-insurance is a form of retention under which an organization records its losses and maintains a formal system to pay for them. A self-insurance plan is usually coupled with the purchase of excess insurance (risk transfer) to cover severe losses, as well as to limit the accumulation of losses.

Self-insurance is best practiced by organizations that have a tolerance for risk retention and a willingness to devote capital and resources to financing and administering a self-insurance program. It is best applied to losses that are of both low severity and high frequency. Because self-insurance involves certain overhead costs and other expenses as well as the assumption of risk of loss, an organization should have the financial resources and a sufficient amount of loss exposures for self-insurance to be economically feasible.

Self-insurance plans can be implemented for one organization (individual self-insurance) or for more than one organization (group self-insurance plans). Individual self-insurance plans involve a single organization. Group self-insurance involves several similar employers that have formed a not-for-profit association or corporation to which they pay premiums to manage self-insurance of their workers compensation or healthcare benefits loss exposures.

The administration of a self-insurance plan involves activities such as funding, recordkeeping, claim adjusting, loss reserving, litigation management, making regulatory filings, and maintaining excess insurance. To self-insure workers' compensation and/or automobile liability in most states, an organization must qualify as a self-insurer. This can be complex and time consuming, because each state has its own unique set of requirements.

A self-insurance plan has many advantages and disadvantages that are similar to those of all retention plans. However, some are unique to self-insurance. The major advantages of using self-insurance plans include control over claims, loss control, long-term savings, and cash flow benefits. The major

disadvantages of using self-insurance plans include uncertainty of retained loss outcomes, administrative requirements, deferral of tax deductions, and contractual requirements.

Knowing which factors to consider when deciding whether an organization can and should self-insure certain losses is an essential skill of an organization's risk management professional. Initially, the risk management professional must determine whether the organization can meet requirements to implement a self-insurance plan; then, he or she must analyze the advantages and disadvantages of such a plan.

ASSIGNMENT NOTES

1. Self-Insurance Institute of America, www.siia.org/i4a/pages/Index.cfm?pageID=4547 (accessed November 1, 2011).
2. Self-Insurance Institute of America, www.siia.org/i4a/pages/Index.cfm?pageID=4546 (accessed November 1, 2011).

Segment B

Assignment 5
Retrospective Rating Plans

Assignment 6
Reinsurance

Assignment 7
Captive Insurance

Assignment 8
Contractual Risk Transfer

Direct Your Learning

5

Retrospective Rating Plans

Educational Objectives

After learning the content of this assignment, you should be able to:

- Describe the purpose and operation of retrospective rating plans.
- Given a case, calculate the premium for a retrospective rating plan.
- Describe the following types of retrospective rating plans:
    - Incurred loss retrospective rating plan
    - Paid loss retrospective rating plan
- Describe the administration of retrospective rating plans.
- Describe the advantages and disadvantages of retrospective rating plans.
- Given a case, justify a retrospective rating plan that can meet an organization's risk financing needs.

Outline

Retrospective Rating Plans

5

PURPOSE AND OPERATION OF RETROSPECTIVE RATING PLANS

Organizations that desire more risk retention while still keeping an insurance program often consider a retrospective rating plan that provides an alternative means for insurance pricing. Because a retrospective rating plan is an optional pricing plan applied to insurance, the insurance professional needs to know the types of losses covered by the plan and how the retrospective rating insurance premium is determined.

The purpose of a **retrospective rating plan** is to adjust the premium for guaranteed-cost insurance to reflect the insured organization's current losses. Rather than using industry-wide loss experience to determine premiums, a retrospective rating plan uses the insured organization's own losses from the current policy period to price the current policy period. To the extent that the insurer assumes the insured organization's losses above specified monetary limits, the retrospective rating plan is a risk transfer plan.

Retrospective rating plan
A rating plan that adjusts the insured's premium for the current policy period based on the insured's loss experience during the current period; paid losses or incurred losses may be used to determine loss experience.

Because the retrospective premium reflects losses incurred during the policy period, the retrospective rating plan provides an incentive to the insured organization to use risk control and thereby reduce losses. To the extent that the insured controls losses, it is rewarded through lower premiums.

Lines of Business and Characteristics of Losses

Organizations commonly use retrospective rating plans for losses arising from their liability loss exposures that are covered by workers compensation, auto liability, and general liability insurance policies. Organizations can also use retrospective rating plans for auto physical damage, crime, and glass loss exposures. A single retrospective rating plan can be used for more than one type of loss exposure. For example, workers compensation, auto liability, and general liability are commonly combined under a single retrospective rating plan.

In general, organizations use retrospective rating plans to finance their low- to medium-severity losses.[1] These types of losses usually have a high frequency and are therefore somewhat predictable in total. See the exhibit "Characteristics of Losses Usually Covered by a Retrospective Rating Plan."

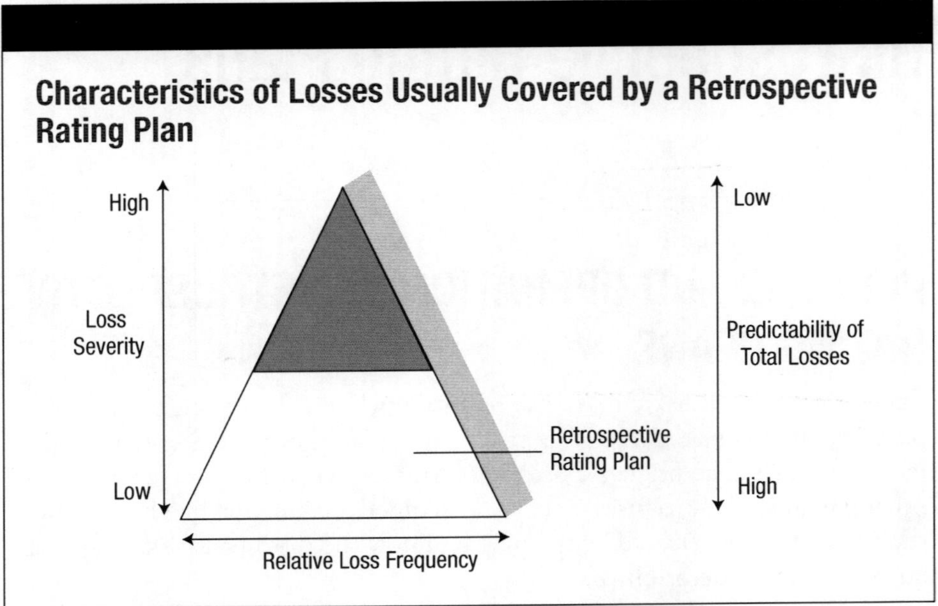

[DA01348]

Other characteristics of organizations that are typically not suited for retrospective rating plans include these:

- Small premium size
- Wide premium fluctuations
- Financial problems

Insurers generally use retrospective rating plans developed by the National Council on Compensation Insurance (NCCI) for workers compensation and by the Insurance Services Office (ISO), Inc., for coverages other than workers compensation. Both organizations have developed eligibility rules, pricing procedures, and retrospective rating premium endorsements that are filed with and authorized for use by the state insurance departments. When a retrospective rating plan is used, the insurer attaches the appropriate retrospective rating premium endorsement to the policy. If multiple insurance policies are subject to the same insurance plan, a retrospective rating premium endorsement is attached to each.

Premium Determination

As with any insurance plan, the insured organization under a retrospective rating plan pays a premium to the insurer. The insurer uses the premium to reimburse claimants for losses and to pay other expenses, such as premium taxes, residual market loadings, loss adjustment costs, and legal defense fees. The premium also includes an amount to cover the insurer's overhead and profit.

Comparing Guaranteed-Cost and Retrospective Rating Insurance Plan Premiums

Under a guaranteed-cost insurance plan, the premium for the policy period does not vary with the insured's losses that occur during the policy period. Therefore, guaranteed-cost insurance is a risk transfer technique.

In contrast, under a retrospective rating plan, the insured organization pays a deposit premium at the beginning of the policy period, and the insurer (using a rating formula agreed on before the policy period) adjusts the premium after the end of the policy period to include a portion of the insured organization's covered losses that occurred during the policy period. Because the premium is adjusted upward or downward based directly on a portion of covered losses, the insured organization is, in effect, retaining a portion of its own losses.

Retrospective Rating Versus Experience Rating

Retrospective rating plan rating is frequently confused with **experience rating**, because both consider the insured organization's loss experience.

Experience rating
A rating plan that adjusts the premium for the current policy period to recognize the loss experience of the insured organization during past policy periods.

In contrast, retrospective rating plans adjust the premium for the current policy period to recognize the insured's loss experience during the *current* policy period. The insured organization's past loss experience is not completely ignored in the retrospective rating plan because past loss experience is reflected in the standard premium. However, past lost experience is less important relative to current losses.

Maximum and Minimum Premiums

The adjusted premium under a retrospective rating plan is subject to a maximum amount and a minimum amount agreed to in the policy. The **maximum premium** is the most an insured organization is required to pay under a retrospective rating plan, regardless of the amount of incurred losses. By agreeing to limit the amount by which the premium can be adjusted upward based on covered losses, the insurer accepts the risk that total losses during the policy period could exceed a maximum amount. The adjusted premium is also often subject to a minimum amount, called a **minimum premium**.

Maximum premium
The most an insured organization is required to pay under a retrospective rating plan, regardless of the amount of incurred losses.

Minimum premium
The least an insured organization is required to pay under a retrospective rating plan, regardless of the amount of incurred losses.

For example, the maximum and minimum premiums for a retrospective rating plan might be $1,000,000 and $200,000, respectively. If during the policy period the insured organization experiences a total of $1,400,000 in losses subject to the policy's loss limit, the premium is limited to the maximum premium of $1,000,000. If the insured organization experiences no losses during the policy period, the minimum premium of $200,000 still applies.

Provided the insured organization has a sufficiently large premium, the retrospective rating plan can be designed to cap losses and thereby minimize the insured organization's retention by using a loss limit. A **loss limit** is the level at which each individual accident or occurrence is limited for the purpose of calculating a retrospective rating insurance premium. The use of a loss limit is

Loss limit
The level at which a loss occurrence is limited for the purpose of calculating a retrospectively rated premium.

another optional factor in a retrospective rating plan. When used, the amount and its cost are negotiated between the insurer and the insured organization.

For example, if the loss limit under a retrospective rating plan is $100,000 per occurrence, only the first $100,000 of each covered loss occurrence is included in the retrospective rating insurance premium. The amount of each loss occurrence that exceeds $100,000 and that is less than the policy limit is transferred to the insurer. See the exhibit "Retained and Transferred Losses Under a Retrospective Rating Plan."

Retained and Transferred Losses Under a Retrospective Rating Plan

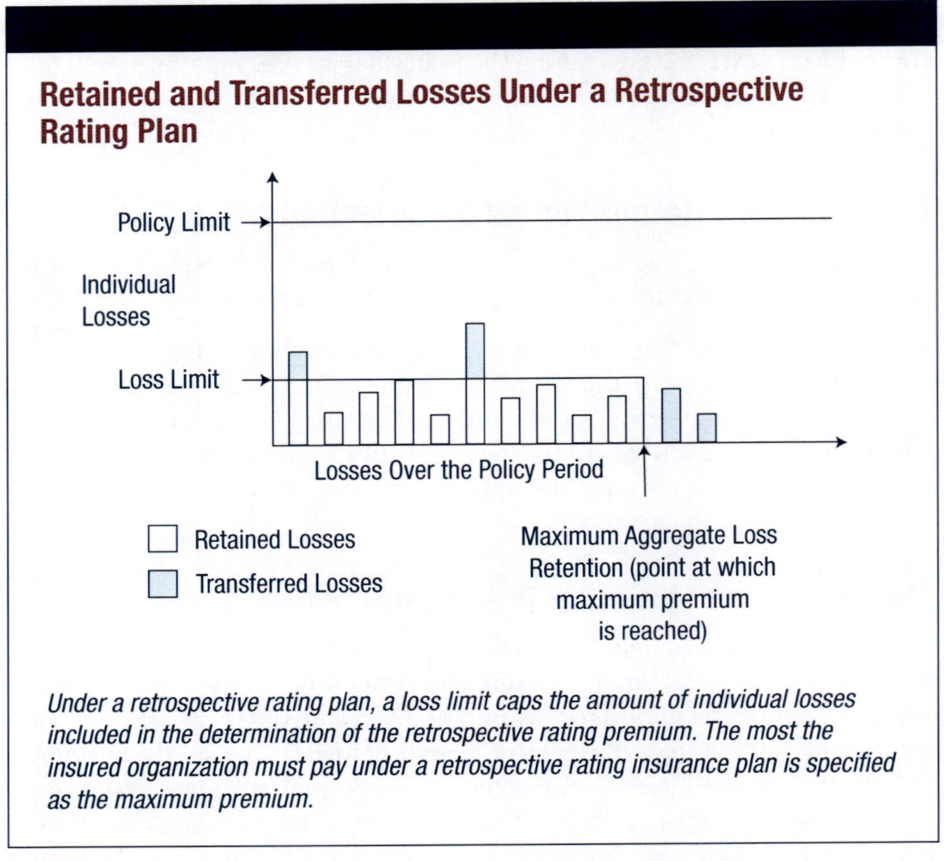

Under a retrospective rating plan, a loss limit caps the amount of individual losses included in the determination of the retrospective rating premium. The most the insured organization must pay under a retrospective rating insurance plan is specified as the maximum premium.

[DA08335]

Other Costs Incorporated Into the Premium

The premium under a retrospective rating plan includes costs other than retained losses, such as insurer overhead and profits, residual market loadings, and premium taxes. The retrospective rating plan premium also includes a risk transfer premium that compensates the insurer for accepting the risk that either or both of these scenarios might occur:

- An individual loss will fall between the loss limit and the policy limit. (The premium component that covers this risk is called an excess loss premium.)
- The total of losses subject to the loss limit during the policy period will exceed the aggregate amount that causes the retrospective rating plan pre-

mium to reach the maximum premium. (The premium component that covers this risk is called an insurance charge.)

The purpose of the risk transfer portion of a retrospective rating plan premium is to compensate the insurer for limiting the amount of an insured's covered losses included in the retrospective rating insurance premium adjustments. The exhibit shows the relationship between losses and premium for a typical retrospective rating plan. Note that the premium is limited by both the maximum and minimum premiums. See the exhibit "Relationship Between Losses and Premium for a Retrospective Rating Plan."

Relationship Between Losses and Premium for a Retrospective Rating Plan

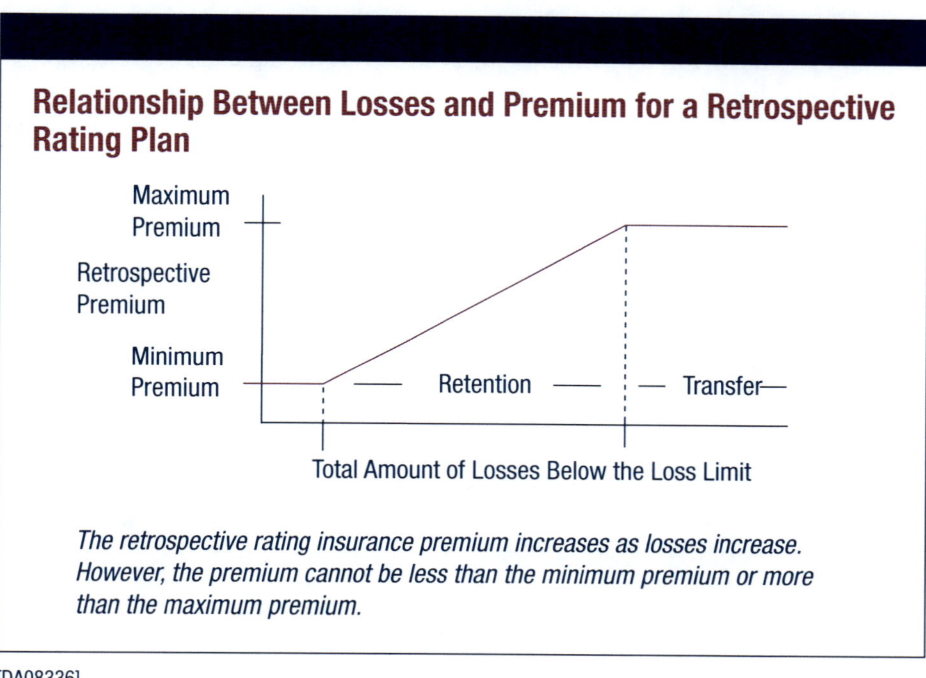

The retrospective rating insurance premium increases as losses increase. However, the premium cannot be less than the minimum premium or more than the maximum premium.

[DA08336]

CALCULATING A RETROSPECTIVE RATING PLAN PREMIUM

Understanding the retrospective rating premium formula is central to obtaining the benefits of this pricing approach.

A retrospective rating premium is calculated using a formula whose factors are agreed upon by the insurer and the insured organization. The retrospective rating plan premium can be expressed as a mathematical formula called the retrospective rating premium formula.

Retrospective Rating Premium Formula

The formula for calculating premium, or the retrospective rating premium formula, is:

$$\text{Retrospective rating plan premium}^{*} = \left(\text{Basic premium} + \text{Converted losses} + \text{Excess loss premium}\right) \times \text{Tax multiplier}$$

*Subject to maximum and minimum amounts

To understand the retrospective rating premium formula, each of its components should be analyzed separately.

Standard Premium

An underlying component of the retrospective rating formula is the standard premium. Standard premium is a premium that is calculated by using state insurance department-authorized rating classifications, applying them to an insured organization's estimated exposures for the policy period, and allowing for various adjustments.

Standard premium is the amount the insured organization would pay for insurance coverage under a guaranteed-cost insurance plan. The standard premium reflects a combination of industry-wide loss experience for a class of organizations (exposure rating) and the insured organization's actual loss experience (experience rating). The calculation of standard premium is:

$$\text{Manual premium} = \frac{\text{Exposure units}}{\text{Exposure base}} \times \text{Manual rate}$$

$$\text{Standard premium} = \text{Manual premium} \times \text{Experience modification factor}$$

The manual rate (the exposure rating component) is developed from industry-wide exposure data. For a guaranteed-cost insurance plan, a premium discount to the standard premium may be available, depending on the size of the insured organization's premium. Insurers provide a premium discount because the relative cost of servicing the policy does not increase proportionately with the size of the premium. Some of the components of the retrospective premium formula are based on an insured's standard premium without an allowance for the premium discount.

At the beginning of the policy period, the standard premium is estimated based on an insured organization's projected exposures for the period. The standard premium is adjusted after the end of the policy period based on the insured organization's actual exposures for the period. Therefore, if an insured organization's exposures, such as sales, turn out to be greater than estimated at the beginning of the policy period, its standard premium is adjusted upward.

Basic Premium

The **basic premium** is a component of the retrospective rating premium formula that covers insurer acquisition expenses, administrative costs, overhead, and profit, as well as the insurance charge. The **insurance charge** is a component of the basic premium that provides the insurer with premium to compensate it for the risk that the calculated retrospective rating premium may be higher than the maximum premium or lower than the minimum premium. The insurance charge reflects both of these possibilities.

The basic premium is expressed as a percentage of the insured organization's standard premium. Therefore, when the standard premium is adjusted after the end of the policy period based on actual exposures, the dollar amount of the basic premium automatically adjusts as well.

Converted Losses

Converted losses is a component of the retrospective rating premium formula that is the product of incurred losses and an applicable **loss conversion factor**.

For example, if an insured organization had annual incurred losses of $500,000 and its retrospective rating premium formula contained a loss conversion factor of 1.25, the converted losses would be $625,000 ($500,000 × 1.25). The formula for converted losses is:

Converted losses = Loss conversion factor × Incurred losses

A high loss conversion factor implies there is a high cost for the insurer to provide claims services for which the cost is not allocated to individual claims. Consequently, a retrospective rating plan with a high loss conversion factor is more expensive for the insured organization than one with a lower loss conversion factor.

The losses included in the determination of converted losses are those below the loss limit applicable to individual losses. The losses include allocated loss adjustment expenses but not unallocated loss adjustment expenses.

Excess Loss Premium

The **excess loss premium** is a component of the retrospective rating premium formula that compensates the insurer for the risk that an individual loss will exceed the loss limit.

For example, assume that the loss limit is $250,000 per occurrence and that the policy limit is $1 million per occurrence. The excess loss premium compensates the insurer for the risk that losses will fall in the layer between $250,000 and $1 million per occurrence.

Basic premium

A fixed cost element of the retrospective rating formula that includes acquisition expenses, loss control services, premium audit, general administration of the insurance, an adjustment for limiting the retrospective premium to a stated maximum, and a provision for the insurer's profits and contingencies.

Insurance charge

A component of the basic premium that provides the insurer with premium to compensate it for the risk that the calculated retrospective rating insurance premium may be higher than the maximum premium or lower than the minimum premium.

Converted losses

An element of the retrospective rating formula that includes the actual losses incurred increased by a factor (loss conversion factor) that reflects loss adjustment expenses.

Loss conversion factor

A factor applied to incurred losses so that the converted losses reflect unallocated loss adjustment expenses.

Excess loss premium

A component of the retrospective rating insurance premium formula that compensates the insurer for the risk that an individual loss will exceed the loss limit.

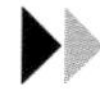

The excess loss premium is the product of the standard premium, the excess loss premium factor, and the loss conversation factor. The formula for the excess loss premium is:

Excess loss premium = Standard premium × Excess loss premium factor × Loss conversion factor

For example, if the standard premium is $600,000, the excess loss premium factor is 15 percent, and the loss conversion factor is 1.25, the excess loss premium is $112,500 ($600,000 × 15 percent × 1.25). When the standard premium is adjusted after the end of the policy period based on actual exposures, the dollar amount of the excess loss premium automatically adjusts as well.

The excess loss premium factor, and consequently the excess loss premium amount, varies with the amount of the loss limit. In the preceding example, the excess loss premium factor would be higher if the loss limit were $100,000 per occurrence rather than $250,000 per occurrence, because the insurer's risk of loss would be greater. The loss conversion factor is included in the formula for the excess loss premium to compensate the insurer for claims handling expenses from the potential losses that exceed the loss limitation and would not be included in the retrospective premium calculation.

Tax Multiplier

Tax multiplier
An element of the retrospective rating insurance premium formula that covers the insurer's cost for state premium taxes, licenses fees, insurance organization assessments, and residual market loadings that the insurer must pay on all written and collected premiums.

The **tax multiplier** is a component of the retrospective rating premium formula that covers the insurer's cost for state premium taxes, licenses fees, insurance organization assessments, and residual market loadings that the insurer must pay on all collected premiums.

The tax multiplier is expressed as a factor that, when multiplied by the other premium components, adds a specified percentage to them. For example, if the amount to be added is 4 percent, the tax multiplier is 1.04.

Maximum and Minimum Premiums

Maximum and minimum premiums are expressed as a percentage of the standard premium. For example, an insured organization and the insurer may agree to a 150 percent maximum premium and a 50 percent minimum premium.

If the standard premium is $900,000, the maximum premium is $1,350,000 ($900,000 × 1.50), and the minimum premium is $450,000 ($900,000 × 0.50). When the standard premium is adjusted after the end of the policy period based on actual exposures, the dollar amounts of the maximum and minimum premiums automatically adjust as well.

Premium Adjustments

Under a retrospective rating plan, insurers generally require the insured organization to pay a deposit premium at the beginning of the policy term that is subsequently adjusted when exposures and losses are known. The deposit premium is usually equal to the standard premium. Some insurers permit the insured organization to pay the deposit premium in installments throughout the policy period. In some cases, the insurer allows the insured organization to pay the standard premium over a period that extends beyond the policy period.

As discussed, the initial standard premium for the retrospective rating plan is based on estimated exposures. Sometime after the end of the policy period, the insurer adjusts the standard premium based on actual exposures for the policy period.

At about the same time (after the end of the policy period), the insurer applies the retrospective rating premium formula to the adjusted standard premium, considering the insured organization's incurred losses (paid and reserved losses) for the policy period. The result is an adjusted retrospective rating plan premium that also accounts for what the insured organization has already paid in premium.

In subsequent periods, usually annually, further adjustments are made to the retrospective rating plan premium by applying the retrospective rating premium formula to subsequent evaluations of incurred losses that occurred during the policy period. If the evaluation of incurred losses for the policy period shows an increase in cumulative incurred losses from one adjustment to the next, an additional premium is due. If the evaluation shows that cumulative incurred losses for the policy period have decreased, premium is returned to the insured organization.

This series of premium adjustments, which can go on for several years after the policy period, continues until all retained losses are paid or until the insurer and the insured organization agree that no further retrospective rating premium adjustments are required. Therefore, a retrospective rating plan premium for a single policy period usually is not finalized until many years after the policy period.

The exhibit illustrates the relationship between incurred losses and premium adjustments for an incurred loss retrospective rating plan. The standard premium is paid during the policy period and, in this example, is adjusted at two evaluation points, Evaluation Point #1 and Evaluation Point #2. Because this example assumes that the cumulative incurred losses at Evaluation Point #1 were less than those anticipated by the standard premium, a return premium is due to the insured organization at Evaluation Point #1. See the exhibit "Relationship Between Incurred Losses and Premium Adjustments for an Incurred Loss Retrospective Rating Plan."

This example assumes that at Evaluation Point #2 cumulative incurred losses further increased, so the insured organization pays an additional premium. Although the exhibit shows only two evaluation points, usually there are many subsequent evaluation points, each of which causes corresponding adjustments to the cumulative premium.

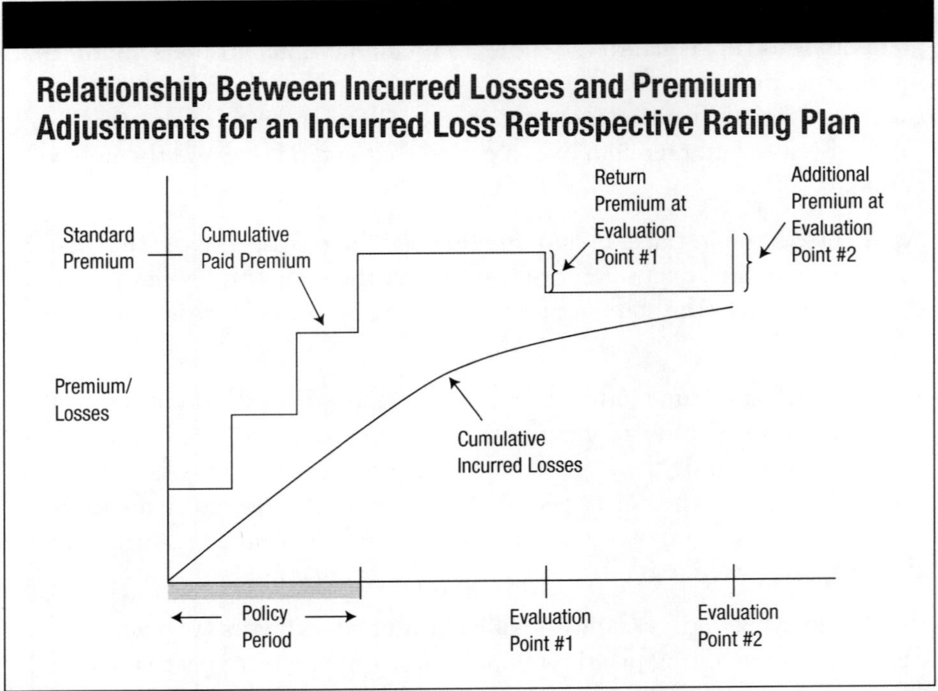

Relationship Between Incurred Losses and Premium Adjustments for an Incurred Loss Retrospective Rating Plan

[DA01330]

Retrospective Rating Plan Premium Calculation Case Study

Case Facts

Assume that Canston Manufacturing Company (Canston) has these cost factors for its incurred loss retrospective rating plan:

- Policy limit: $1,000,000 per occurrence
- Standard premium: $700,000
- Premium discount: $50,000
- Basic premium: 20% of standard premium
- Loss conversion factor: 1.10
- Loss limit: $500,000 per occurrence
- Excess loss premium factor: 5%
- Tax multiplier: 1.04
- Maximum premium: 150% of standard premium
- Minimum premium 40% of standard premium

Analysis

This analysis is used to develop Canston's retrospective rating plan premium:

- The standard premium of \$700,000 minus the premium discount of \$50,000 (\$650,000) is the amount that Canston would pay for a guaranteed-cost insurance plan.
- The basic premium is 20 percent of standard premium, or \$140,000. (The basic premium includes an insurance charge.)
- The excess loss premium is 5 percent of the standard premium times the 1.10 loss conversion factor, or \$38,500.
- The maximum premium is 150 percent of standard premium, or \$1,050,000, and the minimum premium is 40 percent of standard premium, or \$280,000.
- Using the retrospective rating insurance premium formula, the retrospective rating plan premium is calculated as follows:

= [\$140,000 + (Losses × 1.10) + \$38,500] × 1.04

Using the retrospective rating plan premium formula, the table shows retrospective rating plan premium for various incurred loss amounts.

Incurred Losses	Premium	
\$ 50,000	\$ 280,000	Minimum Premium Applies
100,000	300,040	
200,000	414,440	
300,000	528,840	
400,000	643,240	
500,000	757,640	
600,000	872,040	
700,000	986,440	
800,000	1,050,000	Maximum Premium Applies

Further analysis of this table determines losses of \$50,000 or less cause the minimum premium to apply, whereas losses of \$800,000 or more cause the maximum premium to apply. Canston pays the standard premium of \$700,000 as a deposit during the policy period. The premium is adjusted upward or downward as incurred losses for the policy period are evaluated at subsequent annual intervals. For example, if at the first evaluation date Canston's incurred losses are \$600,000, then an additional premium of \$172,040 is due (\$872,040 – \$700,000).

Periodic Audits

Because a portion of a retrospective rating plan premium includes the insured organization's covered losses, the insured organization should periodically audit the insurer's claim handling, loss-payment, and loss-reserving practices. Often, a broker or a risk management consultant performs this audit function on the insured organization's behalf.

TYPES OF RETROSPECTIVE RATING PLANS

Retrospective rating plans allow insured organizations to retain funds to serve other business needs that would otherwise be spent on insurance premiums. Some insurers allow insured organizations even greater cash flow flexibility by using a paid loss retrospective rating plan instead of an incurred loss retrospective rating plan.

With an incurred loss retrospective rating plan, an insured organization pays a deposit premium during the policy period. After the end of the policy period, the insurer adjusts the premium based on the insured organization's actual incurred losses. Because it pays premiums when losses are incurred rather than when they are paid, the insured organization does not receive the cash flow available on its loss reserves, which the insurer holds.

With a paid loss retrospective rating plan, the insured organization pays a deposit premium at the beginning of the policy period and reimburses the insurer for its losses as the insurer pays for them. The total amount paid is subject to the minimum and maximum premiums. Present value analysis can be used to compare the two plans to determine which plan is best for the insured organization.

Incurred Loss Retrospective Rating Plan

Incurred loss retrospective rating plan

A retrospective rating plan in which the insured pays a deposit premium during the policy period; after the end of the policy period, the insurer adjusts the premium based on the insured's actual incurred losses.

An **incurred loss retrospective rating plan** is the type of retrospective rating plan generally offered by insurers. Incurred losses are the sum of paid losses, reserved losses, and loss adjustment expense reserves.

Under an incurred loss retrospective rating plan, the insured organization pays the insurer a premium based on incurred losses, even though those losses may not be paid to a claimant until much later. Because it pays a premium when losses are incurred rather than when they are paid, the insured organization does not receive the cash flow available on its loss reserves, which the insurer holds.

The exhibit shows the relationship between losses and premium payments for an incurred loss retrospective rating plan. Note that the premium payments track the incurred losses rather than the paid losses, providing less cash flow benefit to the insured organization than would be case if premium payments tracked paid losses. See the exhibit "Relationship Between Losses and Premium Payments for an Incurred Loss Retrospective Rating Plan."

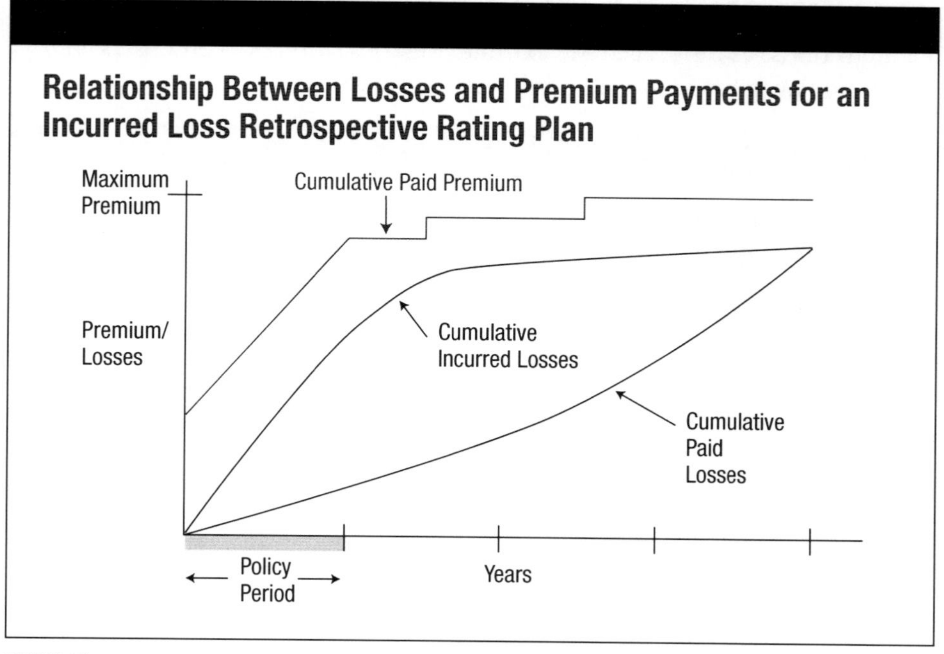

[DA01342]

Paid Loss Retrospective Rating Plan

A **paid loss retrospective rating plan** is a retrospective rating plan in which the insured organization pays a deposit premium at the beginning of the policy period and reimburses the insurer for its losses as the insurer pays for them and in which the total amount paid is subject to the minimum and maximum premiums.

Paid loss retrospective rating plan
A retrospective rating plan in which the insured pays a deposit premium at the beginning of the policy period and makes additional payments, usually monthly, to reimburse the insurer for the insured's losses as they are paid and in which the total amount paid is subject to the minimum and maximum premium.

For most liability losses, the insurer's loss payments are made over a period of several years after the losses occur. Therefore, the insured organization benefits from the cash flow available on the funds it retains rather than paying them to the insurer.

Relative to an incurred loss retrospective rating plan, the insurer generally requires a smaller deposit premium, thereby further enhancing the insured organization's cash flow. The insured organization must provide the insurer with security, such as a letter of credit, to guarantee future premium payments on losses that have occurred but have not yet been paid by the insurer. The need to provide acceptable forms of security is one of the factors that make paid loss retrospective rating plans more complex to administer than guaranteed-cost insurance.

The exhibit shows the relationship between losses and premium payments for a paid loss retrospective rating plan. Note that the cumulative paid premium tracks the cumulative paid losses rather than the cumulative incurred losses, providing a sizable cash flow benefit to the insured organization because premium is not fully paid until several years after the policy period. Just as with any retrospective rating plan, the paid loss amounts are subject to a loss limit

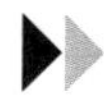

and a maximum premium, so a paid loss retrospective rating plan also has an element of risk transfer. See the exhibit "Relationship Between Losses and Premium Payments for a Paid Loss Retrospective Rating Plan."

Relationship Between Losses and Premium Payments for a Paid Loss Retrospective Rating Plan

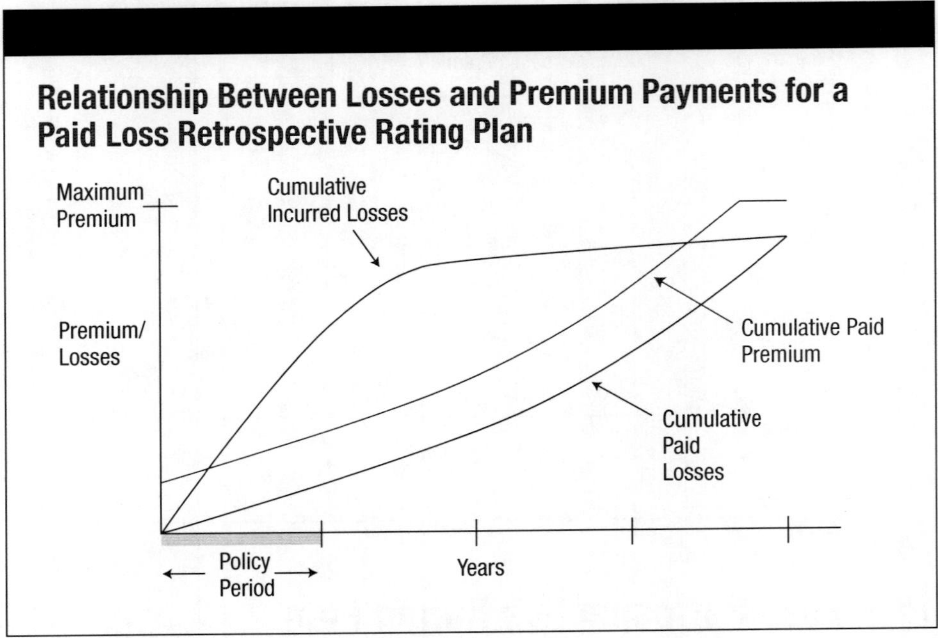

[DA01343]

Comparison of Paid Loss With Incurred Loss Retrospective Rating Plans

Given the previous discussion of paid loss and incurred loss retrospective rating plans, it would seem that an insured would always favor a paid loss over an incurred loss retrospective rating plan. With both plans, the insured organization pays for the insurer's estimated expenses, but with the paid loss plan the insured organization pays premium only as its retained losses are paid rather than incurred, benefiting from the cash flow on retained funds. Under an incurred loss plan, even being able to take a tax deduction on the premium based on incurred rather than paid losses does not compensate for the disadvantage of not benefiting from the cash flow on the insurer's loss reserves.

However, under a paid loss retrospective rating plan, an insurer usually adds an amount to the basic premium to compensate itself for not having use of the cash flow on the loss reserves. Therefore, an insured organization should not automatically choose a paid loss plan over an incurred loss plan, because the decision depends on the relationship between the amount that the insurer adds to the basic premium and the value of the cash flow benefit to the insured.

For example, assume Parne Manufacturing (Parne) is trying to decide between an incurred loss retrospective rating plan and a paid loss retrospective rating plan with the cost factors shown in the table. See the exhibit "Parne Manufactoring Incurred Loss Plan vs. Paid Loss Plan."

Parne Manufactoring Incurred Loss Plan vs. Paid Loss Plan

	Incurred Loss Retrospective Insurance Plan	Paid Loss Retrospective Insurance Plan
Policy limit	$1,000,000 per occurrence	Same
Standard premium	$700,000	Same
Basic premium	20% of standard premium	28% of standard premium
Loss conversion factor	1.10	Same
Loss limit	$500,000 per occurrence	Same
Excess loss premium factor	5%	Same
Tax multiplier	1.04	Same
Maximum premium	150% of standard premium	158% of standard premium
Minimum premium	40% of standard premium	Same

[DA01345]

Note that the difference between the two plans is the charge for the basic premium, which is higher under the paid loss plan. The maximum premium is also adjusted upward to account for the influence of the higher basic premium as part of the retrospective rating insurance premium formula. This higher charge for the basic premium is meant to compensate the insurer for its loss of use of cash flow on the loss reserves under the paid loss retrospective rating plan.

Present value analysis should be used to compare the paid loss and incurred loss plans. The cash flow benefit from paying premium as the losses are paid under the paid loss plan may or may not offset the additional amount loaded into the basic premium.

Another factor to consider when choosing between a paid loss and an incurred loss retrospective rating plan is the additional administrative tasks associated with a paid loss retrospective plan.

ADMINISTRATION OF RETROSPECTIVE RATING PLANS

Retrospective rating plans require the insured organization to perform only a moderate amount of administration.

Because retrospective rating plans are based on insurance, the insurer, rather than the insured organization, is responsible for many of the tasks of administering such plans, such as adjusting losses, making necessary filings with the state regulatory authorities, and paying applicable premium taxes and residual market loadings.

The insured organization's responsibility is limited to making premium payments and arranging for any required security (collateral), such as letters of credit, to guarantee future loss payments under a paid loss retrospective rating plan.

Collateral Requirements

Paid loss retrospective rating plans enable the insured organization to retain funds until the insurer has actually paid the claimant. For many types of losses, particularly workers compensation, for which some benefits are paid periodically over time, the contractual relationship between the insured organization and the insurer can last many years beyond the policy expiration. Consequently, insurers require the insured organization to provide collateral to guarantee that future premium adjustments will be paid. Examples of acceptable forms of collateral include letters of credit, certificates of deposit, or first rights to an escrow account.

Maintaining collateral can be expensive and time consuming for the insured organization. For example, banks charge a fee for providing a letter of credit, even if the credit promised is never accessed. The cost of the letter of credit is relative to the creditworthiness of the insured organization and the bank's expectation that it will be used. Letters of credit need to be periodically renewed, particularly for long-term commitments typical of the obligations the insured organization assumes under a retrospective rating plan.

As the insured organization uses retrospective rating plans over a period of years, the risk management professional needs to keep track of a letter of credit for each policy term. Consequently, maintaining a retrospective rating plan involves expenses and administrative work that are not present when guaranteed-cost insurance is used.

Financial Accounting Issues

For financial accounting purposes, an organization must recognize its retained losses as they are incurred. Therefore, it follows that an organization using a retrospective rating plan should recognize any future premium payments that are due based on current retained losses that have been incurred. These payments must be posted as a liability on the organization's balance sheet and charged as an expense on its income statement.

For example, assume that an organization pays a deposit premium for an incurred loss retrospective rating plan and discovers at the end of the policy period that its incurred losses are much higher than expected. When it prepares its next set of financial statements, the organization should recognize the additional premium that is due at the next adjustment by using the retrospective rating plan premium formula and applying it to the incurred losses. The higher-than-expected incurred losses create an obligation (liability) on the insured organization's part.

With a paid loss retrospective rating plan, premium payments are based on paid rather than incurred losses. However, for financial accounting purposes, the insured organization must calculate what the premium would be at any time if incurred losses rather than paid losses were used. The difference between the amount of premium using incurred losses and the amount currently paid should be recognized as a liability on the organization's balance sheet and as an expense on its income statement.

With either type of retrospective rating plan, an organization may need to recognize an amount for incurred but not reported (IBNR) retained losses. If an IBNR amount can be estimated with reasonable accuracy, then the organization should use it when applying the retrospective rating insurance premium formula to its losses. The insured organization should include any additional premium resulting from IBNR losses as a liability on its balance sheet and as an expense on its income statement.

Tax Treatment

An important tax issue for risk financing is the timing of expense deductions from an organization's taxable income. In general, under a retrospective rating plan, an organization can take a tax deduction on premiums when they are paid. Therefore, an incurred loss retrospective rating plan, in effect, allows an organization to deduct its reserves for the retained portion of its losses, because premiums are paid based on incurred losses.

This favorable timing of the tax deduction helps offset some of the cash flow disadvantage of paying premium based on incurred rather than paid losses. A paid loss retrospective rating plan does not allow an organization to deduct funds set aside for retained losses because, in general, premiums are paid, and therefore deductible for tax purposes, only when losses are paid.

Exit Strategy

As with guaranteed-cost insurance, an insured organization can terminate a retrospective rating plan at any time, although a financial penalty may apply if the insurance policy is cancelled before its normal termination date.

Because the final retrospective rating plan premium is subject to adjustment, particularly with a paid loss retrospective rating plan, terminating a retrospective rating plan is more cumbersome than terminating a guaranteed-cost insurance plan.

Because retrospective rating plans are insurance plans, they are easy to administer relative to other risk financing plans. The extent to which retrospective rating plans are not considered an administrative burden should be weighed along with the advantages and disadvantages of retrospective rating plans.

ADVANTAGES AND DISADVANTAGES OF RETROSPECTIVE RATING PLANS

As with all risk financing plans, the organization and its risk management professional must weigh the advantages with the disadvantages presented by retrospective rating plans to determine whether a plan is suited for the organization.

Because they are hybrid risk financing plans, retrospective rating plans have many of the advantages and disadvantages of both retention and transfer. The degree to which these advantages and disadvantages apply to a specific retrospective rating plan depends on the plan's design—that is, the degree of retention versus the degree of transfer built into the plan.

Advantages of Retrospective Rating Plans

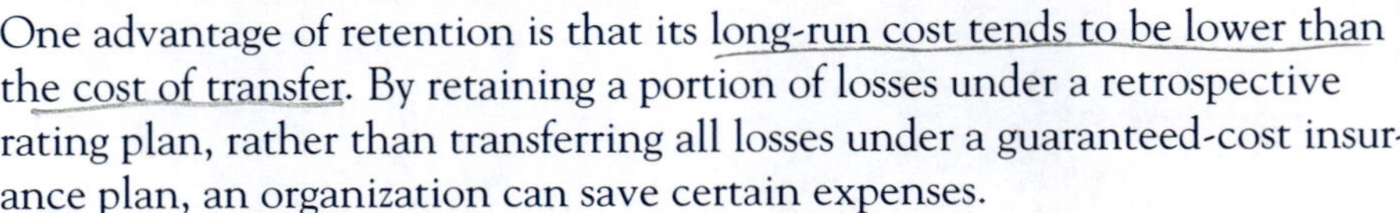

One advantage of retention is that its long-run cost tends to be lower than the cost of transfer. By retaining a portion of losses under a retrospective rating plan, rather than transferring all losses under a guaranteed-cost insurance plan, an organization can save certain expenses.

One significant expense saved is insurer risk charges, which are extra charges that an insurer includes as part of its guaranteed-cost premium to cover the chance that losses will be higher than expected. In addition, savings result from the cash flow gained by retaining losses under a paid loss retrospective rating plan.

Retrospective rating plans also encourage risk control. With a retrospective rating plan, an organization that is able to reduce its losses quickly realizes a premium savings compared with what it would pay under a guaranteed-cost insurance plan. This direct link between losses and premium is a major incentive for an insured organization to control its losses.

If designed properly, a retrospective rating plan also provides many of the advantages of risk transfer. If the loss limit and the maximum premium are set to reduce the uncertainty of the insured organization's retrospective rating plan premium adjustments to a level it can tolerate, then the insured organization benefits from the relative stability that the retrospective rating plan provides in earnings, net worth, and cash flow. A retrospective rating plan that covers more than one type of loss exposure provides stability through diversification by allowing the insured organization to retain losses from different types of loss exposures under a single plan.

Disadvantages of Retrospective Rating Plans

If a retrospective rating plan is not properly designed, it can make financial planning difficult for the insured organization. For example, if the loss limit and maximum premium are set at a high level, the insured organization may not be able to tolerate the uncertainty created by the possibility of upward premium adjustments that reduce its earnings, net worth, and cash flow.

If the insurer sets unrealistically high reserves for the retained portion of losses, the insured organization would pay a premium based on inflated loss reserve figures, resulting in a loss of cash flow, an additional disadvantage with a retrospective rating plan. Under this scenario, the premium would eventually be adjusted downward as losses are paid, because the inflated loss reserves would be eliminated. In the meantime, however, the insurer would have use of the insured organization's funds.

An objection raised to retrospective rating plans is that an insurer may not diligently adjust losses when it knows the insured organization is retaining them, resulting in loss payments that are higher than necessary. However, insurers contend that they adjust claims similarly regardless of the type of plan and that the claim representative for a specific loss typically has no knowledge of the type of plan involved.

Another disadvantage of retrospective rating plans is that the losses that the insured organization ultimately retains are initially paid to the insurer as a premium. Because the insured organization pays them as "premium," the losses must be increased so that the insurer can pay premium taxes and residual market loadings. Premium taxes and residual market loadings add expenses to retrospective rating plans that do not exist with every risk financing plan.

SELECTING A RETROSPECTIVE RATING PLAN

Retrospective rating plans provide an alternative means for pricing guaranteed-cost insurance coverage. Because a retrospective rating plan contains elements of risk retention and risk transfer, it is considered a hybrid risk financing plan. Unlike guaranteed-cost insurance program pricing, retrospective rating plans respond almost immediately to improvements, as well as deterioration, in the insured organization's loss experience.

This case study illustrates the application of a retrospective rating plan to a specific situation. The proposed plans outlined are realistic for the circumstances shown but are not necessarily the only retrospective plan options

appropriate for the hypothetical organization. Two caveats should be kept in mind when reading these cases:

- Retrospective rating plan selection is a function of insurance marketplace conditions and is influenced by who is assisting the risk management professional in developing the program.
- Retrospective rating plan selection is usually based on an in-depth analysis of the insured organization's historical loss experience and financial condition, as well as such subjective factors as senior management's risk aversion.

Case Facts: Etchley Manufacturing

Etchley Manufacturing (Etchley) makes high-end bedding—sheets, bedspreads, and comforters—which it sells primarily to the major hotel chains. Last year, Etchley sold its subsidiary that manufactured baby cribs. Although other economic factors contributed to the sale, one key factor was the lawsuits brought against Etchley for design defects that resulted in bodily injury to children. Etchley's management structured the terms of the subsidiary's sale so that any future lawsuits would be the responsibility of its new owners.

Steps in Evaluating Retrospective Rating Plans

Etchley's management is concerned that its adverse past loss experience will be part of its loss experience for several more years and has asked its risk management professional to investigate alternatives to its guaranteed-cost insurance plan that may meet its risk financing goals. Because Etchley's management is relatively risk-averse, the risk management professional decides to compare Etchley's current insurance plan with a retrospective rating plan.

Etchley's risk management professional identifies four steps in evaluating retrospective rating plans relative to its guaranteed-cost insurance plan:

1. Determine which coverages to include in the retrospective rating plan
2. Determine the limit to which the retrospective rating plan will apply
3. Determine the loss limitation, if any
4. Determine the maximum and minimum premiums

Determining Which Coverages to Include in the Retrospective Rating Plan

Etchley's risk management professional first analyzes the organization's loss exposures to determine which to consider including in the retrospective rating plan. The risk management professional is aware that retrospective rating plans are usually used with workers compensation and that retrospective rating plans that combine loss exposures beyond workers compensation, auto liability, and general liability are uncommon.

The risk management professional immediately identifies the organization's workers compensation loss exposure, because its associated losses are relatively stable, and also considers including its general liability loss exposure. Management is most concerned about this loss exposure, and it also offers the potential of a significant premium cost savings. If the retrospective rating plan is effective in reducing Etchley's cost of risk, the risk management professional may consider additional loss exposures in the future.

Determining the Limit to Which the Retrospective Rating Plan Applies

Etchley's risk management professional next analyzes the limit to which the retrospective rating plan will apply. A retrospective rating plan can apply to the total policy limit or a lesser amount. For example, Etchley may have a $1 million limit for its general liability coverage but may choose to apply the retrospective rating plan to a $250,000 limit.

Selecting a lower limit to which to apply the retrospective rating plan is not an option with retrospective rating plans that apply to workers compensation. Workers compensation coverage is provided without coverage limits because state statutes specify benefits.

Etchley's risk management professional decides to apply the retrospective rating plan to the total coverage limit of its general liability coverage, or $1 million.

Determining the Loss Limitation

The next task the risk management professional performs is to determine what, if any, loss limitation should apply. Etchley's standard premium is large enough to permit a loss limitation. Etchley's risk management professional decides that purchasing a loss limit is prudent because it mitigates the losses included in the retrospective rating plan formula and, consequently, the final retrospective rating plan premium.

Etchley's risk management professional considers three loss limitations that apply on a per accident basis: $200,000, $300,000, and $250,000.

Determining the Maximum and Minimum Premiums

Etchley's risk management professional wants to evaluate several maximum and minimum premium combinations with various expected loss scenarios to present to management.

A high maximum premium and a high minimum premium should result in a relatively low basic premium because of the smaller insurance charge that results. Conversely, a low maximum premium and a low minimum premium should result in a relatively high basic premium.

Etchley's insurer will likely want a maximum premium that is large enough to cover expected losses as well as some cushion in case losses are greater than expected. The risk management professional is unwilling to select a high maximum premium because Etchley's management is risk-averse and already concerned about rising insurance costs. Maximum premium factors generally range from 100 percent (a factor of 1.00) to 150 percent (a factor of 1.50).

Selecting a minimum premium is not as cumbersome as selecting a maximum premium because the insurer simply charges more for the lower minimum. Some insurers allow insured organizations to purchase a retrospective rating plan with a minimum that covers the product of the basic premium and the tax multiplier. Minimum premium factors generally range from 60 percent (a factor of 0.60) to 25 percent (a factor of 0.25).

Evaluating the Maximum and Minimum Premium Choices

The risk management professional researches Etchley's options and develops a proposal that compares the three proposed retrospective rating plan alternatives. Etchley's guaranteed cost insurance premium is determined to be $1.2 million. The three compared options should be considered relative to management's expectation for losses. See the exhibit "Comparison of Etchley's Retrospective Rating Plan Alternatives."

Etchley's management should evaluate these options while considering the organization's past loss experience. The proposal shows what Etchley's premiums would be for three levels of losses—$600,000, $800,000, and $1,000,000. If, for example, Etchley's management could predict that its losses would be $600,000 or less, then the retrospective rating plan with the $300,000 loss limitation would be the most economical choice. However, the uncertainty of ultimate losses makes plan selection challenging.

Comparison of Etchley's Retrospective Rating Plan Alternatives

Loss limitation	$200,000 each accident	$300,000 each accident	$250,000 each accident
Plan factors:			
Basic	0.375	0.325	0.360
Tax multiplier	1.090	1.090	1.085
Loss conversion factor	1.110	1.120	1.090
Maximum premium	1.500	1.814	1.500
Minimum premium	Basic × tax	0.35425	0.500
Estimated premiums:			
Excess loss premiums	$25,000	$15,000	$22,500
Standard premiums	$1,200,000	$1,200,000	$1,200,000
Estimated program cost			
Minimum premium	**$490,500**	**$425,100**	**$600,000**
@ $600,000 losses	$1,243,690	$1,173,930	$1,202,723
@ $800,000 losses	$1,485,670	$1,418,090	$1,439,253
@ $1,000,000 losses	$1,727,650	$1,662,250	$1,675,783
Maximum premium	**$1,800,000**	**$2,176,800**	**$1,800,000**
Other factors	Pay-in: 12 monthly payments @ $103,453	Pay-in: 12 monthly payments @ $97,715	Pay-in: 12 monthly payments @ $100,068

[DA01354]

SUMMARY

The premium for a retrospective rating plan includes a portion of the insured organization's covered losses during the policy period and is subject to maximum and minimum amounts. Therefore, a retrospective rating plan allows an insured organization to effectively retain a portion of its losses.

If an insured organization incurs higher-than-average losses during a policy period, the final adjusted premium under a retrospective rating plan is higher than the premium that the insured organization would pay under a guaranteed-cost insurance plan to cover the same losses. The opposite is true if losses are lower than average.

When used, the loss limit softens the impact of large individual losses on the insured organization. The portion of losses not retained is transferred to the insurer, which is compensated through risk transfer premium charges (the

excess loss premium and the insurance charge) that are built into the retrospective rating plan premium.

The retrospective rating plan premium also includes charges for other components, such as residual market loadings, premium taxes, and insurer overhead and profit. Insurance professionals must understand how the premium components of the plan interact. The retrospective rating plan premium formula specifies the relationship among these premium components.

The components of the formula for calculating retrospective rating plan premium include basic premium, converted losses, excess loss premium, and a tax multiplier. An underlying component of the retrospective rating plan formula is standard premium. The retrospective rating plan premium is subject to maximum and minimum amounts. The insurer periodically adjusts the premium based on evaluations of incurred losses during the policy period.

An incurred loss retrospective rating plan is the type of retrospective rating plan generally offered by insurers. With it, the insured organization pays a deposit premium during the policy period; after the end of the policy period, the insurer adjusts the premium based on the insured organization's actual incurred losses.

With a paid loss retrospective rating plan, the insured organization pays a deposit premium at the beginning of the policy period and reimburses the insurer for its losses as the insurer pays for them and in which the total amount paid is subject to the minimum and maximum premiums.

An insured organization should not automatically choose a paid loss plan over an incurred loss plan because the decision depends on the relationship between the amount that the insurer adds to the basic premium and the value of the cash flow benefit to the insured. Present value analysis should be used to compare the paid loss and incurred loss plans.

Retrospective rating plans require the insured organization to perform only a moderate amount of administration, including making premium payments and arranging for any required security, such as letters of credit to guarantee future loss payments under a paid loss retrospective rating plan. Insurers require the insured organization to provide collateral to guarantee that future premium adjustments will be paid. For financial accounting purposes, an organization that uses a retrospective rating plan should recognize as a liability any future premium payments that will be due based on current retained losses that have been incurred. In general, under a retrospective rating plan, an organization can take a tax deduction on premiums when they are paid, helping offset some of the cash flow disadvantage of paying premium based on incurred rather than paid losses.

Retrospective rating plans offer many of the advantages and disadvantages of both retention and transfer. Under such plans, long-run cost trends are lower than the cost of transfer, leading to savings in insurer risk charges and savings resulting from cash flow gained by retaining losses. Retrospective rating plans also encourage risk control and, if designed properly, provide stability in earnings, net worth, and cash flow. However, retrospective rating plans that are not properly designed can make financial planning difficult and cause premiums to be based on inflated loss reserve figures, resulting in loss of cash flow. In addition, the insured organization's payment of retained losses to the insurer as premium must be high enough to cover the insurer's premium taxes and residual market loadings, an additional expense.

Selecting a retrospective rating plan for an organization entails these steps:

1. Determine which coverages to include in the retrospective rating plan
2. Determine the limit to which the retrospective rating plan will apply
3. Determine the loss limitation, if any
4. Determine the maximum and minimum premiums

ASSIGNMENT NOTE

1. For workers compensation, a retrospective rating plan also covers high-severity losses because a workers compensation policy covers statutory benefits, which are theoretically unlimited in amount.

Direct Your Learning

6

Reinsurance

Educational Objectives

After learning the content of this assignment, you should be able to:

- Describe reinsurance and its principal functions.
- Describe the three sources of reinsurance.
- Describe treaty reinsurance and facultative reinsurance.
- Describe the types of pro rata reinsurance and excess of loss reinsurance and their uses.
- Explain the reinsurance concerns of risk management professionals.

Outline

Reinsurance

6

REINSURANCE AND ITS FUNCTIONS

A single insurer that sells a $100 million commercial property policy and a $100 million commercial umbrella liability policy to the owners of a high-rise office building may appear to be jeopardizing its financial stability. Insurers who provide billions of dollars of property insurance in wind-prone Florida and earthquake-prone California may seem similarly imperiled. However, such transactions are possible when the insurers use reinsurance as a tool to expand their capacity.

No insurer intentionally places itself in a situation in which a catastrophic event could destroy its net worth. Additionally, insurance regulators attempt to prevent insurers from being left in such a position. Reinsurance is one way insurers protect themselves from the financial consequences of insuring others. This section introduces basic reinsurance terms and concepts, including the principal functions of reinsurance.

See the exhibit "Importance of Reinsurance to Risk Management Professionals."

Importance of Reinsurance to Risk Management Professionals

Every insured organization depends on the financial stability of its commercial insurers. Because commercial insurers usually rely on reinsurance to mitigate the potentially adverse effects of a single large loss or an aggregation of smaller losses, any disruption to an insurer's reinsurance network, such as the bankruptcy of a major reinsurer, can threaten an organization's risk financing program.

Furthermore, an organization's risk management professional sometimes deals directly with reinsurers; for example, when he or she purchases reinsurance for a captive insurance subsidiary or places excess insurance layers directly into the reinsurance market.

To understand the importance of reinsurance to a risk financing program, the risk management professional should have a solid understanding of the sources and types of reinsurance.

OV08604

Basic Terms and Concepts

Reinsurance, commonly referred to as "insurance for insurers," is the transfer from one insurer (the **primary insurer**) to another (the **reinsurer**) of some or all of the financial consequences of certain loss exposures covered by the

Reinsurance

The transfer of insurance risk from one insurer to another through a contractual agreement under which one insurer (the reinsurer) agrees, in return for a reinsurance premium, to indemnify another insurer (the primary insurer) for some or all of the financial consequences of certain loss exposures covered by the primary's insurance policies.

Primary insurer

In reinsurance, the insurer that transfers or cedes all or part of the insurance risk it has assumed to another insurer in a contractual arrangement.

Reinsurer

The insurer that assumes some or all of the potential costs of insured loss exposures of the primary insurer in a reinsurance contractual agreement.

primary insurer's policies. The loss exposures transferred, or ceded, by the primary insurer could be associated with a single subject of insurance (such as a building), a single policy, or a group of policies.

An insurer that transfers liability for loss exposures by ceding them to a reinsurer can be referred to as the reinsured, the ceding company, the cedent, the direct insurer, or the primary insurer. Although all these terms are acceptable, "primary insurer" will be used to denote the party that cedes loss exposures to a reinsurer.

Reinsurance agreement
Contract between the primary insurer and reinsurer that stipulates the form of reinsurance and the type of accounts to be reinsured.

Insurance risk
Uncertainty about the adequacy of insurance premiums to pay losses.

Reinsurance premium
The consideration paid by the primary insurer to the reinsurer for assuming some or all of the primary insurer's insurance risk.

Retention
The amount retained by the primary insurer in the reinsurance transaction.

Retrocession
A reinsurance agreement whereby one reinsurer (the retrocedent) transfers all or part of the reinsurance risk it has assumed or will assume to another reinsurer (the retrocessionaire).

Ceding commission
An amount paid by the reinsurer to the primary insurer to cover part or all of the primary insurer's policy acquisition expenses.

Retrocedent
The reinsurer that transfers or cedes all or part of the insurance risk it has assumed to another reinsurer.

Reinsurance is transacted through a **reinsurance agreement**, which specifies the terms under which the reinsurance is provided. For example, it may state that the reinsurer must pay a percentage of all the primary insurer's losses for loss exposures subject to the agreement, or must reimburse the primary insurer for losses that exceed a specified amount. Additionally, the reinsurance agreement identifies the policy, group of policies, or other categories of insurance that are included in the reinsurance agreement.

The reinsurer typically does not assume all of the primary insurer's **insurance risk**. The reinsurance agreement usually requires the primary insurer to retain part of its original liability. This **retention** can be expressed as a percentage of the original amount of insurance or as a dollar amount of loss. The reinsurance agreement does not alter the terms of the underlying (original) insurance policies or the primary insurer's obligations to honor them. See the exhibit "Risk."

Risk

Although "risk" is often defined as uncertainty about the occurrence of a loss, risk has several other meanings that are useful in understanding reinsurance practices. In reinsurance, the term risk often refers to the subject of insurance, such as a building, a policy, a group of policies, or a class of business. Reinsurance practitioners use the term risk in this way and include it in common reinsurance clauses.

[DA05756]

The primary insurer pays a **reinsurance premium** for the protection provided just as any insured pays a premium for insurance coverage, but, because the primary insurer incurs the expenses of issuing the underlying policy, the reinsurer might pay a **ceding commission** to the primary insurer. These expenses consist primarily of commissions paid to producers, premium taxes, and underwriting expenses (such as policy processing and servicing costs, and risk control reports).

Reinsurers may transfer part of the liability they have accepted in reinsurance agreements to other reinsurers. Such an agreement is called a **retrocession**. Under a retrocession, one reinsurer, the **retrocedent**, transfers all or part of the reinsurance risk that it has assumed or will assume to another reinsurer,

the **retrocessionaire**. Retrocession is very similar to reinsurance except for the parties involved in the agreement. The discussions of reinsurance in the context of a primary insurer-reinsurer relationship also apply to retrocessions.[1]

Retrocessionaire

The reinsurer that assumes all or part of the reinsurance risk accepted by another reinsurer.

Reinsurance Functions

Reinsurance helps an insurer achieve several practical business goals, such as insuring large exposures, protecting policyholders' surplus from adverse loss experience, and financing the insurer's growth. The reinsurance that an insurer obtains depends mainly on the constraints or problems the insurer must address to reach its goals. Although several of its uses overlap, reinsurance is a valuable tool that can perform six principal functions for primary insurers:

- Increase large-line capacity
- Provide catastrophe protection
- Stabilize loss experience
- Provide surplus relief
- Facilitate withdrawal from a market segment
- Provide underwriting guidance

Depending on its goals, a primary insurer may use several different reinsurance agreements for these principal functions.

Increase Large-Line Capacity

The first function of reinsurance is to increase **large-line capacity**, which allows a primary insurer to assume more significant risks than its financial condition and regulations would otherwise permit. For example, an application for $100 million of property insurance on a single commercial warehouse could exceed the maximum amount of insurance that an underwriter is willing to accept on a single account. This maximum amount, or **line**, is subject to these influences:

Large-line capacity

An insurer's ability to provide larger amounts of insurance for property loss exposures, or higher limits of liability for liability loss exposures, than it is otherwise willing to provide.

Line

The maximum amount of insurance or limit of liability that an insurer will accept on a single loss exposure.

- The maximum amount of insurance or limit of liability allowed by insurance regulations. Insurance regulations prohibit an insurer from retaining (after reinsurance, usually stated as net of reinsurance) more than 10 percent of its policyholders' surplus (net worth) on any one loss exposure.
- The size of a potential loss or losses that can safely be retained without impairing the insurer's earnings or policyholders' surplus.
- The specific characteristics of a particular loss exposure. For example, the line may vary depending on property attributes such as construction, occupancy, loss prevention features, and loss reduction features.
- The amount, types, and cost of available reinsurance.

Reinsurers provide primary insurers with large-line capacity by accepting liability for loss exposures that the primary insurer is unwilling or unable to

retain. This function of reinsurance allows insurers with *limited* large-line capacity to participate more fully in the insurance marketplace. For example, a primary insurer may want to compete for homeowners policies in markets in which the value of the homes exceeds the amount the primary insurer can safely retain. Reinsurance allows the primary insurer to increase its market share while limiting the financial consequences of potential losses.

Provide Catastrophe Protection

Without reinsurance, catastrophes could greatly reduce insurer earnings or even threaten insurer solvency when a large number of its insured loss exposures are concentrated in an area that experiences a catastrophe. Potential catastrophic perils include fire, windstorm (hurricane, tornado, and other wind damage), and earthquakes. Additionally, significant property and liability losses can be caused by man-made catastrophes, such as industrial explosions, airplane crashes, or product recalls.

The second function of reinsurance is to protect against the financial consequences of a single catastrophic event that causes multiple losses in a concentrated area. For example, an insurer might purchase reinsurance that provides up to $50 million of coverage per hurricane when the total amount of loss from a single hurricane exceeds the amount the insurer can safely retain.

Stabilize Loss Experience

An insurer, like most other businesses, must have a steady flow of profits to attract capital investment and support growth. However, demographic, economic, social, and natural forces cause an insurer's loss experience to fluctuate widely, which creates variability in its financial results. Volatile loss experience can affect the stock value of a publicly traded insurer;[2] alter an insurer's financial rating by independent rating agencies; cause abrupt changes in the approaches taken in managing the underwriting, claim, and marketing departments; or undermine the confidence of the sales force (especially independent brokers and agents who can place their customers with other insurers). In extreme cases, volatile loss experience can lead to insolvency.

Reinsurance can smooth the resulting peaks and valleys in an insurer's loss experience curve. In addition to aiding financial planning and supporting growth, this function of reinsurance encourages capital investment because investors are more likely to invest in companies whose financial results are stable.

Reinsurance can be arranged to stabilize the loss experience of a line of insurance (for example, commercial auto), a class of business (for example, truckers), or a primary insurer's entire book of business. In addition, a primary

insurer can stabilize loss experience by obtaining reinsurance to accomplish any, or all, of these purposes:

- Limit its liability for a single loss exposure
- Limit its liability for several loss exposures affected by a common event
- Limit its liability for loss exposures that aggregate claims over time

The exhibit illustrates how reinsurance can stabilize a primary insurer's loss experience. See the exhibit "Stabilization of Annual Loss Experience for a Primary Insurer With a $20 Million Retention."

Provide Surplus Relief

Insurers that are growing rapidly may have difficulty maintaining a desirable capacity ratio, because of how they must account for their expenses to acquire new policies. State insurance regulation mandates that, for accounting purposes, such expenses be recognized at the time a new policy is sold. However, premiums are recognized as revenue as they are earned over the policy's life. When an insurer immediately recognizes expenses while only gradually recognizing revenue, its policyholders' surplus will decrease as its capacity ratio increases.

Many insurers use reinsurance to provide **surplus relief**, which satisfies insurance regulatory constraints on excess growth. State insurance regulators monitor several financial ratios as part of their solvency surveillance efforts, but the relationship of written premiums to **policyholders' surplus** is generally a key financial ratio and one considered to be out of bounds if it exceeds 3 to 1 or 300 percent. Policyholders' surplus (also called "surplus to policyholders" or simply "surplus") is an insurer's net worth as reported on the financial statement prescribed by state insurance regulators. It represents the financial resource the primary insurer can draw on to pay unexpected losses.

Surplus relief

A replenishment of policyholders' surplus provided by the ceding commission paid to the primary insurer by the reinsurer.

Policyholders' surplus

Under statutory accounting principles (SAP), an insurer's total admitted assets minus its total liabilities.

Some reinsurance agreements facilitate premium growth by allowing the primary insurer to deduct a ceding commission on loss exposures ceded to the reinsurer. The ceding commission is an amount paid by the reinsurer to the primary insurer to cover part or all of a primary insurer's policy acquisition expenses. The ceding commission immediately offsets the primary insurer's policy acquisition expenses for the reinsured policies and often includes a profit provision, or an additional commission, if the reinsurance ceded is profitable.

Because the ceding commission replenishes the primary insurer's policyholders' surplus, the surplus relief facilitates the primary insurer's premium growth and the increase in policyholders' surplus lowers its capacity ratio.

Facilitate Withdrawal From a Market Segment

Reinsurance can also facilitate withdrawal from a market segment, which may be a particular class of business, geographic area, or type of insurance.

Stabilization of Annual Loss Experience for a Primary Insurer With a $20 Million Retention

(1) Time Period (Year)	(2) Actual Losses ($000)	(3) Amount Reinsured ($000)	(4) Stabilized Loss Level ($000)
1	15,000	—	15,000
2	35,000	15,000	20,000
3	13,000	—	13,000
4	25,000	5,000	20,000
5	40,000	20,000	20,000
6	37,000	17,000	20,000
7	16,500	—	16,500
8	9,250	—	9,250
9	18,000	—	18,000
10	10,750	—	10,750
Total	$219,500	$57,000	$162,500

The total actual losses are $219.5 million, or an average of $21.95 million each time period. If a reinsurance agreement were in place to cap losses to $20 million, the primary insurer's loss experience would be limited to the amounts shown in the stabilized loss level column. The broken line that fluctuates dramatically in the graph below represents actual losses, the dotted line represents stabilized losses, and the horizontal line represents average losses.

A primary insurer may want to withdraw from a market segment that is unprofitable, undesirable, or incompatible with its strategic plan. When withdrawing from a market segment, the primary insurer has these options:

- Stop writing new insurance policies and continue in-force insurance until all policies expire (often referred to as "run-off")
- Cancel all policies (if insurance regulations permit) and refund the unearned premiums to insureds
- Withdraw from the market segment by purchasing portfolio reinsurance

To withdraw from a market segment, an insurer can stop writing new business or, to the extent permitted by applicable cancellation laws, cancel all policies in effect and return the unearned premiums to its insureds. However, these approaches can be unwieldy and expensive and could create ill will among insureds, producers, and state insurance regulators. They also create

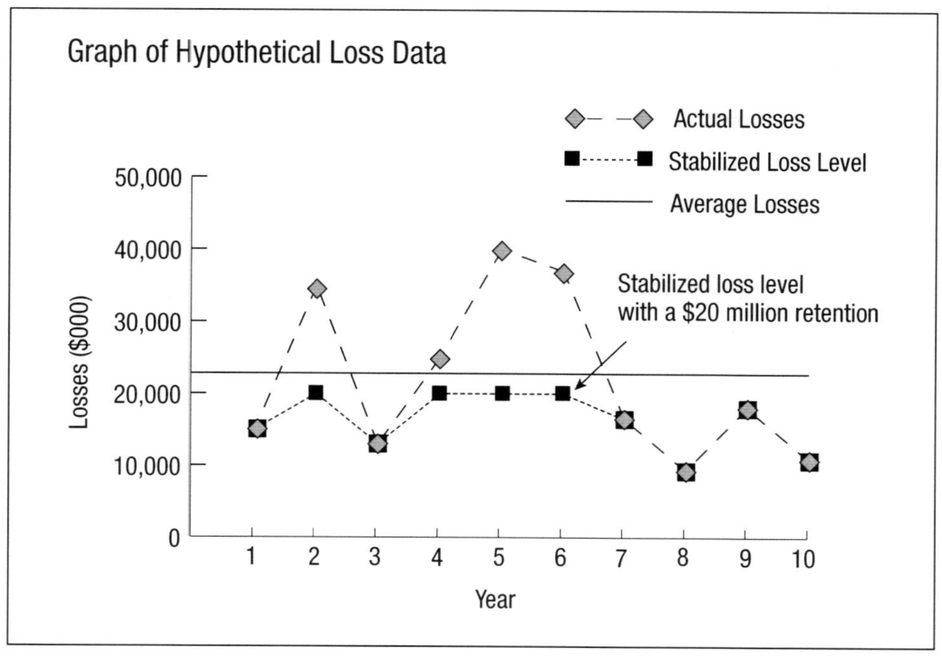

[DA03016]

uncertainty about the insurer's outstanding claims, which must be settled, and about new claims, which might continue to be filed even after the insurer ceases operations.

Another approach available to the primary insurer is to transfer the liability for all outstanding policies to a reinsurer by purchasing **portfolio reinsurance**. Portfolio reinsurance can facilitate withdrawal from a market segment and prevent the formation of ill will due to policy cancellation. It is an exception to the general rule that reinsurers do not accept all of the liability for specified loss exposures of an insurer.

Portfolio reinsurance
Reinsurance that transfers to the reinsurer liability for an entire type of insurance, territory, or book of business after the primary insurer has issued the policies.

In portfolio reinsurance, the reinsurer accepts all of the liability for certain loss exposures covered under the primary insurer's policies, but the primary insurer must continue to fulfill its obligations to its insureds. For example, the primary insurer may decide to use portfolio reinsurance to withdraw from the errors and omissions insurance market. In this situation, the reinsurer typically agrees to indemnify the primary insurer for all losses incurred as of, and following, the date of the portfolio reinsurance agreement. However, the primary insurer continues to pay claims to (or on behalf of) its insureds who are covered by the underlying insurance.

Portfolio reinsurance can be expensive, particularly if the portfolio has been unprofitable and is expected to incur additional losses for the reinsurer. In many states, portfolio reinsurance must be approved by the state insurance department.

Sometimes a primary insurer wants to completely eliminate the liabilities it has assumed under the insurance policies it has issued. This can be

Novation

An agreement under which one insurer or reinsurer is substituted for another.

accomplished through a **novation**. A novation is not considered portfolio reinsurance because the substitute insurer assumes the direct obligations to insureds covered by the underlying insurance. Usually, the approval of state insurance regulators or the insured is required to effect a novation.

Provide Underwriting Guidance

Reinsurance may also provide underwriting guidance. Reinsurers work with a wide variety of insurers in the domestic and global markets under many different circumstances. Consequently, reinsurers accumulate a great deal of underwriting expertise. A reinsurer's understanding of insurance operations and the insurance industry can assist other insurers, particularly inexperienced primary insurers entering new markets and offering new products. For example, one medium-size insurer reinsured 95 percent of its umbrella liability coverage over a period of years and relied heavily on the reinsurer for technical assistance in underwriting and pricing its policies. Without such technical assistance, certain primary insurers would find it difficult to generate underwriting profits from coverages with which they have limited expertise.

Reinsurers that provide underwriting assistance to primary insurers must respect the confidentiality of their clients' proprietary information. Reinsurers often learn about the primary insurer's marketing and underwriting strategies but should not reveal insurer-specific information to other parties.

REINSURANCE SOURCES

The reinsurance market is international in scope, with many participants. In the United States, licensed insurers can market reinsurance unless prohibited by statute or charter. Few such prohibitions exist, and many primary insurers sell some reinsurance. If an insurer is too small to provide reinsurance on its own, it can participate in various reinsurance pools and syndicates.

Reinsurance can be purchased from three sources:

- Professional reinsurers
- Reinsurance departments of primary insurers
- Reinsurance pools, syndicates, and associations

Additionally, the reinsurance business has several professional and trade associations that serve member companies and provide information to interested parties.

Professional reinsurer

An insurer whose primary business purpose is serving other insurers' reinsurance needs.

Professional Reinsurers

The first source of reinsurance is **professional reinsurers**, which interact with other insurers either directly or through intermediaries as primary insurers do.

A reinsurer whose employees deal directly with primary insurers is called a **direct writing reinsurer**. However, most direct writing reinsurers in the U.S. also solicit reinsurance business through reinsurance intermediaries.

Direct writing reinsurer

A professional reinsurer whose employees deal directly with primary insurers.

Reinsurance intermediary

An intermediary that works with primary insurers to develop reinsurance programs and that negotiates contracts of reinsurance between the primary insurer and reinsurer, receiving commission for placement and other services rendered.

Reinsurance intermediaries generally represent a primary insurer and work with that insurer to develop a reinsurance program that is then placed with a reinsurer or reinsurers. The reinsurance intermediary receives a brokerage commission—almost always from the reinsurer or reinsurers—for performing other necessary services in addition to placing the reinsurance, such as disbursing reinsurance premiums among participating reinsurers and collecting loss amounts owed to the insurer.

Although the variety of professional reinsurers leads to differences in how those reinsurers are used and what they can offer, some broad generalizations may be made about professional reinsurers:

- Primary insurers dealing with direct writing reinsurers often use fewer reinsurers in their reinsurance program.
- Reinsurance intermediaries often use more than one reinsurer to develop a reinsurance program for a primary insurer.
- Reinsurance intermediaries can often help secure high coverage limits and catastrophe coverage.
- Reinsurance intermediaries usually have access to various reinsurance solutions from both domestic and international markets.
- Reinsurance intermediaries can usually obtain reinsurance under favorable terms and at a competitive price because they can determine prevailing market conditions and work repeatedly in this market with many primary insurers.

Professional reinsurers evaluate the primary insurer before entering into a reinsurance agreement because the treaty reinsurer underwrites the primary insurer as well as the loss exposures being ceded. In evaluating the primary insurer, the reinsurer gathers information about the primary insurer's financial strength by analyzing the primary insurer's financial statements or by using information developed by a financial rating service. Other information about the primary insurer may be obtained from state insurance department bulletins and the trade press.

Reinsurers also consider the primary insurer's experience, reputation, and management. The reinsurer relies on the quality of the management team, and a relationship of trust must underlie any reinsurance agreement. Whether it involves a one-time facultative agreement or an ongoing treaty agreement, the relationship between the primary insurer and the reinsurer is considered to be one of "utmost good faith." This is because each party is obligated to and relies on the other for full disclosure of material facts about the subject of the agreement. It would be considered a breach of this duty of utmost good faith if the primary insurer withheld material facts relevant to the reinsurer's underwriting decision, intentionally underestimated prior losses, or failed to disclose hazardous conditions affecting loss exposures.

Just as the reinsurer should evaluate the primary insurer, the primary insurer should evaluate the reinsurer's claim-paying ability, reputation, and management competence before entering into the reinsurance agreement.

Reinsurance Departments of Primary Insurers

Some primary insurers also provide treaty and facultative reinsurance, and the reinsurance departments of these companies serve as the second source of reinsurance.

A primary insurer may offer reinsurance to affiliated insurers, regardless of whether it offers reinsurance to unaffiliated insurers. To ensure that information from other insurers remains confidential, a primary insurer's reinsurance operations are usually separate from its primary insurance operations.

Many primary insurers are groups of commonly owned insurance companies. Intragroup reinsurance agreements are used to balance the financial results of all insurers in the group. The use of intragroup reinsurance agreements does not preclude using professional reinsurers.

Reinsurance Pools, Syndicates, and Associations

Reinsurance pools, syndicates, and associations
Groups of insurers that share the loss exposures of the group, usually through reinsurance.

Reinsurance pool
A reinsurance association that consists of several unrelated insurers or reinsurers that have joined to insure risks the individual members are unwilling to individually insure.

Syndicate
A group of insurers or reinsurers involved in joint underwriting to insure major risks that are beyond the capacity of a single insurer or reinsurer; each syndicate member accepts predetermined shares of premiums, losses, expenses, and profits.

The third source of reinsurance is **reinsurance pools, syndicates, and associations**. These entities provide member companies the opportunity to participate in a line of insurance with a limited amount of capital—and a proportionate share of the administrative costs—without having to employ the specialists needed for such a venture. Whether a pool is a reinsurance device is determined by the organizational structure, the type of contract issued, and the internal accounting procedures. The terms "pool," "syndicate," and "association" are often used interchangeably, although there are some fine differences.

In a **reinsurance pool**, a policy for the full amount of insurance is issued by a member company and reinsured by the remainder of the pool members according to predetermined percentages. Some pools are formed by insurers whose reinsurance needs are not adequately met in the regular marketplace, while others are formed to provide specialized insurance requiring underwriting and claim expertise that the individual insurers do not have. Reinsurance intermediaries also form reinsurance pools to provide reinsurance to their clients. A reinsurance pool may accept loss exposures from nonmember companies or offer reinsurance only to its member companies. Some reinsurance pools restrict their operations to narrowly defined classes of business, while others reinsure most types of insurance.

In a **syndicate**, each member shares the risk with other members by accepting a percentage of the risk. These members collectively constitute a single, separate entity under the syndicate name. For example, syndicates are a key component of Lloyd's (formerly Lloyd's of London), an association that provides the physical and procedural facilities for its members to write insurance.

Each individual investor of Lloyd's, called a "Name," belongs to one or more syndicates. The syndicate's underwriter, or group of underwriters, conducts the insurance operations and analyzes applications for insurance coverage. Depending on the nature and amount of insurance requested, a particular syndicate might accept only a portion of the total amount of insurance. The application is then taken to other syndicates for their evaluations.

An **association** consists of member companies that use both reinsurance and risk-sharing techniques. In many cases, the member companies issue their own policies; however, a reinsurance certificate is attached to each policy, under which each member company assumes a fixed percentage of the total amount of insurance. One member company is usually responsible for inspection and investigation, while a committee comprising underwriting executives from the member companies establishes the association's underwriting policy. Organizations of this type allow members to share risks that require special coverages or special underwriting techniques, and can increase the primary insurer's capacity to insure extra-hazardous risks.

Association

An organization of member companies that reinsure by fixed percentage the total amount of insurance appearing on policies issued by the organization.

Reinsurance Professional and Trade Associations

Unlike many primary insurers, reinsurers do not use service organizations such as Insurance Services Office, Inc. (ISO) and the American Association of Insurance Services (AAIS) to develop loss costs and draft contract wording. However, the reinsurance field has several associations that serve member companies and provide information to interested parties.

Intermediaries and Reinsurance Underwriters Association (IRU)

The Intermediaries and Reinsurance Underwriters Association (IRU) was founded in 1967 and is composed of intermediaries and reinsurers that broker or assume non-life treaty reinsurance. IRU publishes the *Journal of Reinsurance*, which discusses concepts and research affecting the reinsurance market. IRU conducts claim seminars, sponsors an internship program for college students, and holds conferences for members.[3]

Brokers & Reinsurance Markets Association (BRMA)

The Brokers & Reinsurance Markets Association (BRMA) represents intermediaries and reinsurers that are predominately engaged in U.S. treaty reinsurance business obtained through reinsurance brokers. BRMA seeks to identify and address industry-wide operational issues through various member committees and is described as a forum for treaty reinsurance professionals.

Of particular importance are BRMA's efforts in the area of reinsurance contract wording. The organization has compiled the *Contract Wording Reference Book*, which has become a benchmark for treaty reinsurance contracts. It is available on BRMA's website.[4]

Reinsurance Association of America (RAA)

The Reinsurance Association of America (RAA), headquartered in Washington, D.C., is a not-for-profit trade association of professional reinsurers and intermediaries. All members are domestic U.S. companies or U.S. branches of international reinsurers.

The RAA engages in many activities, serving its members and providing information on reinsurance issues to interested parties outside the industry. In addition to member advocacy and lobbying at both the state and federal levels, the RAA analyzes aggregate data and conducts seminars countrywide.[5]

REINSURANCE TRANSACTIONS

No single reinsurance agreement performs all the reinsurance functions. Instead, reinsurers have developed various types of reinsurance, each of which is effective in helping insurers meet one or more goals. A primary insurer often combines several reinsurance agreements to meet its particular needs. Each reinsurance agreement is tailored to the specific needs of the primary insurer and the reinsurer.

There are two types of reinsurance transactions: treaty and facultative.

Treaty reinsurance

A reinsurance agreement that covers an entire class or portfolio of loss exposures and provides that the primary insurer's individual loss exposures that fall within the treaty are automatically reinsured.

Facultative reinsurance

Reinsurance of individual loss exposures in which the primary insurer chooses which loss exposures to submit to the reinsurer, and the reinsurer can accept or reject any loss exposures submitted.

Treaty reinsurance uses one agreement for an entire class or portfolio of loss exposures and is also referred to as obligatory reinsurance. The reinsurance agreement is typically called the treaty.

Facultative reinsurance uses a separate reinsurance agreement for each loss exposure it wants to reinsure and is also referred to as nonobligatory reinsurance.

Treaty Reinsurance

In treaty reinsurance, the reinsurer agrees in advance to reinsure all the loss exposures that fall within the treaty. Although some treaties allow the reinsurer limited discretion in reinsuring individual loss exposures, most treaties require that all loss exposures within the treaty's terms must be reinsured.

Primary insurers usually use treaty reinsurance as the foundation of their reinsurance programs. Treaty reinsurance provides primary insurers with the certainty needed to formulate underwriting policy and develop underwriting guidelines. Primary insurers work with reinsurance intermediaries (or with reinsurers directly) to develop comprehensive reinsurance programs that address the primary insurers' varied needs. The reinsurance programs that satisfy those needs often include several reinsurance agreements and the participation of several reinsurers.

Treaty reinsurance agreements are tailored to fit the primary insurer's individual requirements. The price and terms of each reinsurance treaty are individually negotiated.

Treaty reinsurance agreements are usually designed to address a primary insurer's need to reinsure many loss exposures over a period of time. Although the reinsurance agreement's term may be for only one year, the relationship between the primary insurer and the reinsurer often spans many years. A primary insurer's management usually finds that a long-term relationship with a reinsurer enables the primary insurer to be able to consistently fulfill its producers' requests to place insurance with them.

Most, but not all, treaty reinsurance agreements *require* the primary insurer to cede all eligible loss exposures to the reinsurer. Primary insurers usually make treaty reinsurance agreements so their underwriters do not have to exercise discretion in using reinsurance. If treaty reinsurance agreements permitted primary insurers to choose which loss exposures they ceded to the reinsurer, the reinsurer would be exposed to **adverse selection**.

Adverse selection

The decision to reinsure those loss exposures that have an increased probability of loss because the retention of those loss exposures is undesirable.

Because treaty reinsurers are obligated to accept ceded loss exposures once the reinsurance agreement is in place, reinsurers usually want to know about the integrity and experience of the primary insurer's management and the degree to which the primary insurer's published underwriting guidelines represent its actual underwriting practices.

Facultative Reinsurance

In facultative reinsurance, the primary insurer negotiates a separate reinsurance agreement for each loss exposure that it wants to reinsure. The primary insurer is not obligated to purchase reinsurance, and the reinsurer is not obligated to reinsure loss exposures submitted to it. A facultative reinsurance agreement is written for a specified time period and cannot be canceled by either party unless contractual obligations, such as payment of premiums, are not met.

The reinsurer issues a **facultative certificate of reinsurance** (or facultative certificate) that is attached to the primary insurer's copy of the policy being reinsured.

Facultative certificate of reinsurance

An agreement that defines the terms of the facultative reinsurance coverage on a specific loss exposure.

Facultative reinsurance serves four functions:

- Facultative reinsurance can provide large-line capacity for loss exposures that exceed the limits of treaty reinsurance agreements.
- Facultative reinsurance can reduce the primary insurer's exposure in a given geographic area. For example, a marine underwriter may be considering underwriting numerous shiploads of cargo that are stored in the same warehouse and that belong to different insureds. The underwriter could use facultative reinsurance for some of those loss exposures, thereby reducing the primary insurer's overall exposure to loss.
- Facultative reinsurance can insure a loss exposure with atypical hazard characteristics and thereby maintain the favorable loss experience of the primary insurer's treaty reinsurance and any associated profit-sharing arrangements. Maintaining favorable treaty loss experience is important

because the reinsurer has underwritten and priced the treaty with certain expectations. A loss exposure that is inconsistent with the primary insurer's typical portfolio of insurance policies may cause excessive losses and lead to the treaty's termination or a price increase. The treaty reinsurer is usually willing for the primary insurer to remove high-hazard loss exposures from the treaty by using facultative reinsurance. These facultative placements of atypical loss exposures also benefit the treaty reinsurer. For example, an insured under a commercial property policy may request coverage for an expensive fine arts collection that the primary insurer and its treaty reinsurer would not ordinarily want to cover. Facultative reinsurance of the fine arts collection would eliminate the underwriting concern by removing this loss exposure from the treaty. Often, the treaty reinsurer's own facultative reinsurance department provides this reinsurance. The facultative reinsurer knows that adverse selection occurs in facultative reinsurance. Consequently, the loss exposures submitted for reinsurance are likely to have an increased probability of loss. Therefore, facultative reinsurance is usually priced to reflect the likelihood of adverse selection.

- Facultative reinsurance can insure particular classes of loss exposures that are excluded under treaty reinsurance.

Primary insurers purchase facultative reinsurance mainly to reinsure loss exposures that they do not typically insure or on exposures with high levels of underwriting risk. Consequently, primary insurers use facultative reinsurance for fewer of their loss exposures than they use treaty insurance. Primary insurers that find they are increasingly using facultative reinsurance may want to review the adequacy of their treaty reinsurance.

The expense of placing facultative reinsurance can be high for both the primary insurer and the reinsurer. In negotiating facultative reinsurance, the primary insurer must provide extensive information about each loss exposure. Consequently, administrative costs are relatively high because the primary insurer must devote a significant amount of time to complete each cession and to notify the reinsurer of any endorsement, loss notice, or policy cancellation. Likewise, the reinsurer must underwrite and price each facultative submission. See the exhibit "Hybrids of Treaty and Facultative Reinsurance."

Hybrids of Treaty and Facultative Reinsurance

Reinsurers sometimes use hybrid agreements that have elements of both treaty and facultative reinsurance. The hybrid agreements usually describe how individual facultative reinsurance placements will be handled. For example, the agreement may specify the basic underwriting parameters of the loss exposures that will be ceded to the reinsurer as well as premium and loss allocation formulas. Although hybrid agreements may be used infrequently, they demonstrate the flexibility of the reinsurance market to satisfy the mutual needs of primary insurers and reinsurers. The two hybrid agreements briefly described next illustrate common reinsurance agreement variations.

- In a *facultative treaty*, the primary insurer and the reinsurer agree on how subsequent individual facultative submissions will be handled. A facultative treaty could be used when a class of business has insufficient loss exposures to justify treaty reinsurance but has a sufficient number of loss exposures to determine the details of future individual placements.
- In a *facultative obligatory treaty*, although the primary insurer has the option of ceding loss exposures, the reinsurer is obligated to accept all loss exposures submitted to it. Facultative obligatory treaties are also called *semi-obligatory treaties*.

[DA05757]

TYPES OF REINSURANCE

Each reinsurance agreement negotiated between a primary insurer and reinsurer is unique because its terms reflect the primary insurer's needs and the willingness of reinsurers in the marketplace to meet those needs. Several forms of reinsurance have been developed to serve the functions of reinsurance and to help insurers meet their goals.

The two types of reinsurance transactions are treaty reinsurance and facultative reinsurance. These types can be further categorized based on the manner in which the primary insurer and the reinsurer divide the obligations under the reinsurance agreements. The principal approaches that reinsurers use to allocate losses are broadly defined as pro rata reinsurance and excess of loss reinsurance. These types of reinsurance reflect how the primary insurer and reinsurer will share premiums, amounts of insurance, and losses.

The exhibit shows the types of reinsurance and their relationships, and augments the description of the subcategories of pro rata and excess of loss reinsurance. In practice, a reinsurance agreement might contain several of the various types of reinsurance agreements to meet the specific needs of a primary insurer. Unlike primary insurance contracts, reinsurance agreements are not standardized. See the exhibit "Types of Reinsurance."

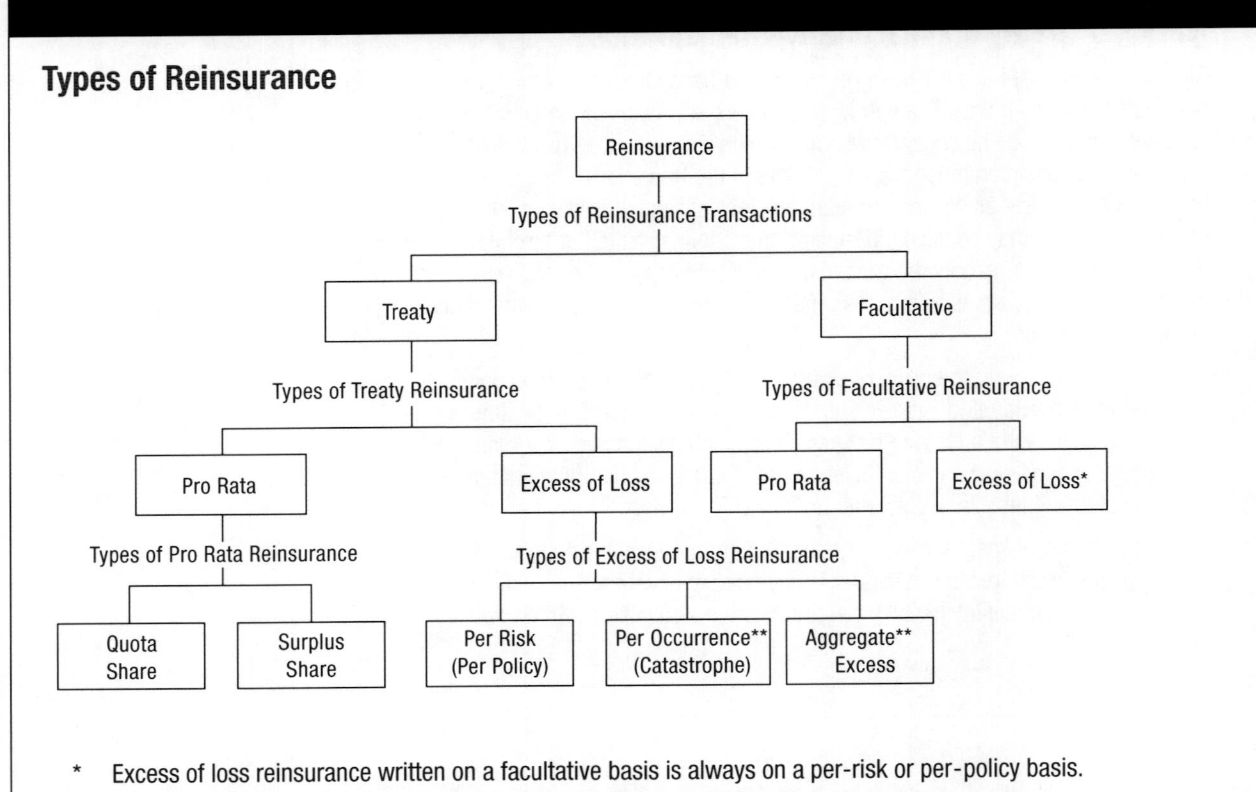

[DA05080]

Pro Rata Reinsurance

Pro rata reinsurance
A type of reinsurance in which the primary insurer and reinsurer proportionately share the amounts of insurance, policy premiums, and losses (including loss adjustment expenses).

Loss adjustment expense (LAE)
The expense that an insurer incurs to investigate, defend, and settle claims according to the terms specified in the insurance policy.

Under **pro rata reinsurance**, or proportional reinsurance, the primary insurer cedes a portion of the original insurance premiums to the reinsurer as a reinsurance premium. The reinsurer usually pays the primary insurer a ceding commission for the loss exposures ceded. The ceding commission reimburses the primary insurer for policy acquisition expenses incurred when the underlying policies were sold. In addition to policy acquisition expenses, insurers incur **loss adjustment expenses.** Loss adjustment expenses that can be related to a specific loss are usually shared proportionately by the primary insurer and the reinsurer.

The amount of insurance, the premium, and the losses (including loss adjustment expenses) are divided between the primary insurer and the reinsurer in the same proportions as the risk. For example, if the reinsurer covers 60 percent of the liability for each loss exposure the primary insurer insures, then the reinsurer would be entitled to 60 percent of the policy premiums and would be responsible for 60 percent of each loss. The amount of the ceding commission paid to the primary insurer is usually negotiated and is taken from the reinsurance premium remitted to the reinsurer. When the ceding commission is a fixed percentage of the ceded premium with no adjustment for the primary insurer's loss experience, it is referred to as a **flat commission**.

Flat commission

A ceding commission that is a fixed percentage of the ceded premiums.

The reinsurance agreement may also include a **profit-sharing commission**, or profit commission, which is negotiated and paid to the primary insurer after the end of the treaty year if the reinsurer earns greater-than-expected profits on the reinsurance agreement. The profit-sharing commission percentage is predetermined and applied to the reinsurer's excess profits; that is, the profits remaining after losses, expenses, and the reinsurer's minimum margin for profit are deducted. Profit commission is also called "contingent commission" because its payment is contingent on the reinsurance agreement's profitability.

Profit-sharing commission

A ceding commission that is contingent on the reinsurer realizing a predetermined percentage of excess profit on ceded loss exposures.

Sometimes, as an alternative to the flat commission and profit-sharing commission, the ceding commission initially paid to the primary insurer may be adjusted to reflect the actual profitability of the reinsurance agreement. This type of commission is called a **sliding scale commission** and could result in the commission being lower than the commission initially paid.

Sliding scale commission

A ceding commission based on a formula that adjusts the commission according to the profitability of the reinsurance agreement.

Pro rata reinsurance is generally chosen by newly incorporated insurers or insurers with limited capital because it is effective in providing surplus relief. Its effectiveness results from the practice of paying ceding commissions under pro rata treaties, a practice not common under excess of loss treaties.

Pro rata reinsurance can be identified as either quota share or surplus share. The principal difference between them is how each one indicates the primary insurer's retention.

Quota Share Reinsurance

The distinguishing characteristic of **quota share reinsurance** is that the primary insurer and the reinsurer use a fixed percentage in sharing the amounts of insurance, policy premiums, and losses (including loss adjustment expenses). Quota share reinsurance can be used with both property insurance and liability insurance but is more frequently used in property insurance.

Quota share reinsurance

A type of pro rata reinsurance in which the primary insurer and the reinsurer share the amounts of insurance, policy premiums, and losses (including loss adjustment expenses) using a fixed percentage.

For example, an insurer may arrange a reinsurance treaty in which it retains 45 percent of policy premiums, coverage limits, and losses while reinsuring the remainder. Such a treaty would be called a "55 percent quota share treaty" because the reinsurer accepts 55 percent of the liability for each loss exposure subject to the treaty.

Most reinsurance agreements specify a maximum dollar limit above which responsibility for additional coverage limits or losses reverts to the primary insurer (or is taken by another reinsurer). With a pro rata reinsurance agreement, that maximum dollar amount is stated in terms of the coverage limits of each policy subject to the treaty. For example, a primary insurer and a reinsurer may share amounts of insurance, policy premiums, and losses on a 45 percent and 55 percent basis, respectively, subject to a $1 million maximum coverage amount for each policy.

In addition to a maximum coverage amount limitation, some pro rata reinsurance agreements include a per occurrence limit, which restricts the primary insurer's reinsurance recovery for losses originating from a single occurrence. This per occurrence limit may be stated as an aggregate dollar amount or as a **loss ratio** cap. The per occurrence limit diminishes the usefulness of pro rata reinsurance in protecting the primary insurer from the effects of catastrophic events. Primary insurers exposed to catastrophic losses usually include **catastrophe excess of loss reinsurance** in their reinsurance programs.

Loss ratio

A ratio that measures losses and loss adjustment expenses against earned premiums and that reflects the percentage of premiums being consumed by losses.

Catastrophe excess of loss reinsurance

A type of excess of loss reinsurance that protects the primary insurer from an accumulation of retained losses that arise from a single catastrophic event.

The exhibit shows how the amounts of insurance, policy premiums, and losses would be shared between a primary insurer and a reinsurer for three policies subject to a quota share treaty. See the exhibit "Quota Share Reinsurance Example."

These observations can be made about quota share reinsurance:

- Because the retention and cession amounts are each a fixed percentage, the dollar amount of the retention and the dollar amount of the cession change as the amount of insurance changes. On policies with higher amounts of insurance, the primary insurer will have a higher dollar retention.
- Because the primary insurer cedes a fixed percentage under a quota share treaty, even policies with low amounts of insurance that the primary insurer could safely retain are reinsured.
- Quota share treaties are straightforward because of the fixed percentage used in sharing premiums and losses. The primary insurer can combine premium and loss amounts and determine the amounts owed to the reinsurer in premiums and owed by the reinsurer in losses.
- Because the primary insurer and the reinsurer share liability for every loss exposure subject to the quota share treaty, the reinsurer is usually not subject to adverse selection. The loss ratio for the reinsurer is the same as that of the primary insurer for the ceded loss exposures.

One type of quota share treaty, a variable quota share treaty, has the advantage of enabling a primary insurer to retain a larger proportion of the small loss exposures that are within its financial capability to absorb, while maintaining a safer and smaller retention on larger loss exposures.

Surplus Share Reinsurance

Surplus share reinsurance

A type of pro rata reinsurance in which the policies covered are those whose amount of insurance exceeds a stipulated dollar amount, or line.

The distinguishing characteristic of **surplus share reinsurance** is that when an underlying policy's total amount of insurance exceeds a stipulated dollar amount, or line, the reinsurer assumes the surplus share of the amount of insurance (the difference between the primary insurer's line and the total amount of insurance). Surplus share reinsurance is typically used only with property insurance.

The primary insurer and the reinsurer share the policy premiums and losses proportionately. The primary insurer's share of the policy premiums and losses

Quota Share Reinsurance Example

Brookgreen Insurance Company has a quota share treaty with Cypress Reinsurer. The treaty has a $250,000 limit, a retention of 25 percent, and a cession of 75 percent. The following three policies are issued by Brookgreen Insurance Company and are subject to the pro rata treaty with Cypress Reinsurer.

- Policy A insures Building A for $25,000 for a premium of $400, with one loss of $8,000.
- Policy B insures Building B for $100,000 for a premium of $1,000, with one loss of $10,000.
- Policy C insures Building C for $150,000 for a premium of $1,500, with one loss of $60,000.

Division of Insurance, Premiums, and Losses Under Quota Share Treaty

	Brookgreen Insurance Retention (25%)	Cypress Reinsurance Cession (75%)	Total
Policy A			
Amounts of insurance	$6,250	$18,750	$25,000
Premiums	100	300	400
Losses	2,000	6,000	8,000
Policy B			
Amounts of insurance	$25,000	$75,000	$100,000
Premiums	250	750	1,000
Losses	2,500	7,500	10,000
Policy C			
Amounts of insurance	$37,500	$112,500	$150,000
Premiums	375	1,125	1,500
Losses	15,000	45,000	60,000

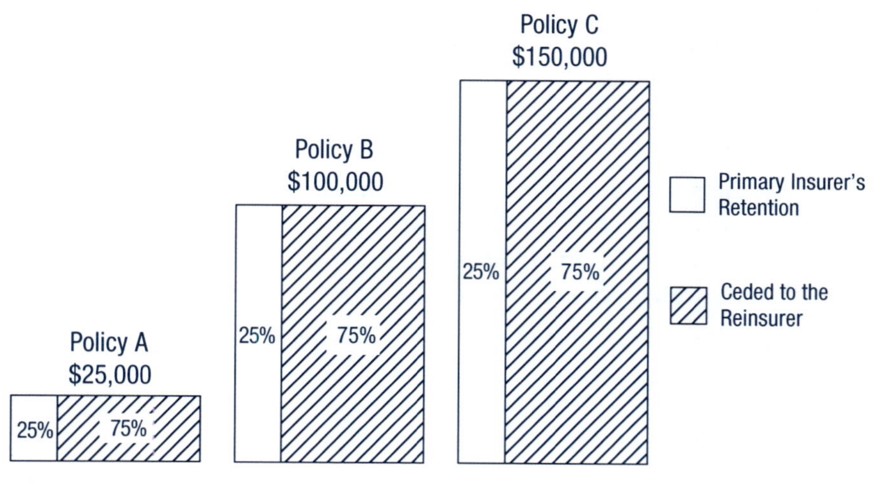

[DA05081]

is the proportion that the line bears to the total amount of insurance. The reinsurer's share of the premiums and losses is the proportion that the amount ceded bears to the total. For example, if the line is $50,000 and the amount ceded is $200,000, the primary insurer would receive 20 percent ($50,000 ÷ $250,000) of the policy premium and pay 20 percent of all losses, while the reinsurer would receive 80 percent ($200,000 ÷ $250,000) of the policy premium and pay 80 percent of all losses.

The exhibit shows how a primary insurer and a reinsurer would share amounts of insurance, policy premiums, and losses under a surplus share treaty using the same three policies shown in the quota share treaty exhibit. See the exhibit "Surplus Share Reinsurance Example."

The reinsurance limit—the total limit or capacity—of a surplus share treaty is expressed in multiples of the primary insurer's line. A primary insurer with a nine-line surplus share treaty has the capacity under the treaty to insure loss exposures with amounts of insurance that exceed its retention by a multiple of nine. For example, if the line is $300,000 for a nine-line surplus share treaty, the primary insurer has a total underwriting capacity of $3 million, calculated as the $300,000 line, plus nine multiples of that $300,000 line. In addition to being expressed as a number of lines, the reinsurance limit of a surplus share treaty can also be expressed as an amount of insurance the reinsurer is willing to provide, such as $2.7 million ($300,000 multiplied by nine lines).

These observations can be made about surplus share reinsurance:

- The surplus share treaty does not cover policies with amounts of insurance that are less than the primary insurer's line. Many primary insurers use surplus share reinsurance instead of quota share reinsurance so that they do not have to cede any part of the liability for loss exposures that can be safely retained.
- The amount of insurance for a large number of loss exposures may be too small to be ceded to the treaty but, in the aggregate, may cause the primary insurer to incur significant losses that are not reinsured. For example, many homeowners policies in the same region that do not exceed the primary insurer's line could incur extensive losses from a single occurrence, such as a hurricane.
- Because the percentage of policy premiums and losses varies for each loss exposure ceded, surplus share treaties are more costly to administer than quota share treaties. Primary insurers must keep records and, in many cases, periodically provide the reinsurer with a report called a **bordereau**.
- Surplus share treaties may provide surplus relief to the primary insurer because the reinsurer usually pays a ceding commission for those policies ceded. Loss exposures with amounts of insurance that are less than the primary insurer's line are not reinsured, so a surplus share treaty typically provides less surplus relief than does a quota share treaty.

Bordereau

A report the primary insurer provides periodically to the reinsurer that contains a history of all loss exposures reinsured under the treaty.

Unlike the simplified example shown in the "Surplus Share Reinsurance Example" exhibit, many surplus share treaties allow the primary insurer to

Surplus Share Reinsurance Example

Brookgreen Insurance Company has a surplus share treaty with Cypress Reinsurer and retains a line of $25,000. The treaty contains nine lines and provides for a maximum cession of $225,000. Therefore, the retention and reinsurance provide Brookgreen with the ability to issue policies with amounts of insurance as high as $250,000. The following three policies are issued by Brookgreen Insurance Company and are subject to the surplus share treaty with Cypress Reinsurer.

- Policy A insures Building A for $25,000 for a premium of $400, with one loss of $8,000.
- Policy B insures Building B for $100,000 for a premium of $1,000, with one loss of $10,000.
- Policy C insures Building C for $150,000 for a premium of $1,500, with one loss of $60,000.

Division of Insurance, Premiums, and Losses Under Surplus Share Treaty

	Brookgreen Insurance Retention	Cypress Reinsurance Cession	Total
Policy A			
Amounts of insurance	$25,000 (100%)	$0 (0%)	$25,000
Premiums	400	0	400
Losses	8,000	0	8,000
Policy B			
Amounts of insurance	$25,000 (25%)	$75,000 (75%)	$100,000
Premiums	250	750	1,000
Losses	2,500	7,500	10,000
Policy C			
Amounts of insurance	$25,000 (16.67%)	$125,000 (83.33%)	$150,000
Premiums	250	1,250	1,500
Losses	10,000	50,000	60,000

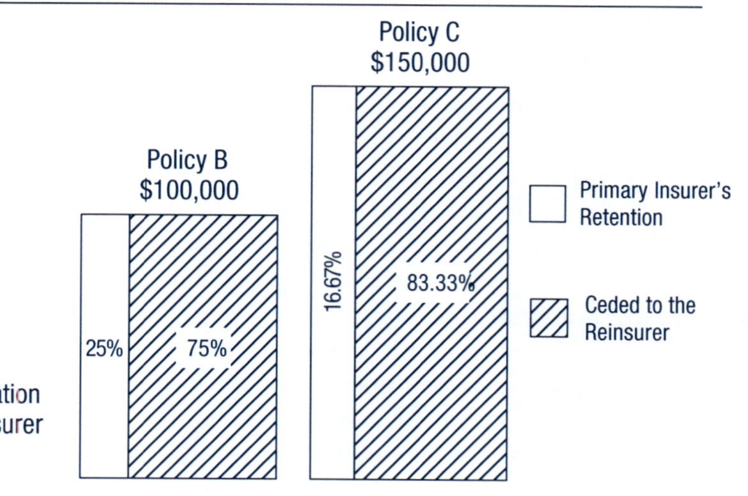

[DA05082]

increase its line from a minimum amount to a maximum amount, depending on the potential loss severity of the exposed limit. For example, Brookgreen Insurance Company's surplus share treaty may allow the company to increase its line on a "superior" loss exposure from $25,000 to $50,000. In this case, the nine-line surplus share treaty would give Brookgreen Insurance Company the large line capacity to insure loss exposures with amounts of insurance as large as $500,000, which is calculated as the $50,000 line plus nine multiplied by the $50,000 line. The primary insurer's ability to vary its line also allows it to retain some loss exposures it may otherwise be required to cede. The flexibility provided by the reinsurer in the surplus share treaty is usually communicated to the primary insurer's underwriters through a **line guide**, or line authorization guide.

Line guide

A document that provides the minimum and maximum line a primary insurer can retain on a loss exposure.

When the total underwriting capacity of the primary insurer's surplus share treaty is insufficient to meet its large-line capacity needs, the primary insurer can arrange for additional surplus share reinsurance from another reinsurer. When a primary insurer arranges more than one surplus share treaty, the surplus share treaty that applies immediately above the primary insurer's line is referred to as the first surplus. Other surplus share treaties are referred to in the order that they provide additional large-line capacity, such as second or third surplus treaties.

Excess of Loss Reinsurance

In an **excess of loss reinsurance** agreement, also called "non-proportional reinsurance," the reinsurer responds to a loss only when the loss exceeds the primary insurer's retention, often referred to as the **attachment point**. The primary insurer fully retains losses that are less than the attachment point, and will sometimes be required by the reinsurer to also retain responsibility for a percentage of the losses that exceed the attachment point.

Excess of loss reinsurance (nonproportional reinsurance)

A type of reinsurance in which the primary insurer is indemnified for losses that exceed a specified dollar amount.

Attachment point

The dollar amount above which the reinsurer responds to losses.

Excess of loss reinsurance can be visualized as a layer, or a series of layers, of reinsurance on top of the primary insurer's retention. See the exhibit "How Excess of Loss Reinsurance Is Layered."

An excess of loss reinsurer's obligation to indemnify the primary insurer for losses depends on the amount of the loss and the layer of coverage the reinsurer provides. The reinsurer providing the first layer of excess of loss reinsurance shown in the exhibit would indemnify the primary insurer for losses that exceed $250,000 (the attachment point) up to total incurred losses of $500,000. This reinsurer describes its position in the primary insurer's excess of loss reinsurance program as being "$250,000 in excess of (denoted as 'xs') $250,000." The reinsurer in the second layer of the excess of loss reinsurance program would indemnify the primary insurer for losses that exceed $500,000 up to total incurred losses of $1 million, or "$500,000 xs $500,000." Losses that exceed the capacity of the primary insurer's excess of loss reinsurance remain the primary insurer's responsibility unless otherwise reinsured.

▶▶

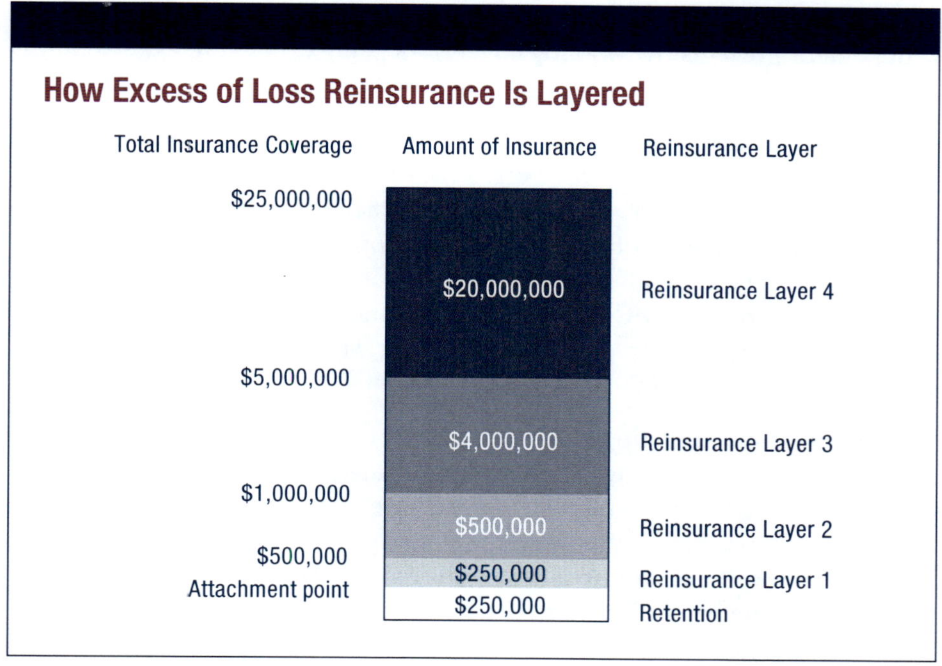

[DA05084]

In the exhibit, loss amounts in excess of $25 million are the primary insurer's responsibility.

Excess of loss reinsurance premiums are negotiated based on the likelihood that losses will exceed the attachment point. The reinsurance premium for excess of loss reinsurance is usually stated as a percentage (often called a rate) of the policy premium charged by the primary insurer (often called the **subject premium** or underlying premium). Therefore, unlike quota share and surplus share reinsurance, the excess of loss reinsurer receives a nonproportional share of the premium.

Subject premium
The premium the primary insurer charges on its underlying policies and to which a rate is applied to determine the reinsurance premium.

Generally, reinsurers do not pay ceding commissions under excess of loss reinsurance agreements. However, the reinsurer may reward the primary insurer for favorable loss experience by paying a profit commission or reducing the rate used in calculating the reinsurance premium.

The primary insurer's attachment point is usually set at a level where claims that are expected are retained. However, if the primary insurer's volume of losses is expected to be significant, an excess of loss reinsurance agreement may have a low attachment point. This type of reinsurance agreement is sometimes referred to as a **working cover**. A working cover enables the primary insurer to spread its losses over several years. The primary insurer and the reinsurer anticipate that profitable years will offset unprofitable ones. Primary insurers selling a type of insurance with which they have little expertise may choose to purchase a working cover until they better understand the frequency and severity of losses that the portfolio for that particular type of insurance produces. Reinsurers typically require a working cover to contain

Working cover
An excess of loss reinsurance agreement with a low attachment point.

an occurrence limitation of two or three times the reinsurance limit. This requirement prevents the working cover from being exposed to catastrophic events, such as an earthquake.

Co-participation provision
A provision in a reinsurance agreement that requires the primary insurer to retain a specified percentage of the losses that exceed its attachment point.

Sometimes a **co-participation provision** is contained within an excess of loss reinsurance agreement. The purpose of this provision is to provide the primary insurer with a financial incentive to efficiently manage losses that exceed the attachment point. A co-participation provision is usually denoted by specifying a percentage before the position of its layer. For example, if the fourth layer in the "How Excess of Loss Reinsurance is Layered" exhibit had a 5 percent co-participation provision, that layer would be specified as "95% of $20,000,000 xs $5,000,000."

In addition to indemnifying losses in a layer of coverage, the reinsurer's obligation may also extend to payment of loss adjustment expenses. Loss adjustment expenses are often a substantial insurer expense, especially for insurance for liability loss exposures. Therefore, excess of loss reinsurance agreements are usually very specific regarding how loss adjustment expenses attributable to specific losses are handled. In rare circumstances, they may be excluded from the reinsurance agreement, but these are the two most common approaches to handling loss adjustment expenses:

- Prorate the loss adjustment expenses between the primary insurer and the reinsurer based on the same percentage share that each is responsible for the loss. This approach is commonly referred to as "*pro rata* in addition."
- Add the loss adjustment expenses to the amount of the loss when applying the attachment point of the excess of loss reinsurance agreement. This approach is commonly referred to as "loss adjustment expense included in the limit."

If loss adjustment expenses are prorated, the primary insurer pays all of the loss adjustment expenses when the loss amount does not exceed the attachment point. If loss adjustment expenses are added to the loss amount, the reinsurer may have to pay a claim in which the loss amount alone does not exceed the attachment point. Primary insurers and reinsurers usually assess the potential for loss adjustment expenses independent of the actual loss potential when negotiating the excess of loss reinsurance agreement. Commonly, reinsurance agreements provide that loss adjustment expenses are prorated for property insurance and most types of liability insurance. However, excess of loss reinsurance covering liability insurance that usually involves substantial litigation often specifies that loss adjustment expenses are added to the amount of the loss when applying the attachment point. For instance, medical malpractice insurance often involves substantial loss adjustment expenses in the form of legal fees even if the claim can be settled with a nominal loss payment or no payment at all.

There are five types of excess of loss reinsurance, each of which usually has a specific use. See the exhibit "Five Types of Excess of Loss Reinsurance."

Five Types of Excess of Loss Reinsurance

1. Per risk excess of loss
2. Catastrophe excess of loss
3. Per policy excess of loss
4. Per occurrence excess of loss
5. Aggregate excess of loss

[DA05083]

Per Risk Excess of Loss

The first type of excess of loss reinsurance is **per risk excess of loss reinsurance**, which is often referred to as property per risk excess of loss and is generally used with property insurance. It applies separately to each loss occurring to each risk, with the primary insurer usually determining what constitutes one risk (loss exposure).

Per risk excess of loss reinsurance
A type of excess of loss reinsurance that covers property insurance and that applies separately to each loss occurring to each risk.

The exhibit indicates how a reinsurer would respond if the primary insurer defined three separate buildings under a per risk excess of loss reinsurance agreement as three separate risks. In this example, a tornado damaged all three buildings in one occurrence. Because each building is a risk, the attachment point and reinsurance limit apply separately to each. The attachment point and reinsurance limit are stated as a dollar amount of loss. See the exhibit "Example of Per Risk Excess of Loss Reinsurance Applying $950,000 xs $50,000."

Example of Per Risk Excess of Loss Reinsurance Applying $950,000 xs $50,000

Building Number	Loss Amount	Primary Insurer's Retention	Reinsurer's Payment
1	$ 500,000	$ 50,000	$ 450,000
2	350,000	50,000	300,000
3	700,000	50,000	650,000
Total	$1,550,000	$150,000	$1,400,000

[DA05086]

Per occurrence limits are commonly included with per risk excess of loss reinsurance agreements. A per occurrence limit restricts the amount that the reinsurer pays as the result of a single occurrence affecting multiple risks. Had a per occurrence limit of $1 million been imposed in the example in the exhibit, the reinsurer would have been responsible for only $1 million of losses (instead of $1.4 million) because the three losses arose out of the same occurrence (the tornado). Catastrophe excess of loss reinsurance is usually purchased in conjunction with per risk excess of loss reinsurance to protect the primary insurer from one occurrence affecting multiple risks.

Catastrophe Excess of Loss

The second type of excess of loss reinsurance is catastrophe excess of loss reinsurance, which protects the primary insurer from an accumulation of retained losses that arise from a single catastrophic event. It may be purchased to protect the primary insurer and its reinsurers on a combined basis but is more frequently purchased to protect the primary insurer on a net basis after all other reinsurance recoveries are made. Examples of catastrophic events include tornadoes, hurricanes, and earthquakes. Such events, especially major hurricanes, can result in losses totaling billions of dollars.

As with per risk excess of loss reinsurance, the attachment point and reinsurance limit for catastrophe excess of loss reinsurance are stated as dollar amounts of loss. The attachment point is subject to negotiation, but it is usually set high enough so that it would be exceeded only if the aggregation of losses from a catastrophe would impair the policyholders' surplus of a primary insurer. Additionally, losses exceeding the attachment point are usually subject to a co-participation provision.

Loss occurrence clause

A reinsurance agreement clause that defines the scope of a catastrophic occurrence for the purposes of the agreement.

Because the attachment point and reinsurance limit apply separately to each catastrophe occurring during a policy period, the catastrophe excess of loss reinsurance agreement defines the scope of a catastrophic occurrence through a **loss occurrence clause** (sometimes called an hours clause). The loss occurrence clause specifies a time period, in hours, during which the primary insurer's losses from the same catastrophic occurrence can be aggregated and applied to the attachment point and reinsurance limits of the catastrophe excess of loss reinsurance agreement. Such clauses usually specify a time period of 72 consecutive hours (three days) for hurricane losses and 168 consecutive hours (seven days) for earthquake losses. When making a claim against the catastrophe excess of loss reinsurance agreement, the primary insurer can usually choose the date and time when the period of consecutive hours commences to maximize the amount of recovery under the agreement. The exhibit provides an example of the operation of a loss occurrence clause in a catastrophe excess of loss reinsurance agreement and shows how a primary insurer can select the period of coverage to its advantage. See the exhibit "Example of the Operation of a Loss Occurrence Clause in a Catastrophe Excess of Loss Reinsurance Agreement."

Example of the Operation of a Loss Occurrence Clause in a Catastrophe Excess of Loss Reinsurance Agreement

Day	Losses	Period of Coverage Providing Maximum Recovery
1	$1,000,000	
2	1,000,000	$7,000,000 (days 2–4)
3	2,000,000	
4	4,000,000	
Total	$8,000,000	

The total losses that could potentially be applied to the reinsurance agreement are $7 million if the seventy-two-hour period starts on the second day, as opposed to $4 million if the period had started on the first day.

[DA05087]

In this example, the primary insurer sustains $8 million in losses from a hurricane over a four-day period. The primary insurer has a $6 million xs $1 million catastrophe excess of loss reinsurance treaty with a loss occurrence clause that stipulates a period of seventy-two consecutive hours for a hurricane. In this simplified example, selecting the specific hour of the day that coverage begins is not an issue, and no co-participation provision applies. Given the distribution of losses over the four days, the primary insurer should elect to start the seventy-two-hour period on the second day to maximize its reinsurance recovery.

Payments from the reinsurer to the primary insurer for catastrophe losses reduce the reinsurance coverage limits available for future losses, but catastrophe excess of loss reinsurance agreements often include a provision requiring the primary insurer to pay an additional premium to reinstate the limits of the agreement after a loss. This provision allows the reinsurer to obtain additional premiums and gives the primary insurer confidence that sufficient limits are available should another catastrophe occur during the reinsurance agreement's term.

Primary insurers and their reinsurers usually do not anticipate that the catastrophe excess of loss reinsurance will be triggered every year. Catastrophe protection is purchased for the unlikely, but possible, event that may cause unstable operating results or that cannot be absorbed by the primary insurer's policyholders' surplus. A primary insurer's need for catastrophe reinsurance and the amount purchased depends on its catastrophe loss exposures. The exhibit provides an example of how the amount of loss retained by the primary insurer and the amount of loss owed by the reinsurer are determined under catastrophe excess of loss reinsurance. See the exhibit "Catastrophe Excess of Loss Reinsurance Example."

Catastrophe Excess of Loss Reinsurance Example

Brookgreen Insurance Company (Brookgreen) decides to sell earthquake coverage in southern California but wants to limit its losses to approximately $1 million from any one earthquake. Brookgreen conducted a study and estimated that its maximum loss from any one earthquake, given its spread of earthquake loss exposures in southern California, would be $10 million. Brookgreen purchases catastrophe excess of loss reinsurance of 95 percent of $9,250,000 xs $750,000. If Brookgreen were to sustain a $10 million loss from an earthquake, it would retain $1,212,500 and the reinsurer would pay $8,787,500. These figures are calculated as follows:

Step 1—Determination of the loss amount exceeding the attachment point

Amount exceeding the attachment point	=	Amount of loss (subject to the reinsurance limit)	–	Retention
	=	$10,000,000	–	$750,000
	=	$9,250,000		

Step 2—Determination of the co-participation

Amount of co-participation	=	Amount exceeding the attachment point	×	Co-participation percentage
	=	$9,250,000	×	0.05
	=	$462,500		

Step 3—Determination of the amount of loss owed by the reinsurer

Amount owed by the reinsurer	=	Amount exceeding the attachment point	–	Amount of co-participation
	=	$9,250,000	–	$462,500
	=	$8,787,500		

Step 4—Determination of the amount retained by Brookgreen

Amount retained by Brookgreen	=	Retention	+	Amount of co-participation
	=	$750,000	+	$462,500
	=	$1,212,500		

[DA05088]

Per policy excess of loss reinsurance

A type of excess of loss reinsurance that applies the attachment point and the reinsurance limit separately to each insurance policy issued by the primary insurer regardless of the number of losses occurring under each policy.

Per Policy Excess of Loss

The third type of excess of loss reinsurance, **per policy excess of loss reinsurance**, is used primarily with liability insurance.The exhibit provides an example of how a reinsurer would respond under a $900,000 xs $100,000 per policy excess of loss treaty. In this example, three separate general liability policies issued by the same primary insurer incur losses from *separate events*. See the exhibit "Example of Per Policy Excess of Loss Reinsurance Applying $900,000 xs $100,000."

Example of Per Policy Excess of Loss Reinsurance Applying $900,000 xs $100,000

Primary Insurer has a $900,000 xs $100,000 per policy excess of loss treaty. The table below shows three policies for which Primary Insurer is indemnified by Reinsurer because the amount of loss arising out of each of the policies exceeds Primary Insurer's attachment point.

Policy	Loss Amount	Primary Insurer's Retention	Reinsurer's Payment
1	$ 300,000	$ 100,000	$ 200,000
2	500,000	100,000	400,000
3	600,000	100,000	500,000
Total	$1,400,000	$300,000	$1,100,000

[DA05094]

Per Occurrence Excess of Loss

Per occurrence excess of loss reinsurance, the fourth type of excess of loss reinsurance, is usually used for liability insurance. It applies the attachment point and the reinsurance limit to the total losses arising from a single event affecting one or more of the primary insurer's policies. See the exhibit "Example of Per Occurrence Excess of Loss Reinsurance Applying $4,900,000 xs $100,000."

Per occurrence excess of loss reinsurance

A type of excess of loss reinsurance that applies the attachment point and reinsurance limit to the total losses arising from a single event affecting one or more of the primary insurer's policies.

Example of Per Occurrence Excess of Loss Reinsurance Applying $4,900,000 xs $100,000

Primary Insurer has a $4,900,000 xs $100,000 per occurrence excess of loss treaty. The table below shows how losses are accumulated to determine whether the attachment point has been exceeded. Primary Insurer is indemnified by Reinsurer because the total amount of the loss arising out of all three policies exceeds Primary Insurer's attachment point.

Policy	Loss Amount		Primary Insurer's Retention		Reinsurer's Payment
1	$ 300,000				
2	500,000				
3	600,000				
Total	$1,400,000	=	$100,000	+	$1,300,000

[DA05095]

The exhibit provides an example of how a per occurrence excess of loss treaty applies to the three policies used in the "Example of Per Policy Excess of Loss Reinsurance Applying $900,000 xs $100,000" exhibit. In the exhibit, a $100,000 attachment point applies to the total losses of the policies covering the same event, and there is a $4.9 million reinsurance limit. A per occurrence excess of loss treaty covering liability insurance usually has an attachment point that is less than the highest liability policy limit offered by the primary insurer.

Clash cover

A type of per occurrence excess of loss reinsurance for liability loss exposures that protects the primary insurer against aggregations of losses from one occurrence that affects several insureds or several types of insurance.

Clash cover, a type of per occurrence excess of loss reinsurance for liability loss exposures, can be provided for a combination of different types of liability insurance, including auto liability, general liability, professional liability, and workers compensation. Clash cover has an attachment point higher than any of the limits of the applicable underlying policies.

For example, a primary insurer could issue a workers compensation policy and a general liability policy with an each occurrence limit of $1 million. To obtain higher limits of coverage for an occurrence that may involve injury to both employees and nonemployees, a clash cover could be purchased in layers. If an explosion results in both workers compensation and general liability claims, the primary insurer would be covered by the clash cover because the claims arise from a single occurrence (the explosion). The clash cover retention is not in addition to the retention of any other applicable per occurrence excess of loss reinsurance; it is net of those retentions.

As another example, Brookgreen Insurance Company (Brookgreen) insures the general liability loss exposure of six contractors working on a single job site. Each of the six contractors' policies has a limit of $1 million. Brookgreen has per occurrence excess of loss reinsurance of $3 million xs $250,000. Brookgreen also has a clash cover of $3 million xs $1 million. An explosion injures employees and nonemployees. The injured parties are awarded damages that total $6 million from the six contractors' policies. The losses from this single occurrence are paid as indicated in the exhibit. See the exhibit "Application of a Clash Cover to One Occurrence Involving Multiple Claims."

Brookgreen exhausted its per occurrence excess of loss reinsurance retention ($250,000) with payment of the $1 million loss from Policy 1. The per occurrence excess of loss reinsurer paid the remaining losses until the per occurrence limit of $3 million was exhausted. Brookgreen paid the remaining $750,000 under Policy 4 to fulfill its $1 million retention under the clash cover. The clash cover reinsurer then paid the remaining losses.

Both catastrophe excess of loss reinsurance (for property insurance) and clash cover (for liability insurance) are also referred to as pure risk covers because they are expected to cover only rare events, not common claims covered by other excess of loss treaties.

Clash cover may be useful for types of liability insurance in which loss adjustment expenses are likely to be very high and the underlying per occurrence

Application of a Clash Cover to One Occurrence Involving Multiple Claims

Policy	Damages	Brookgreen Insurance Co. Retention	Per Occurrence Reinsurer	Clash Cover Reinsurer
1	$1,000,000	$ 250,000	$ 750,000	$ 0
2	1,000,000	—	1,000,000	0
3	1,000,000	—	1,000,000	0
4	1,000,000	750,000	250,000	0
5	1,000,000	—	Limit exhausted	1,000,000
6	1,000,000	—	—	1,000,000
Total	$6,000,000	$1,000,000	$3,000,000	$2,000,000

[DA05096]

reinsurance limits include these expenses rather than pro rate them. Examples include professional liability (such as medical malpractice, directors and officers liability, and accountants professional liability) and expenses associated with environmental claims (for example, asbestos and pollution liability). Primary insurers also use clash cover when they want protection from extracontractual damages and excess of policy limits losses.

Extracontractual damages are damages awarded to an insured as a result of an insurer improperly handling a claim. This improper behavior is known as bad faith, and it implies that the insurer has failed to deal fairly with the insured. Damages awarded to an insured for an insurer's bad faith in claim handling are usually not considered to be a loss covered by the underlying policy and therefore are usually not subject to indemnification by a reinsurer unless the reinsurance agreement specifically provides coverage.

Extracontractual damages
Damages awarded to the insured as a result of the insurer's improperly handling a claim.

Excess of policy limits losses result when an insured sues an insurer for failing to settle a claim within the insured's policy limits when the insurer had the opportunity to do so. Excess of policy limits losses are also extracontractual obligations of the insurer but are usually distinguished from extracontractual damages by reinsurers because they are covered losses that, as a result of a mistake of the primary insurer, exceed policy limits. As with other extracontractual obligations, the reinsurance agreement specifies whether excess of policy limits losses are subject to indemnification by the reinsurer.

Excess of policy limits loss
A loss that results when an insured sues an insurer for failing to settle a claim within the insured's policy limits when the insurer had the opportunity to do so.

Aggregate Excess of Loss

The fifth type of excess of loss reinsurance is **aggregate excess of loss reinsurance**. This type of excess of loss reinsurance can be used for property or

Aggregate excess of loss reinsurance
A type of excess of loss reinsurance that covers aggregated losses that exceed the attachment point, stated as a dollar amount of loss or as a loss ratio, and that occur over a specified period, usually one year.

liability insurance and covers aggregated losses that exceed the attachment point and occur over a stated period, usually one year. The attachment point in an aggregate excess of loss treaty can be stated as a dollar amount of loss or as a loss ratio. When the attachment point is stated as a loss ratio, the treaty is called "stop loss reinsurance." With stop loss reinsurance, the primary insurer's retention may be a loss ratio of 90 percent, and the reinsurer would indemnify losses up to a loss ratio of 120 percent. The reinsurance agreement in this instance would specify the attachment point and reinsurance limit as "30% xs 90% loss ratio." The primary insurer retains responsibility for losses above a loss ratio of 120 percent.

Aggregate excess of loss treaties are less common and can be more expensive than the other types of excess of loss reinsurance. The treaty usually specifies an attachment point and reinsurance limit that does not result in the primary insurer earning a profit on the reinsured policies when the policies were unprofitable overall. Most aggregate excess of loss treaties also contain a coparticipation provision of 5 to 10 percent to provide the primary insurer with an incentive to efficiently handle claims that exceed the attachment point. See the exhibit "Aggregate Excess of Loss Reinsurance Example."

Aggregate Excess of Loss Reinsurance Example

Brookgreen Insurance Company (Brookgreen) offers liability insurance to a tavern. This general liability policy has an each occurrence limit of $1 million and a general aggregate limit (capping the number of per occurrence dollars the insurer will pay during the policy period) of $2 million.

Brookgreen purchases facultative per occurrence excess of loss reinsurance for this policy in excess of $500,000. This insurance protects Brookgreen against any loss above $500,000 but would not respond to any loss below $500,000. If the tavern suffered three separate losses of $450,000 each, Brookgreen would not recover from the reinsurer even though the total of all losses under the policy during the policy period exceeded $500,000.

Because of concern about aggregation of losses from this and similar loss exposures, Brookgreen decides to purchase a $7 million xs $3 million aggregate excess of loss treaty that is applicable to all of its liability insurance. This treaty further stabilizes losses by indemnifying Brookgreen for accumulations of losses exceeding $3 million. For example, Brookgreen insures a cosmetics manufacturer whose wrinkle cream causes an increase in susceptibility to skin cancer. Brookgreen settles a class action suit brought by customers who used the product for $15 million. Brookgreen's net loss is $8 million (the $3 million retention plus $5 million loss amount that exceeds the $7 million limit).

[DA05097]

Because of the stabilizing effect of aggregate excess of loss reinsurance on a primary insurer's loss ratio, it may be argued that it is the only type of reinsurance needed. However, aggregate excess of loss reinsurance has limited availability. When used, the aggregate excess of loss reinsurer usually expects

to pay losses only after the primary insurer has been reimbursed under its other reinsurance agreements.

While a catastrophe excess of loss reinsurance agreement only protects against catastrophe losses (loss severity), an aggregate excess of loss reinsurance agreement provides the reinsured with broader protection. This is because the aggregate excess of loss reinsurance agreement includes catastrophes and unforeseen accumulations of non-catastrophic losses during a specified period (addressing both loss severity and loss frequency).

REINSURANCE CONCERNS OF RISK MANAGEMENT PROFESSIONALS

Risk management professionals often are not involved with negotiating reinsurance contracts, because, typically, only insurers and reinsurers enter into reinsurance contracts. However, situations exist in which a risk management professional would deal directly with a reinsurer.

A risk management professional might deal directly with a reinsurer in these situations:

- A reinsurer takes the place of an insurer as a result of a portfolio reinsurance arrangement.
- A reinsurer takes the place of an insurer through a cut-through endorsement added to an insurance policy.
- An organization establishes a subsidiary that insures or reinsures the organization's loss exposures.
- An organization purchases reinsurance for a pool of which it is a member.
- A reinsurer or several reinsurers team up with an insurer or several insurers to provide coverage.

Portfolio Reinsurance Arrangements

As a means through which an insurer can transfer all of the liability of specified loss exposures, portfolio reinsurance is commonly used by insurers who are withdrawing from a type of insurance or market segment. Portfolio reinsurance is not a legal substitution of one insurer for another. However, after the portfolio reinsurance transaction, the original insurer only provides services, while all losses are paid by another insurer.

A risk management professional whose insurance plan has been reinsured through a portfolio reinsurance arrangement should learn the details of the transaction in order to ascertain that the insured organization's coverage is maintained and that the reinsurer is at least as financially sound as the retiring insurer.

Portfolio reinsurance arrangements usually satisfy an immediate need of the insurer and pay minimal regard to the underlying insureds. Consequently, most risk management professionals would likely reconsider an insurance placement that is included as part of a portfolio reinsurance transaction and change insurers either immediately or at the expiration of the policy period.

Cut-Through Endorsements

The usefulness of insurance depends on the financial solvency of the insurer. Consequently, when the insured organization or its lenders become concerned about the insurer's financial solvency (evidenced by the insurer's financial rating) the organization may change insurers or seek additional security from the insurer. One means of accomplishing this is through the addition of a **cut-through endorsement** to the organization's insurance policy.

Cut-through endorsement
An endorsement that provides that, in the event of the insolvency of the primary insurer, the reinsurer directly assumes the obligations of the primary insurer.

An insured's or a third party's right of recovery from an insurer "cuts through" directly to the reinsurer.

The insured is not a party to the reinsurance agreement and, without the endorsement, has no right to recover directly from the reinsurer. Normally, the insured organization needs no such right because the solvent primary insurer fulfills its obligation under the underlying policy and is indemnified by the reinsurer to the extent specified in the reinsurance treaty.

However, the liquidator of an insolvent primary insurer is not able to treat insurance claimants any differently than any other creditor of the primary insurer in satisfying unmet obligations. The cut-through endorsement provides the insured with direct rights against the reinsurer, bypassing the primary insurer's insolvency proceedings.

A cut-through endorsement is usually requested when the primary insurer does not satisfy the financial standards established by the insured organization's lender. The endorsement can take many forms, depending on the needs of the parties and the applicable state law. Typically, the cut-through endorsement states that reinsurance proceeds will be paid directly to the payee in the event that the primary insurer is unable to pay a loss. The payee may be the insured organization, the lender, or both. The reinsurer will respond to the insured organization and the lender, as their interests may appear, up to the limit of the reinsurance treaty.

The insolvent primary insurer's liquidator sometimes contests the enforcement of the cut-through endorsement because it reduces available funds that can be directed to other creditors. In some instances, reinsurers have been forced to pay claims twice—once on behalf of the insured under the terms of the cut-through endorsement, and again to the liquidator of the insolvent primary insurer.

Reinsurers prefer to avoid cut-through endorsements because of the administrative expenses involved in tracking them and the potential for third-party liability. However, reinsurers usually will accommodate an insurer's requests

for cut-through endorsements because it is in both the insurer's and reinsurer's best interests to retain the insured organization's business.

Reinsurance Through a Subsidiary

Many organizations form subsidiaries called captive insurers as a risk financing technique. However, captive insurers often rely on reinsurance as the primary means to transfer risk from the organization's economic family. Captive insurers can directly insure the organization's loss exposures, or they can operate as a reinsurer for the commercial insurer that provides the organization's primary insurance.

Reinsuring a Pool

Risk management representatives of pool participants often serve on governing committees of the pool and as informal advisers to the pool's management. Consequently, they must be concerned with the financial strength, integrity, and operating efficiency of the pool's reinsurer, which all affect the pool's reliability, and consequentially, the solidity and effectiveness of the organization's risk financing program.

Pools often purchase excess of loss reinsurance to provide large-line capacity to their insureds and to stabilize their net underwriting results. Although this excess of loss reinsurance is usually purchased on a treaty basis, it is sometimes purchased on a facultative basis. Reinsurers can help the management of a pool by providing underwriting expertise. In many cases, reinsurers assist a pool in underwriting unrelated third-party business (business not related to its owners).

Cooperation Between Insurers and Reinsurers to Provide Capacity

Insurers and reinsurers sometimes cooperate to provide the capacity an insured requires. In these situations, the insured's coverage needs are often divided into layers to which insurers and reinsurers both subscribe. For example, insurers and reinsurers jointly participated to fulfill the property coverage needs of the owners of the World Trade Center in New York City.

SUMMARY

Reinsurance is the transfer of insurance risk from one insurer to another through a contractual agreement under which the reinsurer agrees, in return for a reinsurance premium, to indemnify the primary insurer for some or all the financial consequences of the loss exposures covered by the reinsurance contract. Reinsurance performs these principal functions for primary insurers: increase large-line capacity, provide catastrophe protection, stabilize loss

experience, provide surplus relief, facilitate withdrawal from a market segment, and provide underwriting guidance.

Reinsurance is available from professional reinsurers; reinsurance departments of primary insurers; and reinsurance pools, syndicates, and associations. A direct writing reinsurer is a professional reinsurer that deals directly with primary insurers. Reinsurers also may deal with primary insurers through reinsurance intermediaries. Some primary insurers also serve as reinsurers, either only to affiliates or to both affiliated and unaffiliated insurers.

Reinsurance pools, syndicates, and associations are groups of insurers that share the loss exposures of the group. Several reinsurance professional and trade associations serve member companies and provide information to interested parties.

The two types of reinsurance transactions are treaty reinsurance and facultative reinsurance. Treaty reinsurance agreements provide coverage for an entire class or portfolio of loss exposures and involve an ongoing relationship between the primary insurer and the reinsurer. Treaty reinsurance agreements are usually obligatory; loss exposures must be ceded to and accepted by the reinsurer. Facultative reinsurance agreements insure individual loss exposures. Under a facultative agreement, the reinsurer is usually not obligated to accept the loss exposure submitted by the primary insurer.

Reinsurance agreements can be categorized as either pro rata (proportional) or excess of loss (nonproportional) reinsurance. Pro rata reinsurance involves the proportional sharing of amounts of insurance, policy premiums, and losses (including loss adjustment expenses) between the primary insurer and the reinsurer. Pro rata reinsurance can be either on a quota share basis or on a surplus share basis. With excess of loss reinsurance, the reinsurer responds to a loss only when the loss exceeds the primary insurer's retention (often referred to as the attachment point).

Reinsurance is an essential element of the insurer's financial security and, consequently, of the financial security of the organizations that insurers insure. Because reinsurance can affect the availability and affordability of primary insurance as well as other aspects of a risk financing plan, risk management professionals should understand how reinsurance operates. Also, reinsurance is often a key component of a captive insurance plan, another tool a risk management professional can use to manage an organization's risks.

ASSIGNMENT NOTES

1. Many of the definitions of terms in this section were adapted from the Reinsurance Association of America's (RAA) *Glossary of Terms*. The RAA's website is www.reinsurance.org (accessed March 31, 2010).
2. Insurers that are publicly traded are usually referred to as "stock insurers" to differentiate them from "mutual insurers," which are owned by their policyholders.

3. Intermediaries and Reinsurance Underwriters Association, www.irua.com (accessed May 12, 2010).
4. Brokers & Reinsurance Markets Association, www.brma.org (accessed May 12, 2010).
5. Reinsurance Association of America, www.reinsurance.org (accessed May 12, 2010).

Direct Your Learning

7

Captive Insurance

Educational Objectives

After learning the content of this assignment, you should be able to:

- Describe the purpose and characteristics of captive insurance plans.
- Describe the types of captive insurance plans available.
- Describe the advantages and disadvantages of using a captive insurance plan.
- Describe the following considerations for forming and operating a captive insurance plan:
  - Conducting a feasibility study
  - Operating as a reinsurer or a direct writing captive insurer
  - Selecting lines of business
  - Setting premium arrangement
  - Determining captive domicile

Outline

Captive Insurance

7

PURPOSE AND CHARACTERISTICS OF CAPTIVE INSURANCE PLANS

Organizations that are willing to retain a significant share of their own losses in exchange for greater flexibility often form their own insurer to address their risk financing needs. This once-novel approach to handling hazard risk, called a captive insurance plan, is now a relatively common way for organizations to reduce their overall cost of risk.

A **captive insurer's** primary purpose usually is to reduce the parent's cost of risk. The captive insurer's relationship with its parent is just like any other insurer's. A captive insurer collects premiums, issues policies, and pays covered losses (both first-party and third-party losses). See the exhibit "The Relationship of a Captive Insurer to Its Parent(s) (Insured)."

Captive insurer, or captive
A subsidiary formed to insure the loss exposures of its parent company and the parent's affiliates.

The Relationship of a Captive Insurer to Its Parent(s) (Insured)

[DA01363]

Most captive insurers purchase reinsurance, usually on an excess of loss basis, to transfer some of their loss exposures to another insurer. Reinsurance provides a captive insurer with many benefits, including the ability to cover large losses.

Retaining and Transferring Losses

Captive insurers often retain losses up to a certain point and then transfer them beyond that point. The exhibit regarding retained and transferred losses illustrates these losses under a hypothetical captive insurance plan in which the captive insurer issues policies and purchases both per occurrence and annual aggregate excess of loss reinsurance. (Aggregate excess of loss reinsurance is usually difficult to obtain, even in a soft market, so most captive insurers don't purchase it.) See the exhibit "Retained and Transferred Losses Under a Hypothetical Captive Insurance Plan."

Retained and Transferred Losses Under a Hypothetical Captive Insurance Plan

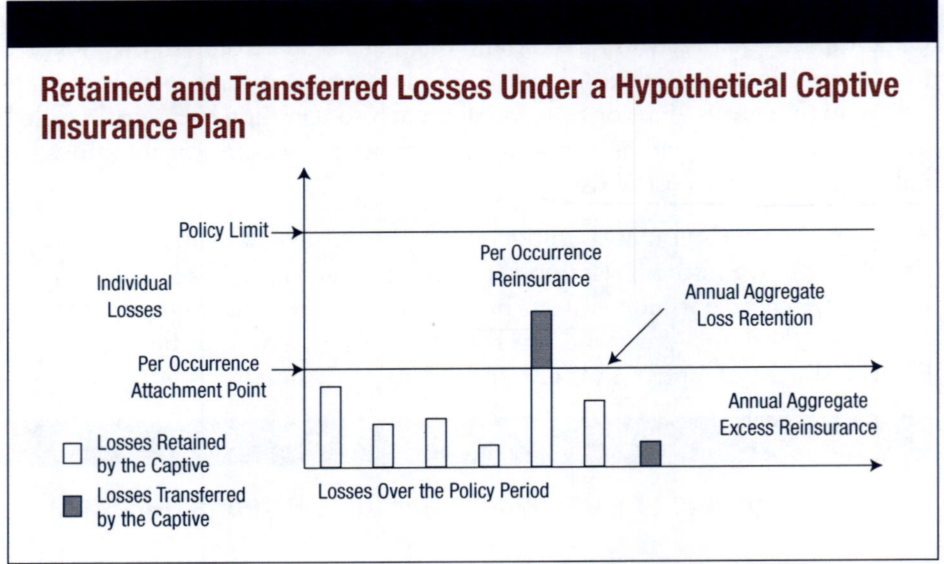

[DA01364]

The net retention of the captive for each occurrence is the amount below the per occurrence attachment point of the reinsurance. This is similar in concept to a loss limit under a retrospective rating plan. If the captive insurer can purchase annual aggregate excess reinsurance, then its annual retained losses are capped at an annual maximum amount. This is similar in concept to a maximum premium under a retrospective rating plan.

Combining a Captive Insurance Plan With Transfer and Hybrid Risk Financing Plans

An organization's risk financing program that includes a captive insurance plan usually combines the captive insurance plan with a hybrid or transfer plan. As with a retrospective rating plan, the captive insurance plan generally is used for the first layer of losses, where there is a relatively high loss frequency and low-to-medium loss severity, with a transfer or a hybrid plan above it that covers the higher-severity losses.

For example, assume that an organization establishes a captive insurer to cover its general liability loss exposures. The captive insurer issues an insurance policy with a limit of $1 million per occurrence to its parent organization. Further, assume that the captive insurer purchases excess of loss reinsurance of $750,000 excess of $250,000 per occurrence.

Excess insurance may be above the $1 million layer of loss covered by the captive insurer. The exhibit shows how the organization could combine excess insurance with the captive insurance plan just described. See the exhibit "Captive Insurance Plan Combined With Excess Insurance."

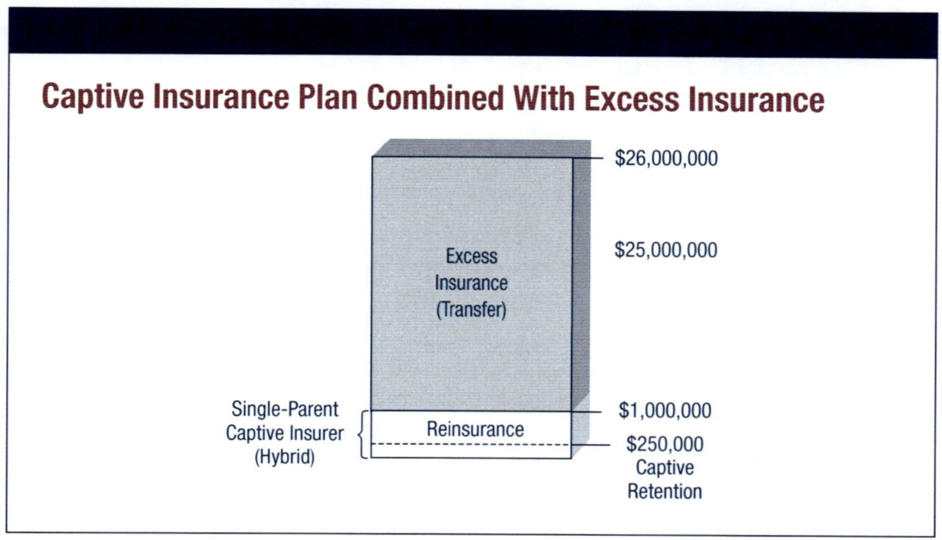

[DA01366]

The organization purchases excess insurance on a guaranteed-cost basis with a limit of $25 million per occurrence to sit directly above the $1 million per occurrence layer of loss covered by the captive insurer. Therefore, the total limit of insurance available to the organization per occurrence is $26 million.

The organization, in effect, retains the first $250,000 per occurrence because its captive insurer retains $250,000 per occurrence, net of reinsurance. The portion of each covered loss that exceeds $250,000 per occurrence up to the policy limit of S1 million per occurrence is transferred to reinsurers through the organization's captive insurer.

To transfer risk, an organization might purchase excess insurance instead of purchasing reinsurance through its captive. For example, with the captive insurance plan just described, the organization might decide to purchase insurance for $750,000 per occurrence excess of $250,000 per occurrence, rather than have the captive purchase reinsurance for the same layer of loss. In this case, the captive would issue a policy with a limit of $250,000 per occurrence rather than $1 million per occurrence. See the exhibit "Purchasing Excess Insurance Instead of Reinsuring a Captive Insurer."

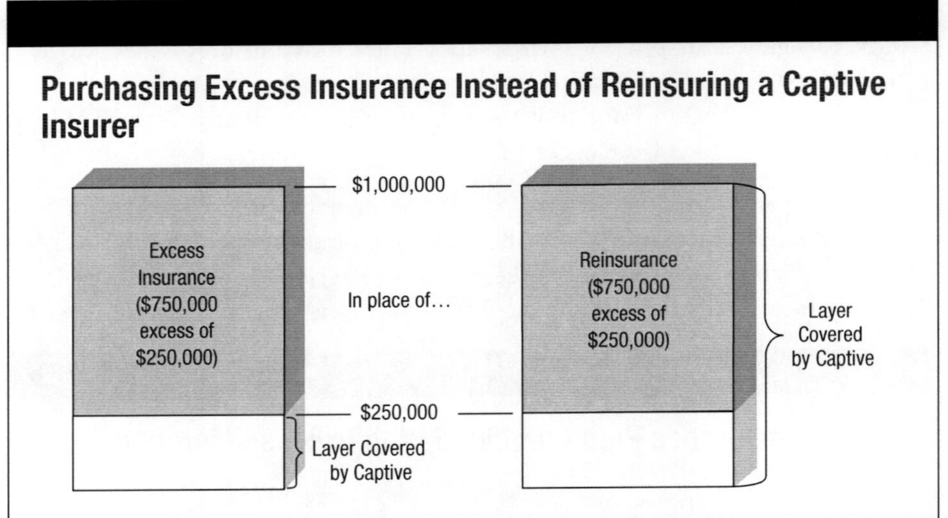

[DA01367]

The characteristics of a captive insurer normally involve both retention and transfer. Therefore, captive insurance often is a hybrid risk financing plan. The severity of the losses covered by a captive insurer, because losses are partially retained, is typically low to moderate. Further, because a captive insurer acts as any other insurer does, the losses are funded.

Because the captive owner/parent is ultimately responsible for expenses—such as claim administration, loss control, and underwriting—the administrative requirements of a captive insurance plan are substantial. The exhibit summarizes the general characteristics of a common captive insurance plan. Several of these general characteristics change from one type of captive insurance plan to another. See the exhibit "General Characteristics of a Common Captive Insurance Plan."

General Characteristics of a Common Captive Insurance Plan

Retention/ Transfer	Severity of Losses	Funded/ Unfunded	Administrative Requirements
Hybrid (usually)	Low to medium	Usually funded	High

[DA01368]

TYPES OF CAPTIVE INSURANCE PLANS

An organization's decision to use a captive insurance plan is the result of a process that considers the advantages and disadvantages of using such a plan relative to other risk financing alternatives.

Each type of captive insurance plan has unique features that address situations faced by an owner/insured(s). Captive insurance plan types include:

- Single-parent (or pure) captive
- Group captive
- Risk retention group
- Agency captive
- Rent-a-captive
- Protected cell company

Single-Parent (or Pure) Captive

A **single-parent captive, or pure captive,** is a captive insurer owned by one company that insures all or part of the loss exposures of that company. Because a captive is an insurer, it requires an investment of capital by its parent(s), as well as expenditures to manage the company and to pay accounting, auditing, legal, and underwriting expenses.

Single-parent captive (pure captive)
A captive insurer owned by one company that insures all or part of the loss exposures of that company or its subsidiaries.

For a captive insurer to be economically viable, it has to insure loss exposures that generate substantial premium revenues to cover these expenditures. Consequently, single-parent captive insurers generally require a minimum annual premium of $2 million.[1]

A single-parent captive is a hybrid risk financing plan because, from its parent's point of view, a single-parent captive usually combines elements of retention and transfer. Because a single-parent captive covers its parent's losses and is part of the same economic family as its parent, losses retained by the captive are, in effect, retained by its parent. For the same reasons, losses transferred by the captive insurer (for example, through reinsurance or some other means) are, in effect, transferred by its parent. Some single-parent captive insurers that do not purchase reinsurance retain all of their losses and therefore should not be considered a hybrid plan.

Group Captive

A **group captive** is a captive insurer owned by a group of companies, usually operating similar businesses, rather than a single parent. A group captive is similar to a mutual insurer except that the insureds (owners) under a group captive exercise significantly more control over the management of the company than do the insureds under a typical commercial insurer.

Group captive
A captive insurer owned by a group of companies, usually operating similar businesses, rather than a single parent.

An **association captive** is a group captive that is sponsored by an association. Many organizations consider the opportunity to obtain insurance through an association captive as one of the benefits of being a member of the association. For example, an association of paint manufacturers might sponsor a captive insurer for the benefit of its members.

Association captive
A group captive sponsored by an association.

A group captive (or an association captive) is considered a hybrid or a transfer plan, depending on its design. If each member (insured) of a group captive retains a portion of its own losses within the captive and shares the balance of its losses with other members, then the group captive is considered a hybrid plan. If each member shares all of its losses with the other members, then the group captive is considered a transfer plan.

Risk Retention Group

Risk retention group
A group captive formed under the requirements of the Liability Risk Retention Act of 1986 to insure the parent organizations.

A **risk retention group** is a group captive formed under the requirements of the U.S. Liability Risk Retention Act of 1986 to provide liability coverage (except personal insurance, employers liability, and workers compensation). To form a risk retention group, all of its owners must be from the same industry and must be insured by the risk retention group. Conversely, all insureds must be owners.

A major benefit of a risk retention group is that it needs to be licensed in only one state in order to provide liability coverage to group members anywhere in the United States. The act supersedes state law that requires an insurer to be licensed in every state in which it sells insurance, thereby saving the risk retention group the expense of complying with regulations in each of the fifty states.

Agency Captive

Agency captive
A type of group captive that is owned by insurance agents or brokers rather than by the organizations insured.

An **agency captive** is a type of group captive that is owned by insurance agents or brokers rather than by the organizations insured. Agency captives are often formed in response to hard markets to insure select accounts for which there is a limited or nonexistent market.

An agency may place a single line of insurance for heterogeneous businesses (such as workers compensation for all commercial insureds) in the captive or multiple lines for homogeneous businesses (such as businessowners policies for retail stores). An agency captive provides a way for agents or brokers to assume a portion of risk and, in turn, generate underwriting and investment income.

Rent-a-Captive

Rent-a-captive
An arrangement under which an organization rents capital from a captive, to which it pays premiums and receives reimbursement for its losses.

A **rent-a-captive** is an arrangement under which an organization rents capital from a captive insurer, to which it pays premium and receives reimbursement for its losses. The organization also receives credit for underwriting profits and investment income. Consequently, the organization benefits from using a captive insurer but is not required to invest its own capital. Each insured keeps its own premium and loss account, so no risk shifting or distribution occurs among the members of a rent-a-captive.

With some types of rent-a-captives, the insured organization must purchase nonvoting preferred stock and receives dividends on the stock equal to its underwriting profit and the investment income earned on its unearned premiums and loss reserves. If a plan does not involve the purchase of nonvoting preferred stock, then the rent-a-captive organization returns underwriting profit and investment income through some other means, such as policyholder dividends. The rent-a-captive organization charges a fee for its services. Rent-a-captives provide a means for an organization to form a captive insurer quickly without tying up capital.

Protected Cell Company

A **protected cell company (PCC)** is a group captive in which each participant pays premiums and receives reimbursement for its losses from, as well as credit for, underwriting profits and investment income, similar to a rent-a-captive. With a PCC, each participant is assured that other participants will not be able to access its capital and surplus in the event the other participants become insolvent. Each participant is also assured that third-party creditors cannot access its assets. This protection does not necessarily exist with a rent-a-captive structure, which involves the purchase of preferred stock by participants.

Protected cell company (PCC)
A corporate entity separated into cells so that each participating company owns an entire cell but only a portion of the overall company.

ADVANTAGES AND DISADVANTAGES OF USING A CAPTIVE INSURANCE PLAN

To evaluate a captive insurance plan, a risk management professional must understand its advantages and disadvantages.

Because single-parent captive insurance plans are usually hybrid risk financing plans, they have many of the advantages and disadvantages of both retention and transfer. The degree to which these advantages and disadvantages apply to a specific single-parent captive insurance plan depends on the design of the plan—that is, the amount of retention versus transfer built into the plan. The same is true of a group captive.

Advantages of a Captive Insurance Plan

Captive insurance plans offer many advantages in comparison with other risk financing plans. Some of the more prominent advantages an organization may experience as a result of forming or joining a captive insurer include these:

- Reducing the cost of risk
- Benefiting from cash flow
- Obtaining insurance not otherwise available
- Having direct access to reinsurers

- Negotiating with insurers
- Centralizing loss retention
- Obtaining potential cash flow advantages on income taxes
- Controlling losses
- Obtaining rate equity

Reducing the Cost of Risk

A captive insurance plan can reduce an organization's cost of risk over the long run when compared to guaranteed-cost insurance because it involves retention; saves the acquisition costs of obtaining insurance; reduces underwriting expenses; saves the cost of the commercial insurer's overhead and profit; and allows for investment income from premium, loss reserve, and collateral investment dollars.

In addition, a group captive, if operated efficiently, can reduce a member organization's cost of risk by distributing the cost of administering the captive insurer among several members. Risk management professionals often consider reducing the cost of risk, and thereby preserving the resources of an organization, to be the most important advantage of a captive insurance plan.

Benefiting From Cash Flow

A captive insurer allows the insured(s) to benefit from the cash flow available on losses that are paid out over time because, as a funded plan, the captive earns investment income on premium funds that have not yet been paid out for claims. This includes investment income on loss reserves and unearned premiums. The insured benefits because it is part of the same economic family as the captive insurer.

However, the return on the capital invested in the captive is likely to be less than the insured's cost of capital. This constitutes an opportunity cost for the insured organization because it would realize a net savings if it could invest some or all of the cash tied up in the captive in its main business. The insured organization can retain some of the cash it would otherwise pay in premiums to the captive insurer by using a paid loss retrospective rating plan when paying premiums to its captive insurer. Also, some jurisdictions allow a captive insurer to lend funds back to its parent (the insured). This arrangement also overcomes the opportunity cost problem.

Obtaining Insurance Not Otherwise Available

Another advantage of a captive insurance plan is that its parent organization can obtain insurance coverage that is not available from commercial insurers. Such coverage includes liability insurance for environmental, products, and professional loss exposures. To obtain these kinds of coverage, the parent pays a premium to its captive, which then issues an appropriate insurance policy.

One could argue that using a single-parent captive to insure hard-to-place coverages does not constitute insurance because the parent owns the captive and, therefore, retains the premium and losses arising from its own loss exposures. However, in such cases, the captive may be able to negotiate a favorable reinsurance arrangement, which, in effect, transfers the parent's loss exposures just as a traditional insurance arrangement would.

Having Direct Access to Reinsurers

A captive insurer provides the insured organization with direct access to the international market of reinsurers, which can be more flexible than insurers in terms of underwriting and rating. A captive insurer that uses reinsurance can capture any ceding commission on the reinsurance that would otherwise be paid to a commercial insurer.

In addition, by removing the primary commercial insurer, the insured organization saves substantial markup costs. However, the advantage of gaining direct access to reinsurers is not as significant as it once was, because risk management professionals can often now deal directly with reinsurers, even in the absence of a captive insurance arrangement.

Negotiating With Insurers

The existence of a captive insurer can improve an insured's negotiating power with commercial insurers. Assume, for example, that an airline forms a single-parent captive insurer to retain a quota share percentage of its aircraft hull insurance. If premiums increase in the aircraft hull insurance market, the airline might increase the share it places in its captive. However, the fact that the airline has this option might increase its bargaining power with its commercial insurers, who might lower the airline's premium so as not to lose business to the captive.

Centralizing Loss Retention

Another advantage of a captive insurance plan is that the insured organization can use it to centralize retained losses that are spread throughout its subsidiaries. Centralization can result in savings to the insured organization because of the lower long-term cost of retention.

For example, if the management of a large multinational corporation wants to retain a significantly higher level of loss than each of its subsidiaries, it could use a single-parent captive to pool its losses on a worldwide basis and retain more losses than each of its subsidiaries, which purchase insurance from the captive. See the exhibit "Retaining Worldwide Risk of Loss in a Captive."

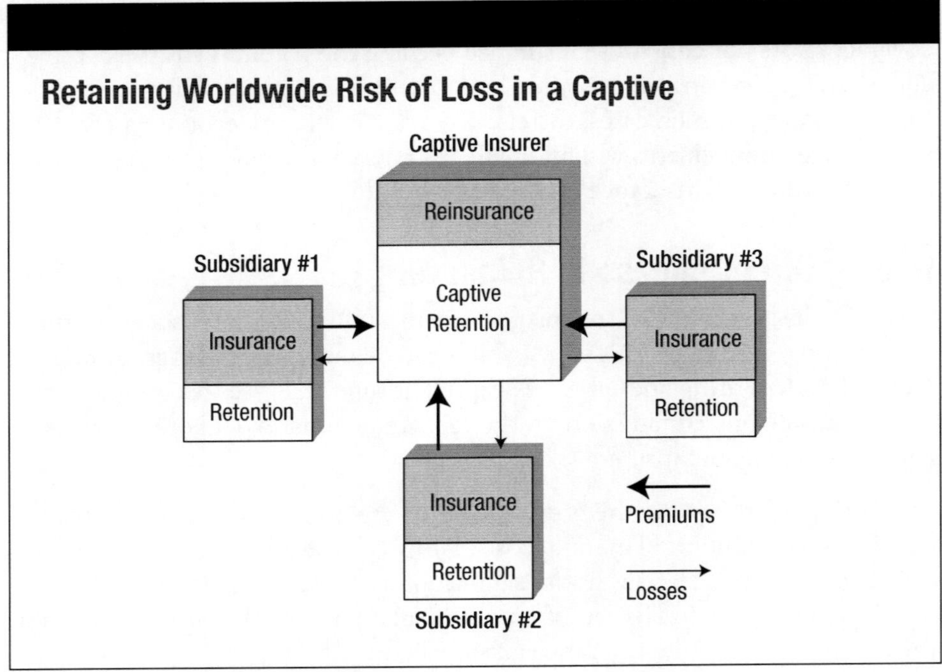

[DA01370]

Obtaining Potential Cash Flow Advantages on Income Taxes

Generally, a parent company may deduct from its taxes only the associated losses and other expenses that are paid by its captive insurer. In some cases, however, a parent company can achieve an even greater tax advantage by deducting from its taxes the premiums that it pays to its captive insurer.

The Internal Revenue Service's (IRS's) determination of whether premiums paid to a captive insurer are tax-deductible is based primarily on two factors: **risk shifting** and **risk distribution**.[2]

Risk shifting
The transfer of risk of loss to an insurer.

Risk distribution
The sharing of risk by an insurer among its insureds.

Determining the tax-deductibility of the premiums paid to a captive insurer is complex. Tax Court cases and IRS rulings will continue to be applied to specific situations that will further define the conditions under which premiums paid to a captive insurer are and are not tax-deductible. See the exhibit "Tax Court Cases Relating to Captive Insurers."

Many captive insurers are domiciled in offshore jurisdictions that have little or no income tax, such as the Bahamas, Bermuda, or Cayman Islands. Establishing a captive insurer in such a location allows a parent located in a high-income-tax country to save taxes if it deducts the premiums it pays to its captive and generates profits from the captive that are, in turn, subject to little or no income tax.

In recent years, however, many countries, including the United States and the United Kingdom, have closed this loophole by requiring the parent company to pay tax in its home country on some or all of the profit generated by its offshore captive, even if the profit has not been paid as a dividend to the parent.

Tax Court Cases Relating to Captive Insurers

The 1989 landmark Tax Court case involving Humana Corporation and its subsidiaries affirmed that the insurance premiums a parent company pays to its captive insurer generally are not tax-deductible. Humana owned a captive insurer to which it and each of its subsidiaries paid premiums. The Tax Court denied a deduction of the premiums paid by Humana to its captive insurer because it was the parent of the captive. The Tax Court did, however, allow a deduction for premiums paid to the captive by each of Humana's subsidiaries. This allowance was based on the Tax Court's conclusion that the relationship between Humana's subsidiaries was a brother-sister relationship—the relationship that exists when subsidiaries are owned by the same parent company. If a brother-sister relationship exists, the risk shifting and distribution of loss exposures to the captive insurer are sufficient to allow the subsidiaries to deduct the premiums they pay to the captive insurer.

Based on prior rulings, a captive may need to insure as many as twelve subsidiaries that share a brother-sister relationship in order for its parent to deduct its premiums, but only if those subsidiaries transfer a roughly equal amount of loss exposures. Specifically, no subsidiary should absorb less than 5 percent or more than 15 percent of the risk distribution (per Ruling 2002-90).

The brother-sister relationship is one of several exceptions to the general rule of the Humana Corporation case that the insurance premium paid by a parent organization to its captive is normally not tax-deductible. Another exception involves third-party business—business that is not directly related to the captive's parent(s) or its subsidiaries. Some early tax rulings determined that if a large percentage of the captive's premiums are derived from third-party business, then the captive is considered to be operating at an arm's length from its parent. In such a case, the premiums paid by the parent to the captive are tax-deductible. However, these early rulings did not determine how much of a captive insurer's premiums must be from third-party businesses in order to render the captive insurer an arm's-length insurer.

In 1991, in three separate cases involving AMERCO, Harper, and Sears, the Tax Court allowed a deduction for premiums paid by each of the parents to their captives. In each case, the captive wrote substantial third-party business, ranging from 99 percent of the premium in the Sears case (Allstate was the insurance subsidiary in question) to less than 30 percent in the Harper case. These cases helped solidify the argument that substantial third-party business should enable a company to take tax deductions for premiums paid to its captive.

In May 2005, the IRS issued Ruling 2005-40, in which it held that a captive insuring one policyholder cannot accomplish adequate risk distribution to allow the premiums paid to the captive to be tax-deductible. In the same ruling, the IRS also stated that if the captive were to insure two policyholders, one of which absorbed a proportionately high amount of risk (a 90/10 split, for example), the premiums paid to the captive would again not be tax-deductible. The ruling did not address situations in which the split was more balanced.

[DA08634]

Controlling Losses

Because a captive insurance plan involves retention, an insured organization that controls its losses is able to save payments for losses and loss expenses. For a premium arrangement with a captive on a guaranteed-cost basis, the savings are immediately captured within the captive. For a premium arrangement with a captive on a retrospectively rated basis, much of the savings accrues directly to the insured organization. In addition, captive insurers can offer specialized risk control services that are similar to other commercial insurers.

Obtaining Rate Equity

An organization may have sufficient historical data to accurately predict its future losses with reasonable confidence.

If the predicted losses are substantially lower than the premium being charged by its commercial insurer (taking into account the acquisition costs, overhead, and profit of the insurer) the risk management professional often concludes that the insured organization's premium is a result of the poor loss histories of other organizations with which it is pooled. In addition, raising the amount of retention does not always result in substantial premium reduction. A captive insurer has the rating flexibility to charge premiums that may more accurately reflect the predicted losses of its parent(s) and affiliates.

Disadvantages of a Captive Insurance Plan

When compared with other risk financing plans, a captive insurance plan presents several disadvantages to the organization using it:

- Capital requirements and start-up costs
- Sensitivity to losses
- Pressure from parent company management
- Payment of premium taxes and residual market loadings

Capital and Start-Up Costs

A captive insurance plan involves a commitment of capital and start-up costs not incurred with other risk financing plans. Initial capital requirements can range from $120,000 to well over $1 million, depending on domicile and lines of business that are written.[3]

Capital must be committed for several years. This requirement can, however, be met by using a letter of credit, which, in a captive insurance market, is a financial instrument issued by a bank at the request of a captive insurer in which the bank agrees to honor a demand for payment made by a third party, which can be the captive's reinsurer or insurance regulator. Some captive domiciles' insurance regulators will allow letters of credit to satisfy the entire capital requirement.

Sensitivity to Losses

Captive insurance plans involve retention of losses, a potential disadvantage of their use. If the losses retained are higher than forecasted and exceed allocated funds, the financial solvency of the captive could be threatened. Financial insolvency would then prevent the payment of the parent company's losses.

This disadvantage is especially relevant when the parent uses a group captive plan. Any of the insured members of a group captive that experience a particularly poor year of losses with high enough coverage limits could financially cripple the captive, regardless of the excellent loss histories of the other members.

This peril of participating in a group captive can, at least partially, be prevented by using a rent-a-captive or a protected cell company captive, which segregate the underwriting account of each member.

Pressure From Parent Company Management

Captive insurers exist for the benefit of the parent organization. Consequently, another of their disadvantages is that they must insure the risks required by their parents. However, the pressure from the parent organization's management to insure risks in an economically advantageous fashion must be moderated.

The IRS requires an arm's-length relationship between the parent and its captive for the premiums paid to the captive insurer to be tax-deductible. Further, the reinsurer of the captive will likely be sensitive to overt pressure from the parent's management that may cause the captive's underwriting standards to be too lenient, its premiums too low, its claim payments too generous, or the lack of cooperation from the parent too easily ignored. This disadvantage may be of greater concern with a single-parent captive than with a group or association captive.

Premium Taxes and Residual Market Loadings

Another disadvantage of a captive insurance plan is that the losses retained by a captive insurer are paid for by the parent company as a premium on which premium taxes and residual market loadings are levied.

FORMATION AND OPERATION OF CAPTIVE INSURANCE PLANS

An organization considering a captive insurance plan must first determine whether forming or joining a captive insurer is feasible. Many of the considerations crucial to operating a captive can be addressed by a feasibility study.

If an organization deems a captive insurance plan feasible, it must resolve some additional considerations, such as whether to operate as a reinsurer or direct writing insurer, selecting lines of business to be covered through the captive, setting premium arrangements, and determining the captive domicile.

Conducting a Feasibility Study

An effective feasibility study should focus on an organization's goals for the captive insurance plan. This allows the organization to optimize the plan's design. As a prelude to conducting the study, an organization's management should carefully consider the decision to enter a captive insurance plan. It involves a multiyear commitment of substantial administrative and capital resources that could be invested at potentially higher rates of return elsewhere. This sacrifice of a possible higher return is often referred to as the opportunity cost. This cost can be measured, at least with respect to the capital resources used, by the parent company's borrowing rate or required rate of return on investment.

The feasibility study should contain an analysis of the parent company's current risk financing structure, which includes the type of insurance coverages used, the amounts of coverage purchased, retention levels, premiums paid, supporting collateral, and type of rating plans applied. The goal is to understand the costs and benefits of the current risk financing plan.

The study should then assess the exposure basis of the parent company, which includes sales, payroll, and property values. This assessment ideally should include several previous years to credibly project trends. Furthermore, the study should consider any management plans, such as a merger or an acquisition, that would affect the organization's loss exposures.

The study must also assess losses. The parent company's history of losses (both retained and transferred) from at least the previous five years should be assessed in terms of its ability to perform risk control and to forecast expected future losses. Entering a captive insurance plan will not resolve a risk control problem that must be separately addressed. Forecasting future expected losses will help the organization determine the recommended level of retention versus transfer per occurrence and in the aggregate when structuring the captive insurance plan's coverage.

The feasibility study should also include the creation of projected pro forma financial statements for the proposed captive. These statements should be prepared by a certified public accountant and include these elements:

- An income statement and balance sheet
- At least five years of projected *pro forma* financial results
- An accounting of the effects of all types of taxation (or an explanation of why a certain tax does not apply)

- At least one scenario that portrays worse-than-expected financial results and that demonstrates management has considered the possibility of financial impairment
- A detailed explanation of each assumption, such as expected loss ratio, interest rates, and year-to-year growth rates
- A model showing the minimum number of participants, premiums, and capital

Operating as a Reinsurer or a Direct Writing Captive Insurer

If the feasibility study supports a decision to form a captive insurer, the organization must decide whether it would like its captive to operate as a reinsurer or a direct writing captive insurer.

Most countries have regulations requiring insurers to be licensed. For example, most U.S. states require an insurer to be licensed to provide insurance for workers compensation and automobile liability loss exposures. Most captive insurers are not licensed to provide these types of insurance in the United States. To save the time and expense of obtaining such licenses, captive insurers usually operate as reinsurers behind U.S.-licensed insurers acting as **fronting companies**.

Fronting company
A licensed insurer that issues an insurance policy and reinsures the loss exposures back to a captive insurer owned by the insured organization.

By having its captive reinsure a fronting company, the insured can benefit from using a captive insurer while also complying with licensing requirements. In addition, a captive insurer that reinsures a fronting company usually satisfies other parties, such as mortgagees, loss payees, and business partners, that require the insured organization to purchase insurance from an established insurer with an acceptable rating from one of the major rating agencies, such as A.M. Best or Standard & Poor's.

However, for some types of insurance, a captive can operate as a **direct writing captive insurer**. For example, to provide many types of property, marine, and liability coverage in the U.S., an insurer does not need to be licensed. Therefore, a captive insurer can issue policies directly to its parent(s) and affiliates. However, the captive insurer must comply with nonadmitted insurer regulations in each state and pay premium taxes. As another example, a captive insurer domiciled in Dublin, Ireland, does not need a license to sell insurance directly for its parent's (and affiliates') operations located throughout the European Union.

Direct writing captive insurer
A captive insurer that issues policies directly to its parent(s) and affiliates and does not use a fronting company.

A major advantage of operating as a direct writing captive insurer is that a captive can save the fees charged by the fronting company, which range from 5 percent to 30 percent of premium.[4] This cost savings can make a direct writing captive insurance plan less expensive than commercial insurance and many other risk financing plans.

Selecting Lines of Business

Captive insurance plans are commonly used to cover lines of business that offer substantial cash flow. A captive insurance plan allows the insured to benefit from the cash flow available on losses that are paid out over time because the captive earns investment income on premium funds that have not yet been paid out for claims. This includes investment income on loss reserves and unearned premiums. Lines of business that offer the greatest cash flow benefit are long-tail lines such as workers compensation, general liability, and automobile liability. Captives may also be used to cover certain types of property losses as well as losses that fall under specialized types of business, such as products and environmental liability.

Setting Premium Arrangement

The premium arrangement between the parent (and subsidiaries) and the captive insurer (with or without a fronting company) can be on a guaranteed-cost basis or a retrospectively rated basis.

Under a guaranteed-cost arrangement, the insured organization pays a fixed premium rate, transferring the entire loss exposure to its captive. However, as mentioned, because the captive is part of the insured's economic family, any risk of loss retained by the captive is, in effect, retained by the insured.

If the premium arrangement is on a retrospectively rated basis, the premium rate adjusts based on a portion of the insured's covered losses during the policy period. In this case, the insured and its captive share the loss exposure (again, with any residual loss retained by the captive in effect retained by the parent).

The retrospectively rated premium can be paid to the captive on a paid loss or an incurred loss basis. If the premium is on a paid loss basis, the benefit of investment income on the loss reserves for the insured's retained losses resides with the insured rather than with its captive insurer. The opposite is true if the premium is on an incurred loss basis. See the exhibit "Using a Retrospective Rating Plan With a Captive Insurer."

A captive insurance plan is funded if a guaranteed cost or an incurred loss retrospective rating plan is used to determine the insured's premium paid by the insured. With these types of premium plans, funds are available within the captive to pay for losses as they become due. When a paid loss retrospective rating plan is used with a captive, the captive is unfunded for the portion of losses that the insured retains.

Determining Captive Domicile

Many jurisdictions encourage captive insurers to locate within their territories by offering favorable regulations and imposing few or no taxes. These jurisdictions see the captive insurance industry as an economic boost that provides employment and other income, such as annual registration fees.

Using a Retrospective Rating Plan With a Captive Insurer

Assume that DKF Manufacturing (DKF) establishes a single-parent captive insurer and uses it to cover losses arising from its automobile liability and general liability loss exposures up to a limit of $1 million per occurrence/accident. To comply with regulatory requirements, DKF's captive insurer reinsures a fronting company, which issues the insurance policies to DKF.

Also assume that the insurance arrangement between DKF and the fronting company is an incurred loss retrospective rating plan with a loss limit of $100,000 per occurrence/accident. Therefore, DKF retains the first $100,000 of its own losses. DKF's captive reinsures the fronting company on the same retrospectively rated basis. Therefore, the deposit premium and retrospective adjustments are passed among DKF, the fronting company, and DKF's captive as follows:

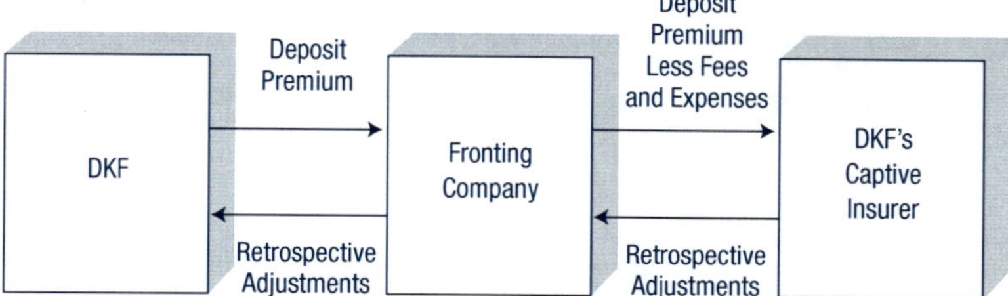

Assume that DKF's captive insurer purchases excess of loss reinsurance of $500,000 excess of $500,000 per occurrence/accident. (It does not purchase aggregate excess of loss reinsurance.) Therefore, the net loss exposure assumed by DKF's captive insurer is $400,000 per occurrence/accident excess of $100,000 per occurrence/accident, which is shown in the following diagram:

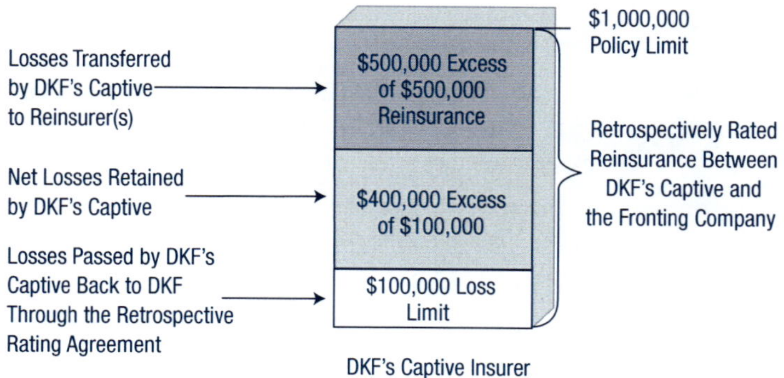

Because all retrospective rating agreements have a maximum premium, DKF's captive assumes the loss exposure that the losses subject to the loss limit of $100,000 will exceed the maximum premium under the retrospective rating plan between the fronting company and DKF.

To cover its reinsurance cost and its net retained loss exposure, DKF's captive builds an insurance charge (to account for the risk that the maximum premium might be exceeded) and an excess loss premium charge (to limit losses subject to retrospective rating to $100,000 per occurrence/accident) into the retrospective premium formula. In addition, DKF's captive includes its administrative costs and overhead in the basic premium, which is part of the retrospective premium formula.

[DA01373]

The top ten captive domiciles in 2010 by number of captives are, in descending order, Bermuda, Cayman Islands, Vermont, Guernsey, Anguilla, Luxembourg, Barbados, British Virgin Islands, Utah, and Hawaii.

Although a captive insurer can be domiciled anywhere, an organization usually places its captive insurer within a favorable jurisdiction for the formation and operation of captives. For example, some states require a single-parent captive to maintain the same minimum capital and surplus of several million dollars that would be required of a commercial insurer. Tying up this much capital would make most single-parent captives uneconomical. By contrast, Vermont has a minimum capital and surplus requirement of $250,000 for a single-parent captive. See the exhibit "Requirements for Forming a Captive Insurer in Utah."

Requirements for Forming a Captive Insurer in Utah

Utah is an onshore domicile for many captive insurers. Some of the requirements for establishing and operating a captive insurer in Utah are these:

Requirement	Details
Capital	Ranges from $100,000 to $500,000 by type of captive, although additional capital may be required (satisfied by cash or an irrevocable letter of credit).
Surplus	Ranges from $150,000 to $1,000,000 by type of captive (satisfied by cash or an irrevocable letter of credit).
Premium tax	$5,000 annual fee.
Examination	All captives must submit to examination by the commissioner every 1-3 years.
Annual reporting	A captive insurer must submit an annual report of its financial condition using generally accepted accounting principles unless the commissioner approves otherwise.
Reinsurance	Captive insurers may take credit for reserves on risks ceded to reinsurers if the captive complies with requirements of the Utah Insurance Code.
Local office	A captive insurer must maintain its principal place of business and hold at least one board of directors meeting each year in Utah. At least one board member must be a resident of the state. Captive insurance companies must appoint a resident agent for service of process.

www.irmi.com/online/rf/ch0apdxb/1lappbut.aspx (accessed November 8, 2011). [DA08515]

When evaluating a domicile for a captive insurer, the organization should consider these factors:

- Minimum premium requirements
- Minimum capitalization
- Solvency requirements
- Incorporation and registration expenses
- Local taxes
- Types of insurance that can be written
- General regulatory environment
- Investment restrictions
- Ease and reliability of communications and travel to and from the domicile
- Political stability
- Support infrastructure in terms of captive managers, claim administrators, bankers, accountants, lawyers, actuaries, and other services

SUMMARY

A captive insurer is a subsidiary that an organization forms to insure its own loss exposures. Organizations that are willing to retain a significant share of losses that offer substantial cash flow, such as those covered by workers compensation, general liability, and automobile liability policies, often pursue a captive insurance plan to finance risk. These losses are usually retained by the captive insurer up to a certain point, beyond which they are transferred. This combination of retention and transfer classifies captive insurance plans as hybrid risk financing plans.

A variety of captive insurance plans exist, each of which is designed to address particular needs of its parent organization. Types of captive plans include single parent (or pure) captives, group captives, risk retention groups, agency captives, rent-a-captives, and protected cell companies.

The advantages of using a captive insurance plan include are primarily financial—for example, reducing the cost of risk and benefiting from cash flow. In addition, a captive insurance plan can enable an organization to obtain insurance that otherwise would not be available. The disadvantages of using a captive insurance plan are likewise primarily financial. For example, the capital requirements and start-up costs for a captive are substantial.

After a feasibility study and resulting decision to pursue a captive insurance plan, the organization should decide whether the captive will operate as a reinsurer or direct writing captive insurer. The lines of business covered will need to be determined along with the premium. Additionally, the organization will select a domicile for the captive, usually based on a jurisdiction's financial and regulatory requirements.

ASSIGNMENT NOTES

1. International Risk Management Institute, Risk Financing: A Guide to Insurance Cash Flow (Dallas: International Risk Management Institute, Inc., 2000), 1st reprint, March 1997, p. IV.K.5.
2. For more information, including links to landmark court cases involving deductibility of premiums paid to captives, see www.assetprotectiontheory.com/captive_cases.htm.
3. Harold Skipper and W. Jean Kwon, Risk Management and Insurance: Perspectives in a Global Economy (Malden, Mass.: Blackwell Publishing, 2007), p 336.
4. Felix H. Kloman, "Captive Insurance Companies," in Harold D. Skipper Jr., International Risk and Insurance (Burr Ridge, Ill.: Irwin/McGraw-Hill, 1998), p. 681.

Direct Your Learning

8

Contractual Risk Transfer

Educational Objectives

After learning the content of this assignment, you should be able to:

- Describe the types of contractual risk transfer for hazard risk.
- Describe contractual risk transfer by type of transaction.
- Explain how contractual risk transfer for hazard risk can alter common-law liabilities.
- Describe the types of statutory limitations on hold-harmless agreements.
- Explain how to manage contractual risk transfer for hazard risk.

Outline

Contractual Risk Transfer

8

TYPES OF CONTRACTUAL RISK TRANSFER

Insurance contracts allow an organization to transfer many of the financial consequences of accidental losses to an insurance company, which pools the risks of many insureds. Contract law allows contracting parties to transfer risks in ways that do not involve insurance. Several types of contractual (noninsurance) risk transfer are available for hazard risk.

Organizations use contractual (noninsurance) risk transfer to transfer many of the same types of hazard risks that are covered by insurance. For example, two parties may agree that one party will reimburse the other for its loss or that one party will undertake an activity (and with it, absorb the accompanying risks) that the other party normally would perform. Under another possible contractual arrangement, a party waives its rights to sue the other party for a tort (a wrongful act or omission, other than a crime or a breach of contract) related to the contracted-for activity.

The transferee in a contractual (noninsurance) risk transfer does not operate as an insurer. Consequently, it does not pool the risks of more than one transferor. However, like insurance, many contractual risk transfers deal with hazard risk; thus they transfer either risk control activities or the cost of recovering from a loss.

Types of Contractual Risk Transfer

A contractual risk transfer is an agreement in which one party (the transferee), not acting as an insurer, accepts another party's (the transferor's) exposure to loss or the financial consequences of the transferor's loss exposures as an incidental aspect of another business transaction. Contractual risk transfers fall into two categories:

- **Noninsurance risk control transfer**—When an organization contractually transfers risk control responsibilities to a party that is not an insurer, it essentially shifts the loss exposures associated with that risk to the transferee. A noninsurance risk control transfer becomes effective only when the transferee performs the action that rids the transferor of risk.
- **Noninsurance risk financing transfer**—When an organization contractually transfers the financial burden of losses, the underlying loss exposures are not transferred between the parties. Noninsurance risk financing transfer provides the transferor with protection only after the funds to restore a loss have been paid. Until a loss occurs, the transferor

Noninsurance risk control transfer

A noninsurance transfer in which the transferor transfers a loss exposure to the transferee, thereby eliminating the possibility that the transferor will suffer a loss from the transferred exposure.

Noninsurance risk financing transfer

A noninsurance transfer in which the transferor transfers to the transferee the financial burden of losses by obligating the transferee to pay money to (or on behalf of) the transferor after the transferor or some third party suffers a loss.

cannot be certain that the transferee will pay. If the transferee fails to provide the expected funds, the financial burden of the risk was never truly transferred.

Contractual risk transfers in both categories can assume a variety of forms, each designed to meet the specific needs of the parties involved. For both types of transfer, a contract is usually formed before any loss occurs.

A critical difference between a noninsurance risk control and a noninsurance risk financing transfer surfaces when a transferee becomes bankrupt or otherwise unable to fulfill the contractual transfer terms. In a noninsurance risk financing transfer, a bankrupt transferee provides no protection to the transferor, who must pay for its own accidental loss. In a noninsurance risk control transfer, a bankrupt or uncooperative transferee may continue to be responsible for losses it caused, preserving the transferor's protection.

Noninsurance Risk Control Transfer

Many risk management professionals are experienced in insurance or financial matters and are therefore accustomed to dealing with contracts that indemnify losses. However, many risk management departments do not handle contractual risk control transfer contracts. For example, some risk management professionals do not manage leases or other similar written contracts that transfer risk of possible loss as an incidental part of the overall transaction.

Examples of noninsurance risk control transfers include these:

- Incorporation
- Leasing
- Contracting for services
- Suretyship and guaranty agreements
- Waiver
- Limitation of liability
- Disclaimer of warranties

Incorporation

Incorporation statutes in many countries stipulate that a corporation is a legal entity distinct from its shareholders and solely responsible for its (or its agents') own wrongs. Therefore, in the absence of fraud, other intentional wrongs, or statutory violation by its founding stockholders, a corporation can lose no more than the value of its assets as a result of a business venture, an accident, or a lawsuit. Incorporation statutes also typically limit any one stockholder's financial loss to the value of his or her own shares, thereby insulating stockholders' personal assets.

A businessowner can insulate the organization from potential losses by designating a separate corporation to conduct each of the organization's major activities. For example, one corporation may manufacture and sell products, while another installs and services them. This practice is known as **segregation**. With segregation, the "divisions" between an organization's exposure units constitute the legal boundaries of separate corporations, thereby limiting loss potentials that arise from business risks, property losses, liability losses, and net income losses.

Segregation

A risk control technique that separates or duplicates an organization's activities or property so that no single cause of loss can simultaneously affect all the organization's activities or property.

Stockholders can control the total value of the corporation's assets by contributing capital to or withdrawing it from the enterprise. The corporation thus serves as a transferee for risk that individual stockholders might otherwise face.

In some cases involving liability claims against corporations, courts have "pierced the corporate veil" by pursuing a major managing stockholder's personal assets. A court may take this approach, for example, when a corporation seeks bankruptcy protection after having apparently manipulated assets to frustrate creditors or when a predominant stockholder or corporate executive uses the corporation to hide personal wrongdoings. Courts in such cases may place greater importance on compensating individuals harmed by the corporation than on maintaining the usual separation between corporate liability and stockholders' personal assets.

Leasing

A **leasehold** right is asserted by a lessee. Before a leasehold is placed in effect and after it expires, the right to occupy or use the property remains with or returns to its owner.

Leasehold

The right to occupy or use real or personal property for a period of time.

Certain risks that attach to property ownership do not accompany its use or occupancy. These risks include loss from property destruction and liability to third parties for dangerous property conditions. A tenant (or lessee) does not normally take on these exposures when leasing the property unless the lease obligates the lessee to return the property to the lessor in the same condition in which it was received or unless the lessee alone has caused a dangerous condition that has harmed others.

An organization that leases property rather than owning it practices risk control by allowing the property owner to retain the risks related to property ownership. Under a **sale-and-lease-back arrangement,** a property owner transfers these risks—often to a corporation or another organization created or selected primarily for risk transferring, risk financing, or property management purposes. If no fraud is involved, courts usually uphold such a transfer (except in cases in which dangerous property conditions were apparent before the property was sold and leased back). A sale-and-leasehold arrangement also allows the former property owner to convert its equity into cash.

Sale-and-leaseback (sale-and-leaseback arrangement)

A transaction through which an organization that owns property transfers its risk by selling the property while retaining the right to occupy or use it under a lease with the new owner.

Contracting for Services

An individual or organization that performs a particular activity is generally held primarily responsible for any losses caused by that activity. An organization that wants to avoid such risk can contract with another organization to perform the activity. This noninsurance risk control transfer method is called contracting for services or simply subcontracting; however, the transferor need not be an independent contractor, and the party that accepts the risk need not be a subcontractor. Any contract requiring another party to perform a service and, implicitly, to assume the risk associated with it, involves the act of subcontracting.

Generally, any property, net income, or personnel loss exposure associated with an activity can be transferred through subcontracting. The transfer agreement must meet the legal requirements for a fairly bargained transfer of both the loss exposures and the actual losses associated with the activity. In this case, both the loss exposure and the burden of financing recovery rest with the subcontractor.

Liability loss exposures associated with an activity are not easily transferred, especially those relating to harm to third parties. For example, if negligence by a high-rise building subcontractor's employees creates a hazard that injures a pedestrian, the employees and the subcontractor would be primarily liable. However, the injured pedestrian would probably sue the landowner as the party responsible for the land's general condition.

Because the courts seek to provide compensation to those who are injured, they favor restricting the general rule that exempts someone who hires an independent contractor from liability for that contractor's torts. As a result, these exceptions have been made to the rule:

- The party that hired the contractor is directly liable for any negligence in selecting the contractor, giving directions, or failing to stop any unnecessary dangerous practices of which the party was aware.
- The responsibility—created by statute, contract, or common law—that certain duties be performed safely cannot be delegated to another party. For example, the duty of common carriers to carry passengers safely is nondelegable.
- If the subcontracted work is inherently dangerous to others (such as blasting and excavating near a public highway), the party that hired the contractor retains liability for a third-party injury caused by the contractor's negligence.

Obligee
The party to a surety bond that receives the surety's guarantee that the principal will fulfill an obligation or perform as promised.

Surety
The party (usually an insurer) to a surety bond that guarantees to the obligee that the principal will fulfill an obligation or perform as required by the underlying contract, permit, or law.

Principal
The party to a surety bond whose obligation or performance the surety guarantees.

Suretyship and Guaranty Agreements

Surety agreements involve three parties—the **surety**; the **obligee**; and the **principal**, or obligor. The surety's contractual guarantee is to perform or hire someone to perform in the principal's place when the principal's failure or inability to perform becomes clear and the obligee demands performance from

the surety. A surety agreement protects the obligee by providing a second source of performance. See the exhibit "Surety Agreements."

Surety Agreements

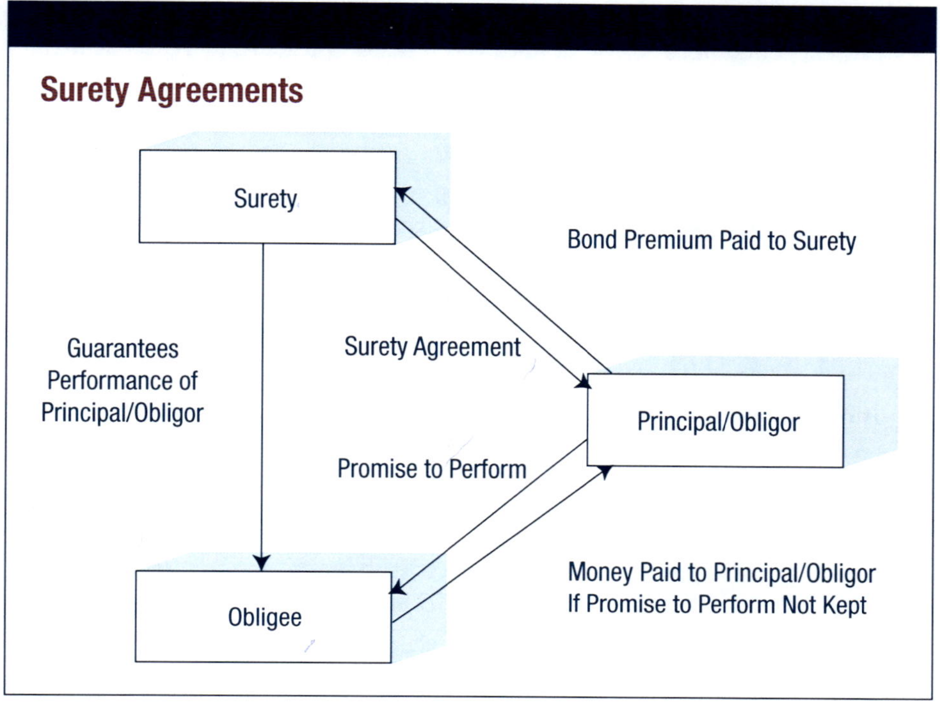

[DA01822]

A guaranty agreement is similar to a surety agreement in that an obligee relies on another party—a **guarantor**—for performance. Unlike a surety, a guarantor is obligated to perform only after the obligee has made every reasonable and legal effort to compel the principal's performance.

Guarantor
A person or organization that has promised to perform a duty in the event the party whose duty it was initially (the principal) fails to perform it.

Both suretyship and guaranty agreements allow the obligee to segregate loss exposures. If the principal does not perform, the obligee can rely on the surety or guarantor for performance. Suretyship law releases the surety from performance if the principal rightly refuses to perform for reasons such as fraud in securing the agreement or other contract defects. Whether a guarantor is released under similar circumstances depends on the wording of the guaranty agreement. See the exhibit "Fidelity Bond."

Fidelity Bond

Insurers that issue performance bonds promising performance of an obligation are acting as sureties, not as insurers. However, insurance written for employee dishonesty is often called a fidelity bond. A fidelity bond is a two-party contract between an employer and an insurer that pays the employer for loss resulting from theft by an employee. This arrangement is not a true bond because an insured's employees are not direct parties to the insurance contract.

[DA08641]

A surety has several rights that protect it against loss from the principal's misconduct or from collusion between the principal and the obligee:

Exoneration
The removal of a duty.

- **Exoneration**—For example, assume that a principal has fallen behind its project schedule, and the obligee has failed to preserve its rights against the principal. In such a case, the surety is released from its liability to the extent that it can show that the obligee's inaction increased the loss of or otherwise harmed the surety.

Subrogation
In a surety agreement, the substitution of one party for another whose debt or performance the substituting party satisfies and that entitles the substituting party to the rights that belonged to the defaulting party.

- **Subrogation**—A subrogation clause in a surety agreement entitles the surety to the same payment the principal would have received. For example, if a surety completes the construction of a building after the default of the building-contractor principal, the building owner (the obligee) must pay the surety for the portion of the work completed on the same basis on which it would have paid the contractor.

Indemnity
In a surety agreement, the right of a surety to seek reimbursement from the principal for the resources the surety expended when it performed the principal's duty.

- **Indemnity**—The surety can proceed directly against the principal to recover the fair value of its effort or any funds it has paid to the obligee as compensation for the principal's inaction. The principal must indemnify the surety for the costs of fulfilling the promise.

Because a surety's contractual commitment is the same as the principal's, any justification (or legal defense) for nonperformance that releases the principal from the underlying contract also releases the surety. The surety can also be legally released if the original contract is modified without the surety's consent.

Waiver

Waiver
The intentional relinquishment of a known right.

Exculpatory clause (exculpatory agreement)
A contractual provision purporting to excuse a party from liability resulting from negligence or an otherwise wrongful act.

An individual or organization can relinquish its right to sue in contract or tort using a **waiver**. By allowing an organization to rid itself of the applicable liability loss exposures, waivers can function as effective risk control mechanisms.

An **exculpatory clause** is similar to a waiver. Both waivers and exculpatory clauses are intended to eliminate one party's liability loss exposure from another party. Many states use the terms "waive" and "exculpate" interchangeably.

Real property leases often contain waivers or exculpatory clauses. For example, common law allows a real property lessee (tenant) to sue a lessor (landlord) for failing to maintain habitable premises. However, if a lessee waives the right to sue, the lessor no longer faces the liability loss exposure from the lessee. Here is a typical lease provision:

> Lessee, as a material part of the consideration to be rendered to the Lessor, hereby waives all claims against Lessor for damages to the goods, wares, and merchandise in, upon, or about said premises and for injuries to Lessee, his agents or invitees in or about said premises....

Unless improperly obtained or nullified by applicable state or local law, this lease provision lessens the landlord's concerns that the tenant will sue for damages to personal property or injuries to the tenant or others who are on the premises at the tenant's request. As worded, the provision is broad, apparently excusing the lessor from liability even for intentional harm to the lessee.

Although this lease provision limits the landlord's loss exposures to the lessee's lawsuits, it does not prevent others—such as the lessee's employees, guests, or other invitees—from suing the landlord. The provision also does not obligate the lessee to hold the lessor harmless from lawsuits—that is, to provide the lessor with a legal defense and to pay any verdicts or judgments levied against the lessor.

An effective waiver agreement is the result of fair bargaining, obtained without deceit or concealment, clear and unambiguous, and supported by legal consideration.

Waivers are generally embodied in original contracts and are signed before the parties begin their contractual dealings or have suffered harm. However, a party may use a **waiver of subrogation** to waive its rights to sue after it has suffered harm. For example, a landlord's insurer may waive its right of subrogation against a tenant who negligently causes a fire that damages the landlord's insured property.

Waiver of subrogation
A special type of waiver that is a pre-loss voluntary relinquishment by an insurer of its right to seek reimbursement of its payment for damages that were caused by a party other than the insured.

Limitation of Liability

When the transferor and transferee have equal bargaining power, the transferor may agree by contract to cap or limit the amount or type of its liability instead of waiving its liability entirely, as in this example of a contractual clause:

> In no event will (transferor) be liable to (transferee) or any third party for any incidental or consequential damages arising out of use or of inability to use (transferor's product which is being sold to transferee), or for any claim by any other party, even if (transferor) has been advised of the possibility of such damages. (Transferor's) total liability with respect to (transferor's product) shall not exceed the purchase price paid by the (transferee). (Transferee) acknowledges that these limitations permit (transferor) to provide this product at a lower cost than it otherwise could, and such limitations on liability are reasonable.

Disclaimer of Warranties

Sellers of property often assert disclaimers of warranties. A disclaimer in a sales contract may deny any express warranties made in conjunction with the property's sale. In addition, it may deny implied warranties, such as the implied warranty for a particular purpose—that the seller is aware of the particular purpose for which the buyer will use the property and that the property is suitable for that purpose—and the implied warranty of merchantability—that the property is suitable for the purpose for which most buyers use it.

This is an example of disclaimer language used in a software sales contract:

> (Seller's property) is provided "as is." To the maximum extent permitted by law, (seller) disclaims all warranties of any kind, either express or implied, including without limitation, implied warranties of fitness for a particular purpose and merchantability.

Noninsurance Risk Financing Transfer

In all forms of noninsurance risk financing transfers, the transferor's protection is only as reliable as the transferee's ability and willingness to pay money when needed to restore the loss. Despite this potential drawback, such transfers can provide dependable protection for a transferor under certain conditions, such as these:

- The transferor has a loss characteristic that places it beyond the scope of typical insurance contracts. For example, the cause of loss might not be covered in the only available or affordable insurance policy.
- The transferee is motivated, by the degree of its commitment to fulfilling the general business contract, to provide more complete indemnity because an insurer might question the indemnitee's right to payment.
- The transferee often has more direct and comprehensive knowledge of the risk it accepts than an insurer's underwriter would have, as is the case for maintenance agreements and guarantees for services.

Noninsurance risk financing contracts transfer the financial burden of losses. If the transferee fails to provide the compensation the contract requires, the financial burden of the loss remains with the transferor. Two prevalent noninsurance risk financing transfers are hold-harmless agreements and transfer of risk to the transferee's insurer.

Hold-Harmless Agreement

A hold-harmless agreement is a contract under which one party agrees to assume the liability of a second party. The parties to the indemnity clause of a hold-harmless agreement are the **indemnitor**—often referred to as the transferee—and the **indemnitee**—often referred to as the transferor. The indemnitor assumes liability for the legal claims that may be brought against the indemnitee because of the activities the contract covers.

Indemnitor

Party in a hold-harmless agreement who assumes the other party's liability.

Indemnitee

Party in a hold-harmless agreement whose legal liability is assumed by the indemnitor.

Hold-harmless agreements contain a broad array of indemnity clauses, which can provide a transferor with funds for restoring accidental losses to property, net income, liability claims, or the loss of the services of the transferor's key personnel. This is an example of a hold-harmless agreement:

> The (transferee) shall hold harmless and indemnify (the transferor) for any losses, claims, damages, awards, penalties, or injuries incurred by any third party, including reasonable attorney's fees, which arise from any alleged breach of such indemnifying party's representations and warranties made under this agreement, provided that the indemnifying party is promptly notified of any such claims. The indemnifying party shall have the sole right to defend such claims at its own expense. The other party shall provide, at the indemnifying party's expense, such assistance in investigating and defending such claims as the indemnifying party may request. This indemnity shall survive the termination of this agreement.

The effect of punitive damages and bankruptcy on hold-harmless and other indemnity agreements varies greatly among jurisdictions. In some jurisdictions, the transferee's payment of punitive damages is included automatically within a hold-harmless agreement. In others, punitive damages are included

only if specified. In still others, contractual transfer of the obligation to pay punitive damages is illegal. Bankruptcy excuses a transferee/indemnitor in some jurisdictions, often depending on the nature of the harm the claimant suffered.

Because noninsurance risk financing transfers are largely unregulated, the provisions and practices of hold-harmless agreements are not standardized. Generally, such transfers are used when one party has the bargaining power to require another party to assume the risk and when such agreements are standard practice for a particular transaction or industry. Any such agreement must be in the form of a legally enforceable contract.

Transfer of Risk to the Transferee's Insurer

Insurance agreements can be modified to allow the transferee's insurer to treat a specified third party as an insured. This can be accomplished through two kinds of endorsements—additional insured and named insured—which obligate the transferee's insurer to pay (or pay on behalf of) the third party after it has suffered a loss.

An **additional insured endorsement** offers a transferor several advantages:

Additional insured endorsement
An endorsement that adds coverage for one or more persons or organizations to the named insured's policy.

- Rights under the policy that are independent of the enforceability of the general business contract between the transferor and the transferee
- Waiver by the transferee's insurer of its right to subrogate against the transferor
- Additional source of funds to pay for the transferor's losses
- The right to demand that the transferee's insurer pay the costs to defend the transferor for a covered liability loss
- Free coverage because the transferor often does not contribute funds toward payment of the transferee's insurance premium

Despite these clear advantages to the transferor, the transferee faces a disadvantage. A request to an insurer to add a transferor as an additional insured to a policy can change the transferee's acceptability to its insurer's underwriter. The underwriter usually has little information about the liability loss exposure presented by the additional insured. An underwriter who identifies correctable problems that present a liability loss exposure may be powerless to make the additional insured take corrective action. The underwriter may be forced to cancel or nonrenew the transferee's policy.

Another disadvantage is that the transferor must still control or finance through another mechanism any loss exposures that are excluded from the policy.

Named insured endorsement

An endorsement that, similar to an additional insured endorsement, adds coverage for one or more persons or organizations to the named insured's policy and elevates the new insured to the status of a named insured, giving it special rights and obligations.

A **named insured endorsement**, by elevating the added insured to the status of a named insured, offers several advantages:

- A transferor's agents, employees, officers, and directors are considered insureds and therefore are included in the transferee's coverage.
- The transferor, as the named insured, is likely entitled to receive notice if the transferee's policy is canceled or endorsed.

Several disadvantages also apply when a transferor is considered a named insured:

- The transferee's insurer may have a right to inspect the transferor's business and financial records.
- By entering the arrangement, the transferor may unknowingly agree to provide periodic reports to the insurer.
- The transferor may become involved in litigation unrelated to relevant insurance coverages.

Risk management professionals must weigh these advantages and disadvantages when considering these kinds of endorsements. Many risk management professionals prefer using the additional insured endorsement.

CONTRACTUAL RISK TRANSFER BY TYPE OF TRANSACTION

Contractual (noninsurance) risk transfers can be so enmeshed in a contract that neither party may be aware of the mutual promise to indemnify the other. This situation creates contract interpretation conflicts that can render both the transfers and each party's attempt to collect indemnity from the other virtually meaningless. To avoid such problems, each organization's risk management professional, legal counsel, and key managers must know how to recognize common forms of contractual (noninsurance) risk transfers within contracts and how to use contractual risk transfer effectively in various types of transactions.

Any written contract can contain a noninsurance transfer of risk control or risk financing. For example, public parking-garage tickets often contain a broad waiver of the car owner's common-law right to bring claims against the garage owner for vehicle and contents damage. Automobile rental agreements require lessees to purchase insurance or otherwise bear the financial consequences of vehicle damage. Finally, two organizations agreeing to the sale, rental, or maintenance of a product can each include a provision in their agreements that makes the other party an indemnitor.

Noninsurance transfers of risk control and of risk financing are typically included in contracts such as these:

- Construction contracts
- Service and maintenance contracts
- Purchase order contracts
- Lease of premises contracts
- Equipment lease contracts
- Bailment contracts
- Sale and supply contracts

Construction Contracts

A building contractor's work creates many loss exposures—principally liability exposures—for the landowner/owner of the building under construction. For example, a contractor's activities can harm its own and its subcontractors' employees, pedestrians, owners of adjoining properties, or even the entire community. As a landowner, the individual or organization for which the building is constructed is ultimately liable for all such harm, as well as harm arising from any breaches of building permit provisions or building codes resulting from contractors' or architects' decisions.

For protection against liability losses, landowners normally require building contractors or architects to hold them harmless from certain construction-related claims. Contractors and architects usually agree to contractual hold-harmless provisions because if they do not, owners may find other contractors or architects who will.

The exact extent of the claims against which the contractor or architect agrees to hold the landowner harmless can be determined only by a careful reading of the hold-harmless agreement. Even then, an agreement may leave some questions regarding scope of application unanswered.

Service and Maintenance Contracts

Unlike construction contracts, which end when buildings are completed, contracts for services, maintenance, and transportation are purchased on a continuing basis. The providers of such services often agree to a generic type of hold-harmless agreement that is both general and broad. Under such agreements, a contractor typically agrees to hold the customer harmless from virtually all property, liability, and other losses (except, most likely, revenue losses) the customer may suffer because of the contractor's errors and to be responsible even for claims arising solely from the customer's negligence.

Purchase Order Contracts

Manufacturers, wholesalers, and retailers can face products liability claims that arise from the raw materials, components, and supplies they purchase and use. For example, items purchased from a vendor may be defective or of the wrong type or grade for the product. Under common law, the ultimate buyer or another product user has the right to sue everyone involved in the product's production or sale, ranging from the raw-material supplier to the retailer.

Any organization in the distribution chain has the right to ask any other party in the chain to provide it with protection against products liability claims. Traditionally, each purchasing organization may require its immediate supplier or vendor to hold it harmless through a contractual provision.

A hold-harmless provision in a purchase order agreement, like an insurance policy, may contain exclusions or conditions. For example, such an agreement may exempt the indemnifying vendor from responding to claims brought against the purchaser based entirely on the purchaser's "sole negligence." An agreement may make the vendor's promise to indemnify conditional on the purchaser's immediately notifying the vendor of any claim. The vendor may be granted authority to manage claims, while the purchaser may be barred from making any separate settlement with a claimant. A hold-harmless agreement does not obligate the purchaser/indemnitee to cooperate with the vendor/indemnitor in the vendor's management of any claim unless this condition is part of the agreement. Insurance contracts typically include this language.

Many hold-harmless agreements also protect the purchaser. This protection is included when the purchaser has enough bargaining power to obtain the vendor's promise of indemnity, and the vendor's eagerness to contract with the purchaser makes the agreement at least tolerable to the vendor. Those relationships can be reversed. An exclusive national manufacturer of a popular product may be able to require each wholesale or retail purchaser of the product to agree to hold the manufacturer harmless from products liability or other claims, or even from other losses. Marketers throughout the distribution chain may have no choice but to promise protection if they want to sell the product.

When several parties in the production-marketing chain enter into a series of hold-harmless agreements, considerable confusion can result. If all agreements transfer the financial consequence of losses one "link" back along the chain, then the original manufacturer (or even the raw-material supplier) could become obligated to finance the losses of all claims against other parties. In the opposite case, when the financial consequence is transferred forward, then the retailer could become burdened with the losses of all the parties in the distribution chain. If a hold-harmless agreement provides for indemnity from purchasers and from vendors, then the aggregate liability of all the producers and marketers could accumulate at various points along the chain. Even greater confusion can exist in construction situations if a contractor

and subcontractors sign agreements holding each other as well as the project owner harmless.

To guard against confusion and to ensure the equitable and efficient distribution of financial responsibility, hold-harmless agreements should be planned so that loss exposures are assumed by those most qualified to control them.

Lease of Premises Contracts

A lease of real or personal property can be used for noninsurance risk control transfer even if it contains no explicit risk transfer provisions. A lease, by nature, allows a lessee to enjoy the use of the property for a specified period without being subjected to many of the loss exposures inherent in property ownership.Although such exposures remain with the lessor, a lessor can attempt to use the lease to transfer the financial burden of some losses to the lessee, resulting in a noninsurance risk financing transfer. In effect, the lessee can use the lease for risk control transfer, and the lessor can use the same lease for risk financing transfer.

Lessees often accept lease agreements prepared by lessors without revision. Consequently, many lease agreements are written to substantially favor the lessor. Although courts often interpret insurance contracts in favor of insureds because they assume that the parties had unequal bargaining power, courts typically interpret leases assuming that the parties had equal bargaining power. This is particularly true if the lessee is an organization renting business space rather than an individual or a family renting personal space.

Leases often include a hold-harmless agreement that obligates the lessee to respond to liability claims that may be brought against the lessor. This broad agreement extends the lessee's financial responsibility not only to the lessor's common-law liabilities but also to its statutory liabilities, including workers compensation claims.

In numerous states, attempts to transfer risk to a lessee's workers compensation insurer or to transfer other statutory liability to a lessee's general liability insurer are highly vulnerable to court challenge by an injured employee of the lessor or a third party injured on the leased premises. The injured party in such a case could claim that the financial security of its statutory protection has been jeopardized significantly by an attempted contractual transfer from the lessor to the presumably less financially able lessee.

Equipment Lease Contracts

An individual or organization that leases equipment usually promises to return it in its original condition, often subject to certain exceptions. That promise protects the lessor against loss to equipment, which is often out of the lessor's direct control for substantial periods. The promise is not burdensome for the lessee for two reasons. First, the lessee assumes no financial responsibility for liability claims against the lessor that may arise from the lessee's posses-

sion or use of the equipment. Second, the lessee is responsible only for the property value of the leased equipment—not for the revenue the lessor could have earned on the equipment had it remained undamaged and available for another rental.

Some equipment leases, however, obligate the lessee to hold the lessor harmless from liability claims related to the equipment while it is in the lessee's possession. The lessee might even be required to maintain insurance that provides the lessor with liability (and often other) protection.

Bailment Contracts

Mutual benefit bailment
An arrangement in which the bailor pays the bailee for work or service related to the bailed property and from which both the bailee and the bailor expect to benefit.

Bailment
The temporary possession by one party (the bailee) of personal property owned by another party (the bailor) for a specific purpose, such as cleaning or repair.

Gratuitous bailment
An arrangement in which the bailee receives no compensation and owes a lower degree of care.

Many business transactions involve placing personal property in the custody of another party—for example, for repair, transportation, or safekeeping. **Bailments** may be **mutual benefit bailments** or **gratuitous bailments**. Under common law, the bailee must exercise ordinary care for the safety of the bailor's property. In most cases, common law requires that a mutual benefit bailee return the property to the bailor in its original condition, excusing the bailee only for damage caused by acts of God and normal wear and tear.

A special class of mutual benefit bailment is a common carriers bailment, under which common carriers transport others' goods in accordance with an established schedule and set fees. Because of the public's interest in safe, efficient, and effective transport of goods, the degree of care required of common carriers exceeds that of an ordinary mutual benefit bailee. The carrier can be liable for any loss that results from an accident or even from a third party's act.

A common carrier is responsible for any damage to a bailor shipper's cargo except that arising from these causes:

- Acts of God
- Warlike activities (usually described as involving acts of a public enemy, but not including rioting or terrorism)
- Exercise of public authority (as when police block the access to a particular neighborhood, thus depriving a business of its usual profits)
- Fault or neglect by the shipper (such as poor packaging or labeling)
- Any inherent vice of the cargo (any potential for the shipper's goods to destroy themselves, as when ice melts or explosives detonate because of improper packaging or labeling)

A bailor and bailee can contractually alter the common-law apportionment of their respective liability. For example, in many business situations, bailees seek to limit their liability through posted notices or contract provisions stating that they are not responsible for damage to bailors' goods. Bailees can also attempt to limit their liability to a specified amount per item or only to the property's value (excluding any profits the bailor would have earned from the property had it not been damaged). In contrast, a bailor can seek to increase

a bailee's liability by, for example, holding the bailee responsible for specified acts of God (such as windstorm).

Either party to a bailment contract can have business reasons for assuming liability that the common law usually places on the other party. Courts respect each party's freedom of contract for fair apportionments of liability. However, they have been reluctant to enforce liability-transferring bailment contract provisions that are contrary to practice within the particular industry, not equitably negotiated, or less than adequately disclosed.

Sale and Supply Contracts

Contracts pertaining to the sale and supply of goods and services offer innumerable opportunities for transferring risk between buyers and sellers. The transfer usually favors the party with the greater bargaining power.

For example, to maintain firm control of their products as they move through marketing channels, some manufacturers and processors sell their goods on consignment. Consignment places title to the property with the manufacturer or processor until the distributor sells the goods to the retailer or ultimate consumer. Ownership, and the loss exposure, move directly from the manufacturer or processor to the retailer or consumer, allowing the distributor to earn revenue only from its distribution. Also, the distributor, having never taken title to the goods, is never exposed to loss from their damage or destruction; however, many consignment agreements require the distributor to indemnify the owner for any loss or damage to the goods during consignment.

Sellers may also use sale and supply contracts to provide additional benefits to buyers, thereby making their products or services more attractive. For example, a seller might agree to protect the buyer or another owner of substantial personal property against specified types of losses to or arising from that property. If the organization promises to provide services only but does not also agree to indemnify the property owner for losses, the agreement is one of risk control, not risk financing. If, in contrast, the organization agrees to hold the owner harmless from liability claims, then the agreement becomes a risk financing transfer.

Organizations become risk transferees under contracts such as these:

- Contracts that provide a customer with a constant fuel supply, which obligate the fuel dealer to pay for any frozen pipes and certain other losses if the customer is ever without fuel
- Contracts to purchase data processing equipment, air conditioners, vehicles, or similar items with guarantees of maintenance and replacement as necessary
- Service contracts under which real estate agents maintain specified equipment, such as heating systems, in homes they sell

Such contracts are similar to insurance if they go beyond guaranteeing the quality of the goods or the reliability of the supplier's performance and extend to other causes of loss. In some situations, courts have found organizations involved in such contracts to be engaged in the business of insurance, making them subject to the provisions of the applicable state insurance code. For example, a tire dealer who agrees to give an allowance for unused mileage if a tire that it sold is damaged by road hazards may be considered to be an insurer. Inadvertently becoming subject to an insurance code can be restrictive and costly for organizations. In effect, the organization can be forced to withdraw from service or maintenance agreements—designed to attract customers—in which they have assumed loss exposures usually borne by customers. Sale and supply contracts can substantially modify the common law that distributes loss exposures between property buyers and sellers. Under common law, the risk of loss, both to the property and from the property's loss of use, moves with the property's title; the owner always bears the exposures. Therefore, special risk transfer provisions aside, the time when ownership changes is important in identifying and managing an organization's loss exposures. The buyer's and seller's bargaining power, as well as industry custom, influence when loss exposures are transferred.

Free on board destination (FOB destination)
A shipping condition in which ownership passes from the seller to the buyer when the carrier delivers the goods to the buyer's premises.

Free on board (F.O.B.) point of origin
A shipping condition in which ownership passes to the buyer as soon as the carrier picks up the goods from the seller's premises.

Cost, insurance, freight (CIF)
Selling terms under which the seller's price includes the cost of insurance and freight charges until the goods reach the foreign port of importation and in which the seller's responsibility for loss or damage to the goods is the same as under Cost and Freight (C&F) terms.

Installment or conditional sales contract
A sales contract in which the seller commonly reserves ownership rights until the buyer meets all the contractual conditions, most notably the buyer's final installment payment.

For example, contract provisions may specify that a sales shipment is to be delivered **free on board (F.O.B.) point of origin** or, in the alternative, **free on board (F.O.B.) destination**. The difference between the two shipping conditions relates to when ownership and associated loss exposures shift from the buyer to the seller.

An alternative sales contract condition, often used in the sale of permanently installed equipment, may specify that the purchaser does not become the owner until the property has been unloaded and installed and has passed a series of operational tests in the buyer's facility. This arrangement allows the seller to maintain control of the property and ensure that it has been appropriately placed in service. In contrast, a seller who wants a buyer to be responsible for any damage to the property throughout its transport may require the buyer to take title to the property at the seller's shipping dock.

Responsibilities for ownership loss exposures can be divided, with different responsibilities being transferred at different times. If goods are shipped under **cost-insurance freight (C.I.F.)** terms, the seller quotes a price that includes the cost of insurance and all transportation charges (freight) incurred to the named destination. The buyer assumes responsibility for loss or damage as soon as the goods are placed into the custody of the ocean carrier or delivered on board the vessel; however, the buyer is the beneficiary of the insurance purchased under the terms of the contract.

Exposures in sales of property can also be divided in **installment or conditional sales contracts**. Although the seller usually retains title, exposure to loss because of property damage can be transferred immediately to the buyer by the sales contract. The transfer can be achieved by a contract provision obligating the buyer to complete the contract by continuing installment payments even though the property might be lost or damaged before the buyer makes the final payment. Such an arrangement preserves the seller's right under an installment contract either to receive the full purchase price or, if the buyer defaults, to repossess the property. The buyer can also obtain insurance or other risk financing to protect its interests and obligations. During the time between the first and last installment payments, therefore, both the buyer and the seller are exposed to loss from damage and have an insurable interest in the property.

A common arrangement is for the seller to retain possession of property that has been sold for later delivery to the buyer. Valuable items of personal property, as well as substantial quantities of **fungible goods**, are often sold in this way. The contract of sale becomes effective as soon as the buyer and seller agree on the particular items or quantity to be sold, the price, and the delivery date. The sales contract commonly specifies that property ownership transfers to the buyer at the time the agreement is reached.

Fungible goods
Commodities or bulk goods, all parts of which are presumed to be uniform.

Although the ownership-related loss exposure to damage thus passes to the buyer, the seller having custody of the property still has a bailee's responsibility for the property's safety. In such cases, both the bailor's ownership interest and the bailee's liability for damage can expose each to loss and support each party's purchase of appropriate insurance or other risk financing arrangements. Exposures might be altered by specific agreement.

Apply Your Knowledge

City Parking Garage, which provides public parking, issues tickets to drivers as they enter the garage to park their cars. Printed on the back of each ticket is a statement indicating that the car owner waives his or her right to bring claims against the garage owner for any damage to the vehicle and its contents while the car is parked in the garage. This contractual risk transfer is part of which one of the following types of transaction?

a. Service and maintenance contract

b. Purchase order contract

c. Equipment lease contract

d. Bailment

Feedback: d. This contractual risk transfer is part of a bailment. City Parking Garage takes temporary possession of cars owned by others. The garage ticket "waiver" may be considered a bailment contract provision that transfers risk to the bailee (the car owner). Many courts are reluctant to enforce liability-transferring bailment contract provisions that are not equitably negotiated or are less than adequately disclosed.

CONTRACTUAL RISK TRANSFER OF COMMON-LAW LIABILITIES

Contractual (noninsurance) risk transfer agreements may define obligations of the transferor and transferee in a way that alters each party's common-law liabilities.

Common-law liabilities affecting a transferor's potential or actual liability loss exposures can be altered by three forms of contract provisions. Categorized by how they alter common law, these provisions can be grouped according to the extent of responsibility they transfer. For example, assume the contracting parties are a building owner (O) and a general contractor (C). They may enter any one of three forms of contractual risk transfer agreement:

- Limited form—Party C holds Party O harmless from responsibility for losses that are exclusively Party C's fault.
- Intermediate form—Party C holds Party O harmless from responsibility for losses resulting from Party C's sole fault and from Party C's and Party O's joint fault.
- Broad form—Party C holds Party O harmless from responsibility for losses resulting from party C's sole fault, both parties' joint fault, and Party O's sole fault.

Although these types of agreements can be applied to any property, net income, liability, or personnel loss exposures, most pertain to a transferor's potential or actual liability loss exposures.

Limited Form

Under the limited form of a hold-harmless agreement, one party (the transferor) transfers its responsibility for the fault of the other party (the transferee) to that party. A common example is a contractor's agreement to hold an owner harmless for harm caused by the contractor's negligence. Without this agreement, the owner could be held responsible for the contractor's negligence under the common-law doctrine of **vicarious liability**.

Vicarious liability
A legal responsibility that occurs when one party is held liable for the actions of a subordinate or associate because of the relationship between the two parties.

Here is an example of a limited-form hold-harmless clause:

> The contractor agrees to indemnify and hold harmless the owner against claims, damages, bodily injury, or property damage arising out of the contractor's work and caused by any act of omission of the contractor, his agents, and his employees.

Intermediate Form

Two or more individuals or organizations working together to fulfill their contract may jointly harm a third party. Or, they may be joined as defendants in a civil suit charging them both with fault for a breach of contract or a tort. Under common law, both parties would be held jointly responsible for the

harm. The facts of the situation may not reveal which party is at fault or the extent to which the parties share fault. Determining who is responsible and to what extent can be a difficult, time-consuming, and contentious process.

However, this process can be eliminated if one contracting party transfers its common-law responsibility for joint civil wrongs to the other contracting party. The one to which joint responsibility is transferred (the transferee) must agree to hold the other party (the transferor) harmless from claims arising from their joint fault.

The intermediate form of hold-harmless agreement transfers sole fault of the transferee as well as joint fault of the transferor and transferee, as shown in this example of such an agreement in a lease contract:

> Lessee shall be liable for, and shall hold the Lessor harmless with respect to, all claims relating to damage or injury to the property or persons of others alleged to have occurred on or have been caused by the condition of the leased premises, if such injury or damage is alleged to have been caused by an act or neglect of the Lessee (including anyone in the Lessee's control or employ) or the joint act or neglect of the Lessee and Lessor.

This agreement is noteworthy because the words at the end of the clause pertaining to joint responsibility are surrounded by many other provisions describing the lessee's responsibility not only for liability claims, but also for damage to the premises.

The words relating to joint liability are designed to transfer the otherwise joint responsibilities for harm, making what was once joint the transferee's sole responsibility. This responsibility could be overlooked easily by the lessee, especially if this part of the agreement is typed or otherwise prepared individually for each agreement and not made a part of the preprinted form. Both the transferor and the transferee must be sure that the agreement expresses their shared intent.

Broad Form

Beginning with a relatively simple restatement of common law, the limited form—and subsequently the intermediate form—of hold-harmless agreement have sought to progressively improve the transferor's position by transferring ever-greater financial consequences to the transferee.

The broad form of hold-harmless agreement attempts to place all financial consequences of potential losses on the transferee—including losses resulting from the sole fault of the transferor. Many state courts refuse to enforce such agreements, holding that including indemnification for acts for which the transferor is solely liable is inappropriate.

Here is an example of a broad-form hold-harmless clause (adapted from the preceding limited-form clause):

> The contractor shall indemnify and hold harmless the owner from and against all claims, damages, bodily injury, or property damage whether or not caused in part by the owner's act or omission.

The words following "whether" do not limit the contractor's duty to respond. In fact, the provision seeks to make the contractor financially responsible for all bodily injury and property damage claims against the owner. The transferee under this agreement, in effect, becomes an insurer by assuming risk of loss for which it bears no fault.

STATUTORY LIMITATIONS ON HOLD-HARMLESS AGREEMENTS

Statutory limitations on hold-harmless agreements seek to protect the public by preventing contracting parties from engaging in unacceptable behavior.

Many state statutes that apply to hold-harmless agreements attempt to preserve fairness and foster economically appropriate allocation of loss exposures and actual losses. These statutes reflect public concern for ensuring that organizations act carefully to prevent harm to others. Some statutes also provide a source of compensation for those harmed—particularly from financially strong organizations that typically have the bargaining power to enforce an unconscionable hold-harmless agreement.

Executives and their legal counsel or risk management professionals draft creative hold-harmless agreements for a broad range of circumstances. Creating a single state law that applies equally and unambiguously to all hold-harmless agreements is unfeasible. Therefore, most statutes regulating hold-harmless agreements include language that describes the specific types of agreement to which they apply. Statutory limitations on hold-harmless agreements vary in the types of contractual (noninsurance) risk transfers to which they apply, the parties regulated, and the scope of loss exposures whose transfer is regulated; each statute must be carefully read to determine how it treats those variables.

The statutes that apply to hold-harmless agreements can be classified into those that entirely prohibit transfer of risk (all-inclusive statutes), those that prohibit particular wording in such agreements, and those that place specific requirements on such agreements.

All-Inclusive Statutes

Some statutes prohibit virtually all hold-harmless agreements. Here is an example of an all-inclusive statute:

> Indemnification Agreements Prohibited. Any agreement or provision whereby an architect, engineer, surveyor, or his agents or employees is sought to be held harmless or indemnified for damages and claims arising out of circumstances giving rise to legal liability therefore on the part of any said persons shall be against public policy, void, and wholly unenforceable.

This statute bars hold-harmless or indemnity agreements that might apply to "circumstances giving rise to legal liability," regardless of the type of wrongdoing or the extent of fault of involved parties. Although its proscription is broad, the statute is also narrow in its application to only architects, engineers, surveyors, and their associates. Any hold-harmless agreement involving, for example, a building owner, contractor, or subcontractor would presumably be valid in this jurisdiction.

Statutes Prohibiting Particular Wording

Some statutes prohibit a narrowly defined class of hold-harmless agreement. For example, by prohibiting hold-harmless agreements that refer to the transferor's "sole negligence," a statute prohibits all agreements that transfer responsibility for losses resulting exclusively from a transferor's negligence.

Other statutes address the wording of risk control and risk financing transfers more directly. For example, several state statutes include this provision:

> No agency of this state nor any political subdivision, municipal corporation, or district, nor any public officer or person charged with the letting of contracts for the construction, alteration, or repair of public works shall draft or cause to be drafted specifications for bids, in connection with the construction, alteration, or repair of public works:
>
> (a) In such a manner as to limit the bidding, directly or indirectly, to any one specific concern or...
>
> (b) In such a manner as to hold the bidder to whom such contract is awarded responsible for extra costs incurred as a result of errors or omissions by the public agency in the contract documents.

This provision prohibits wording that would limit bidding and that would transfer to the bidder any risk resulting from an agency's errors or omissions in the contract document. The provision does not apply to private organizations or individuals, public contracts unrelated to public works, or errors and omissions of the public agency that are not reflected in the contract documents. It is also limited in application only to building/demolition contracts for public works.

Statutes prohibiting particular wording in risk transfer agreements are generally very narrow. Compliance with these statutes primarily involves avoiding the prohibited words and other related phrases. Precise contract wording can usually achieve the contracting parties' intentions almost as fully as if this kind of prohibitory statute did not exist.

Statutes Placing Requirements on Agreements

To prevent a transferee from undertaking burdensome commitments in a hold-harmless agreement, some states specify that if a particular type of contract does include a hold-harmless agreement, it must comply with certain requirements. For example, several states require hold-harmless agreements in construction and design contracts to include a monetary limit on the extent of the indemnification that bears a reasonable commercial relationship to the contract.

MANAGING CONTRACTUAL RISK TRANSFER

An organization's risk management professional should be aware of the legal restrictions that govern the use of contractual (noninsurance) risk transfer and should develop a consistent, feasible program to manage such transfers.

Transferring or assuming risk is not always an organization's best alternative. An organization may instead allow common or statutory law to apportion the loss exposures and financial consequences of specified types of losses.

An organization's risk management efforts should concentrate on establishing an effective program for managing contractual risk transfers. A consistent and effective program includes analysis of factors affecting appropriate use of risk transfers and a clearly written and widely disseminated organizational policy.

Some risk management professionals use the negotiation of contractual transfers, especially those for risk financing, to reduce the organization's liability loss exposures and loss costs. Such an approach is possible because contract provisions, especially liability-related hold-harmless agreements not connected with construction contracts, are largely unregulated.

However, the goal of sound risk management is to use contractual risk transfers in ways that efficiently apportion loss exposures and the loss cost for the transferor, the transferee, and the economy as a whole. With this approach, efficiency refers to both organizational and economy-wide cost of risk. Therefore, the most efficient transfer lowers the cost of risk for each contracting organization.

Legal and Practical Considerations

Parties drafting and using contractual risk transfers often negotiate to achieve the most favorable terms in the transfer agreement. A risk management professional should participate in such negotiations not as a competitor but as a referee, seeking fairness and mutual benefit for all participants. In this role, the risk management professional should consider the legal enforceability of contract provisions, the relative abilities of the parties to manage risk (that is, to keep losses from occurring and to pay for those that do), and the nature and extent of risk transferred.

Legal Enforceability

Legal enforceability is one factor that determines the appropriate use of a contract—or whether it can be used at all. A contract is not enforceable if it is unconscionable or in violation of public policy or statutes. Also, attempts by the contracting parties to rid themselves of the same or related loss exposures or financial consequences could make it difficult to enforce the contract. For example, contracts in which risks have been transferred and retransferred can make it almost impossible for a court to determine who has agreed to accept what risk and may be unenforceable as a result.

Parties' Ability to Manage Risk

Another consideration relating to contractual risk transfer is the parties' ability to manage risk, particularly the transferee's ability to pay major losses when they occur. Construction companies, in particular, are a common target for hold-harmless agreements. As a group, they are also subject to sudden and severe financial strains in the ordinary conduct of their business.

Generally, transferees must receive enough benefits from their contracts to cover the obligations assumed under them. However, a benefit that is fair for the transferee may not always be reasonable for the transferor to offer. In such a case, contractual risk transfer may not be the most efficient method for handling a given loss exposure. Moreover, transfers could make it impractical to handle a loss exposure in a more efficient way or could even preclude such a possibility. For example, the transferee may be unable not only to pay for large losses but also to effectively reduce losses.

Nature and Extent of Risk Transferred

The greatest efficiency is typically achieved when the responsibility for risk financing and the authority for risk control rest with the same party. For example, manufacturers rather than distributors should assume the full financial responsibility for losses arising from faulty products, for defective materials used in the manufacturing process, and for claims arising from their advertising statements. Distributors, then, should have full financial responsibility for claims arising from their own statements in selling and advertising and for their own acts of assembling, disassembling, mixing, storing, and packing products.

Similarly, in building contracts, contractors should have full financial responsibility for their employees; for their agents' activities; and for the condition of their premises, equipment, and materials. The building owner should have full responsibility for losses arising from items such as specifications and from any use the owner makes of the premises on which the contractor is working. Because dividing lines between responsibilities are not always clear, the underlying contract, in the interests of economy and ease of enforcement, should be specifically and carefully worded.

The transfer of the negligence loss exposure, in particular, can violate the principle of assigning authority and its related responsibility to the same party. When liability for the negligence of one's own employees is transferred, the responsibility (and therefore the incentive) to control negligence is disconnected from the authority to do so. The transferor retains the authority to control employee negligence, whereas the transferee acquires the responsibility and the incentive to do so.

In the determination of who can best manage loss exposures and pay for losses, a contractual transfer should not be considered by itself but should be considered in relation to other transfers. This sometimes leads to exceptions to the general rule of merging responsibility and authority. Consider the

responsibility of a single tenant in a large office building for damage to the entire building. The general rule would require the tenant to assume liability for all damage arising from the small portion of the premises the tenant actively controls. But that rule would make it necessary for the tenant to buy insurance against its possible liability for severe fire damage to the building, duplicating the owner's insurance covering the same property.

Strategic and Administrative Considerations

A sound contractual risk transfer control policy rests on both a good general administrative program and specific controls to secure appropriate transfers.

Transfer Strategy

A consistent transfer strategy ensures that the organization transfers or accepts the transfer of risk only when this role serves both the organization and the general economy.

A defensive approach to contractual risk transfer requires an organization to avoid inadvertently becoming a transferee. To do so, the organization should understand the conditions under which it is unwise, and thus economically inefficient for society, to become a transferee.

In contrast, an offensive approach entails taking advantage of other organizations by wielding economic power to impose transfers. An unwavering pursuit of an offensive strategy is inappropriate both for the organization and for society and is regarded by many risk management professionals as unethical. An unduly aggressive strategy could prompt others to consistently follow a defensive strategy and could prompt legislatures and the courts to look suspiciously on transfers that are handled under such circumstances.

An organization using a balanced and productive strategy to manage contractual risk transfer examines the implications of alternative contractual risk transfer arrangements for the contracting organizations and the economy.

General Administrative Controls

Regardless of its size, an organization should have an organized program to control contractual risk transfers. The initial goal of such a program should be to help all contract-related personnel clearly understand the loss exposures that could be hidden in even the simplest contracts and the need to have such documents reviewed by experienced personnel.

In most organizations, contracts are, for the most part, routine and standardized. For example, careful scrutiny over time will probably indicate that purchase orders, service contracts, and other routine contracts contain a standard hold-harmless agreement. Once this has been determined, appropriate decisions can be made about dealing with the liability involved. Those routine contracts can then be left to periodic auditing.

More complex and nonroutine contracts can be troublesome. With these contracts, effective training of all responsible personnel is very important. Contractual risk transfer agreements are not easy to detect or evaluate and can be hazardous to the organization. The risk management professional or another official responsible for controlling such transfers must be given an adequate opportunity to read and interpret each contract. Unlike routine contracts, these types of contracts require more attention than periodic auditing.

Even the most thorough administrative program for controlling contractual risk transfers should be reviewed periodically. Customary procedures can become unnecessarily cumbersome or imprecise over time. Similarly, the cost of administering the program must be known and monitored.

Record Keeping

As part of contractual risk transfer management, an organization should keep detailed, current records of all written contracts it has entered into. These records should include the contracts themselves, the identities of the parties to whom and from whom risk has been transferred (if the contracts include such transfers), and the legal bases (statutes or court cases) for the enforceability of any contractual risk transfers.

Risk management professionals need extensive information to determine the meaning and implications of contractual risk transfers, particularly because of the sheer number of contracts into which an organization enters and the diversity of state and federal laws that may apply. In addition, new contractual risk transfers may be drafted in response to recent court rulings or legislative mandates.

Records and related information regarding contractual risk transfers should be included in the organization's risk management information system (RMIS). An RMIS can help maintain current records of transfers, track recent applicable court decisions and statutes, and generate revised wording for agreements that comply with changes mandated by statutes or courts.

Specific Control Measures

Having identified and evaluated the loss exposures in the contractual transfers, the risk management professional must decide how to treat loss exposures or must present recommendations to management. The risk management professional should review all contracts before they are finally executed and reject inappropriate ones.

When reviewing a contract, the risk management professional should ask these questions:

- To what extent can the assumption of loss exposures be reduced?
- What loss exposures can the organization safely assume?

- To what extent should contractually assumed loss exposures be transferred by insurance?
- Can specific contract provisions be deleted, particularly those involving loss exposures that can be neither safely retained nor transferred?
- Can clearer contract language be negotiated, especially to clarify points that seem likely to be disputed?

An organization may be willing to assume the exposures presented by some transfer agreements without insurance. Such loss exposures usually involve only minor and remote hazards, free of any element of catastrophe. For more severe exposures, retention might be unwise.

For loss exposures to be covered by insurance, the risk management professional must be as certain as possible that coverage is available either under the organization's current coverages or for purchase. The risk management professional must also examine the other contracting party's insurance protection, if any. Whether the exposure is covered under an existing policy or additional coverage will be purchased, the risk management professional should provide a clear description of the coverage that applies, including the insurer's legal defense obligations.

Even the best use of risk control and risk financing can fail to control contractual transfers. Rather than avoid such contracts completely, management can restrict the types of risks it will transfer for example, refusing to transfer liability related to acts of God (a contingency for which no insurance can be obtained) and claims caused entirely by the transferor's alleged fault without wrongdoing by any other party (transferor's sole negligence). The ability to impose such restrictions in a contractual risk transfer agreement depends on the bargaining strengths of the parties and the importance of their contractual relationship. See the exhibit "Fundamental Guidelines of Contractual Risk Transfer Management."

Fundamental Guidelines of Contractual Risk Transfer Management

- Ensure that the indemnitor can fulfill its commitment financially. Legal precedent mandates that the commitment be backed by insurance of at least $1 million per occurrence.
- Require a certificate of insurance for contractual liability coverage before contract operations begin.
- Be named as an additional insured on the transferee's policy. Although being added as an additional insured can pose problems—such as an increased possibility of policy cancellation or nonrenewal—its advantages far outweigh the disadvantages.
- Avoid being too severe. If a contractual transfer is too extreme, courts may construe it as invalid because it is unconscionable or contrary to public policy. The farther apart the two parties are in their bargaining power and knowledge of contract terms, the greater the probability that the contract will be unenforceable.
- Avoid ambiguity. Courts unfavorably view contracts that indemnify individuals or organizations against the consequences of their own negligence or intentional wrongdoing. If contract language is ambiguous, courts generally construe a hold-harmless agreement to make it consistent with common law and public policy. Generally, this means that a person or an organization is indemnified for liability, especially if the person or organization was only passively negligent in causing property damage or bodily injury.
- Become more actively involved in legislation. Many of the current statutes limiting contractual indemnification are the products of lobbying efforts. Risk management professionals have an obligation to their organizations and to the public to present compelling reasons for laws that can benefit an organization, the economy, and society.

[DA08631]

SUMMARY

The two types of contractual (noninsurance) risk transfer are a noninsurance risk control transfer and a noninsurance risk financing transfer. A noninsured risk control transfer rids the transferor of most or all of the possibility of suffering a loss from the transferred exposure. A noninsured risk financing transfer creates the transferee's duty to pay money to (or on behalf of) transferors after the transferor has suffered a loss. Types of noninsurance risk control transfers include incorporation, leasing, contracting for services, suretyship and guaranty agreements, waiver, limitation of liability, and disclaimer of warranties. Types of risk financing transfers include hold-harmless agreements and transfer of risk to a transferee's insurer.

Noninsurance risk transfers can be classified by type of transaction. Examples include transactions involving construction contracts, service and maintenance contracts, purchase order contracts, lease of premises contracts, equipment lease contracts, bailment contracts, and sale and supply contracts.

Contractual (noninsurance) risk transfer agreements may define obligations of the transferor and transferee in a way that alters each party's common-law liabilities. Categorized by how they alter common law, such agreements can be grouped according to whether they transfer responsibility for the transferee's sole fault (limited form), all responsibility for the transferee's sole fault and the joint fault of both parties (immediate form), or all of the parties' responsibility, regardless of fault (broad form).

The statutes that apply to hold-harmless agreements can be classified into those that prohibit transfer (all-inclusive statutes), those that prohibit particular wording, and those that place requirements on the provisions the contracting parties include in their agreement.

When negotiating contractual risk transfers, a risk management professional should consider the enforceability of the transfer, the parties' ability to manage risk, and the nature and extent of risk that is transferred. The first and most important element of a sound contractual risk transfer control program is to develop a consistent transfer strategy.

Segment C

Direct Your Learning

9

Transferring Financial Risk

Educational Objectives

After learning the content of this assignment, you should be able to:

- Describe the various types of financial risk.
- Explain how an organization can use derivatives such as forwards, futures, options, and swaps to transfer financial risk.
- Explain how an organization can use securitization to transfer financial risk.
- Given information on an organization's financial risk, recommend ways to transfer the risk.

Outline

Transferring Financial Risk

9

TYPES OF FINANCIAL RISK

To comprehensively identify an organization's risks, a risk management professional should know the types of financial risk that could potentially harm an organization.

Whenever an organization owns or uses a financial instrument, it becomes exposed to financial risk. A financial instrument is a check, a bond, a share of stock, or another document with monetary value. A financial instrument could also be a binding agreement between parties for payment of money. Financial risk refers to the uncertainty arising from the effect of market forces on a financial asset or liability. Three key categories of financial risk are market risk, credit risk, and price risk.

Market Risk

Market risk is the risk that the value of an investment or a portfolio of investments will decrease or increase due to changes in the market for that investment. Associated market risks include these:

- **Interest rate risk**
- **Exchange rate risk**
- **Liquidity risk**

Interest Rate Risk

Interest rate risk involves uncertainty over the movement of volatile interest rates and the effect that has on the value of an investment. Movement in the interest rate could raise the value of an organization's assets or lower the value of its liabilities. The interest rate moving can also cause an organization's assets to decrease in value or its liabilities to increase in value. For example, suppose an organization takes out a $1 million loan for two years and invests it in assets with a one-year maturity. If it pays 6 percent interest on the loan but earns 7 percent interest on the assets, the organization will make a 1 percent profit. The organization must reinvest the funds in new assets at the end of the year. If the interest rate earned on the new assets declines to 5 percent, the organization will lose money at 1 percent for the second year. The change in interest rate could, in effect, cancel the profit made in the first year.

Market risk

Uncertainty about an investment's future value because of potential changes in the market for that type of investment.

Interest rate risk

The risk that a security's future value will decline because of changes in interest rates.

Exchange rate risk

Uncertainty about an investment's value because of potential changes in the exchange rate between currencies.

Liquidity risk

The risk that an asset cannot be sold on short notice without incurring a loss.

Exchange Rate Risk

Exchange rate risk is a concern to an organization with cash flows denominated in a foreign currency. Changes in the exchange rate can lower the value of an organization's assets or raise the value of its liabilities. (Changes in the exchange rate could also raise the value of an organization's assets or lower the value of its liabilities.) For example, if an Italian ship builder agrees to accept payment in four yearly installments in United States (U.S.) dollars as a ship is being built, the ship builder is accepting the risk that the dollar may depreciate in value in relation to the euro. If that happens, the U.S. company's payments to the ship builder may be reduced when they are converted from dollars to euros (using the current exchange rate) on the days the yearly installments are made. However, the U.S. payer is accepting the risk the dollar will appreciate in value in relation to the euro. If the dollar appreciates, the payments to the ship builder may be increased when they are converted from dollars to euros. It is possible the dollar may appreciate in some years and depreciate in others in relation to the euro, thereby cancelling the exchange rate's effect on the payment.

Liquidity Risk

Liquidity risk involves the uncertainty over an organization having enough cash or other assets that can be converted to cash and maintain value should there be an immediate demand for cash. Typically, the amount of cash needed during a given time period can be reasonably estimated. However, if an unusual event occurs, there may be a sudden and large increase in demand for the organization's cash. Once the cash on hand is spent, the organization may try to borrow additional funds or sell those assets that can be converted to cash with little loss in value. If there is still not enough to meet the demands for cash, the organization may be forced to sell those assets that can only be sold in a short time period at a substantial discount. The discount represents a loss in value in the organization's assets, which must also be shown as a loss in value in the organization's net worth.

An example of a liquidity problem is an organization losing its insurance coverage when its policy is nonrenewed due to a high frequency of claims. Maintaining insurance coverage is a requirement in the loan agreement of a large bank loan. When the bank is notified by the insurer that the coverage has been nonrenewed, the bank demands that the loan be repaid immediately.

Credit Risk

Credit risk
The risk that customers or other creditors will fail to make promised payments as they come due.

Credit risk (which is also referred to as counterparty risk) occurs due to the uncertainty about a party who is obligated to pay money per a binding agreement. The uncertainty concerns whether the party will actually pay all of the money it owes and pay it on time. The party who is obligated to pay could be a customer who bought the organization's products or services on credit. If every customer paid the amount owed on time, there would be no credit risk.

However, if a customer defaults on the credit agreement, the income from the sale of the products or services is at risk.

Similarly, if the obligated party received a loan from the organization and then defaulted on the loan agreement, the principal loaned and the interest that was to be paid are at risk. For example, if an organization discovers that a $50,000 loan is in default and uncollectable due to the deteriorated financial condition of the obligated party, the organization will have to adjust its balance sheet. The asset account for loans made by the organization will have to be reduced by $50,000, and, to maintain balance, the net worth account will also be reduced by the same amount.

Price Risk

Price risk occurs due to the uncertainty of setting the price of an organization's product correctly. Potential loss of revenue can occur as a result of input price risk or output price risk. Input price risk is the uncertainty of the price of the resources that are used to produce an organization's product. An increase in the price of a resource, such as copper for a wire manufacturer, will lower the manufacturer's margin on wire unless it increases the price of the wire. Output price risk is the uncertainty of what price the organization can charge for its product. A competitor's pricing may force an organization to lower the price for its product to one with a very thin margin for profit. For example, a baker might have to lower the price of his baked goods if there are several other bakers in the same town.

Price risk

The potential for a change in revenue or cost because of an increase or a decrease in the price of a product or an input.

Apply Your Knowledge

ABC Insurance is trying to determine what premium to charge an insured for liability insurance in a competitive market. What financial risk is ABC exposed to in this situation, and what makes setting the premium particularly difficult for an insurer?

Feedback: ABC is exposed to price risk in this situation as competitors may underprice the product to gain market share. A unique challenge for insurers such as ABC is that they don't know the costs of the product (input price risk) until after all the claims have been closed on the policy sold.

DERIVATIVES

Knowing the characteristics of financial contracts based on the derivative concept will help a risk management professional identify the best method to use when transferring financial risk for an organization.

A derivative is a financial contract that derives its value from another asset, such as a commodity, or that can derive its value from the yields on another

asset or the level of an index, such as the Standard & Poor's 500 Stock Index. Forward contracts and futures contracts are two of the four major categories of derivatives and are common financial contracts used in financial risk management. The other two major categories of derivatives are options and swaps.

An option is an agreement that gives its holder the right, but not the obligation, to buy or sell an asset at a specific price over a period of time. The strike price is the specific price at which the holder of an option can buy or sell the asset associated with the option. A swap is an agreement between two organizations to exchange payments based on changes in the value of an asset, yield, or index over a specific period.

Forward Contracts

Forward contract

A contract that obligates one party to buy and another party to sell a specific financial instrument or physical commodity at a specified future date and price.

A **forward contract** is the simplest form of derivative for financial risk management. A futures contract is a forward contract that is exchange-traded and therefore standardized, openly available, and transferable. Because a forward contract enables a buyer and seller of a commodity or financial instrument to know its price prior to delivery, it can serve to reduce the risk of price fluctuations of the commodity or financial instrument, subject to the futures contract. Consequently, futures contracts enable organizations to plan and budget activities with less concern regarding price changes.

For example, in June, a small crude oil producer might enter into a forward contract with a refinery to sell 1,000 barrels of production for delivery in November at a price of $80 per barrel. In entering into the forward contract, the crude oil producer forgoes additional revenue if the November open market price of crude oil exceeds $80 per barrel, but is protected against decreased revenue if the November open market price is below $80 per barrel. Regardless of variations in the price of crude oil between June and November, the sales price for the producer's 1,000 barrels will be $80 per barrel. The forward contract enables the crude oil producer to effectively manage its financial risk by eliminating the uncertainty of sales price at delivery.

Options

Options are available for stocks, commodities, foreign exchange rates, and other traded securities; the holder of an option can buy or sell the associated asset for a specific price, or strike price. A **call option** is an option that gives the holder the right to buy an asset. A **put option** is an option that gives the holder the right to sell an asset.

Call option

An option to buy a set amount of the underlying security at any time within a specified period.

Put option

An option giving the holder the right to sell a set amount of the underlying security at any time within a specified period.

When the value of a call option's underlying asset exceeds the strike price, the buyer can exercise the option and realize a gain. If the value of the underlying asset is less than the strike price, the buyer cannot realize a gain by exercising the option.

The seller is the party that issues the option and receives an up-front payment from the buyer. The payment compensates the seller for accepting the risk

that it will have to pay cash to the buyer if the buyer exercises the option. As an example, assume ABC Corporation has an option to purchase 100 shares of stock at a strike price of $70 per share over the next year, and the current market price is $60 per share. If, during the year, the market price of the stock rises to $80 per share, ABC will likely exercise the option. By exercising the option, ABC can purchase 100 shares at $70 each for $7,000 and immediately sell those shares for $8,000 ($80 x 100) in the market. ABC would realize a $1,000 profit on the transaction.

Swaps

Swaps are frequently structured so that no money is paid up front between counterparties for the contract. Instead, cash flows are exchanged back and forth between the organizations throughout the term of the swap. Swaps are commonly used to manage interest rate and currency rate of exchange risk.

As an example of an interest rate swap, ABC Company might be required to pay CBA Company interest at a fixed rate of 2 percent on a principal amount of $5 million. In return, CBA Company might be required to pay ABC Company on the basis of a three-month London Inter-Bank Offer Rate (LIBOR), a frequently changing or "floating" interest rate that banks charge each other for loans, for the same principal amount. This means that ABC Company will make interest payments based on a fixed rate and receive interest payments based on a floating rate, while CBA Company will make interest payments based on a floating rate and receive interest payments based on a fixed rate. All payments will be made on a quarterly basis. The schedule of payments that the swap might follow is shown in the exhibit. See the exhibit "Schedule of Payments in an Interest Rate Swap."

Schedule of Payments in an Interest Rate Swap

Date	LIBOR	Floating Payment	Fixed Payment	Net Cash Flow for ABC Co.
1st Quarter	1.50%	$75,000	$100,000	-$25,000
2nd Quarter	1.75%	$87,500	$100,000	-$12,500
3rd Quarter	2.75%	$137,500	$100,000	$37,500
4th Quarter	3.25%	$162,500	$100,000	$62,500

[DA08716]

SECURITIZATION

Organizations maintain liquidity by generating cash. So knowing how to convert an income-producing asset to a cash asset is valuable, particularly for an organization that needs additional cash quickly.

Securitization is the process of creating a marketable investment security based on a financial transaction's expected cash flows. Using an intermediary allows investors to decide whether to invest in a security based solely on the risk presented by the income-producing asset and not the credit risk of the organization who owned the asset before transferring it to the intermediary. Because some securitizations have been used improperly in the past, these transactions are scrutinized by regulators, auditors, and investors.

Securitization

An organization can use securitization to exchange income-producing assets for cash provided by the purchaser of the security, assuming that a market exists for the asset. This exchange allows the organization to convert the asset to cash on its balance sheet.

For example, a bank can securitize its mortgage loans. Individuals who have received mortgage loans are expected to pay them back. Therefore, the loans are recognized as an asset and are referred to as mortgage receivables on the bank's balance sheet. Cash, however, is often a more desirable asset because of its versatility. For example, the bank could use cash to make more mortgage loans to individuals. Also, unlike mortgage receivables, cash does not carry credit risk, such as the possibility that the mortgage loan will not be repaid. If the bank wishes to convert the mortgage receivables asset to cash, it could sell it to an intermediary.

Special Purpose Vehicle (SPV)

The intermediary that enables the bank to convert its mortgage receivables asset into a cash asset is referred to as a special purpose vehicle (SPV), a facility established for the purpose of purchasing income-producing assets from an organization, holding title to them, and then using those assets to collateralize securities that will be sold to investors.

The SPV securitizes the mortgage receivables by using them as collateral for securities it sells to investors. The SPV then uses the interest and principal repayments on the mortgage receivables to fund the interest and principal repayments to the security investors. The securities carry the risks of the mortgage receivables held by the SPV. These risks include the possibility of default by the mortgagors (the borrowers) and the risk that the mortgagors might cancel their mortgages in order to refinance them at lower interest rates elsewhere. In essence, securitization transfers the risk inherent in the mortgage receivables from the bank to the security investors.

Income-Producing Assets

A major benefit of involving an SPV in a securitization transaction is that investors can decide whether to invest in the securities based solely on the risk presented by the income-producing assets held as collateral by the SPV. If an organization directly securitized its income-producing assets without using an SPV as an intermediary, investors would need to consider not only the risks presented by the income-producing assets but also the overall credit risk of the organization.

Analyzing overall credit risk is complex because an organization holds many different types of assets and incurs many different types of liabilities. Even expert investors frequently have difficulty accurately analyzing the credit risk of an organization. An SPV reduces this associated credit risk.

Securitization Model

The exhibit depicts a generic securitization model. The organization sells income-producing assets to an SPV in exchange for cash. The income-producing assets are no longer owned by the organization but instead are owned by the SPV to sell to investors.

The investors purchase the securities for cash and receive a return on their investment commensurate with the risk inherent in the income-producing assets that back the securities, not in the organization's credit risk. See the exhibit "Generic Securitization Model."

Generic Securitization Model

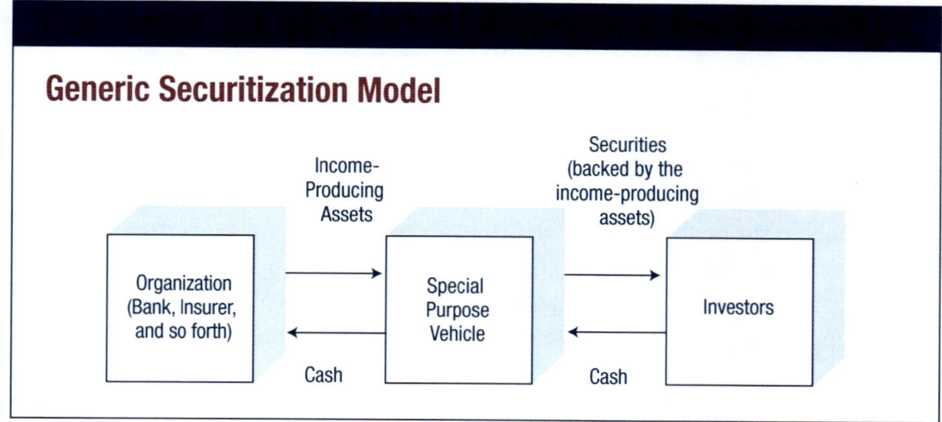

[DA02520]

Regulatory Requirements

Regulators, auditors, and potential investors scrutinize the use of SPVs because they have been used to manipulate organizations' income statements and balance sheets. Therefore, a firm that uses an SPV for securitization must take the utmost care to meet all regulatory requirements and maintain a high level of disclosure regarding the SPV's assets, finances, purpose, and management.

Insurers can participate in a securitization transaction in a number of ways. For example, an insurer can securitize its financed premium receivables by transferring them to an SPV in exchange for cash. The SPV could then use those premium receivables to collateralize securities it sells to investors.

Apply Your Knowledge

ABC Insurance has endured several years of operating at a loss and needs an immediate cash payment to meet current debts. It holds a large amount of financed premium receivables that provide income, but the income is paid to it over an extended period of time. ABC has decided to sell its premium receivables to an SPV. What concerns would an investor have regarding purchasing a security collateralized by ABC's premium receivables?

Feedback: The process of securitization normally narrows down the risk to investors to the risks presented by the income-producing asset itself, which in this case are whether the insureds of ABC keep their policies in force for the full policy term and whether the insureds pay their finance charges and premiums in a timely manner. The credit risk of ABC, as an organization that sold its income-producing asset to an SPV for cash, would typically not be an issue for investors, directly or indirectly. However, if ABC were to become insolvent, the percentage of insureds who continued to pay their premiums as they were due would likely plummet because they might question whether ABC would be able to pay their potential claims.

TRANSFERRING FINANCIAL RISK

Being able to identify the types of financial risk and how to use derivatives and securitization to manage them in a given case is an important skill for a risk management professional. By carefully considering the facts provided in this activity and applying each step for the types of financial risk identified, you can transition from knowing the exposures from financial risk to knowing how to apply the risk treatment tools of derivatives and securitization to those exposures.

Case Facts

Wonderful Fit Clothing (WFC) Company is a new clothing manufacturer. A popular celebrity was recently spotted wearing WFC's products, causing sales to rise quickly—so quickly, in fact, that the company is now unable to keep up with demand. Recognizing that the tastes of its consumers can change quickly, WFC is trying to raise cash so it can increase production and sell more of its products while demand is high.

WFC management wants to raise cash using two methods. The first is to take out a loan. However, it was only able to obtain short-term financing at a reasonable interest rate and is concerned that when the time comes to refinance the debt, the interest rate could rise, creating an expense it cannot afford.

The second method of raising cash involves converting past sales into cash. Past sales have resulted in a large accounts receivable account, which contains the amounts due from retail stores that have sold WFC products but not yet paid for them. Several investors have expressed an interest in paying cash for WFC's accounts receivable as long as the company remains financially solvent and is able to forward retail-store payments to the investors.

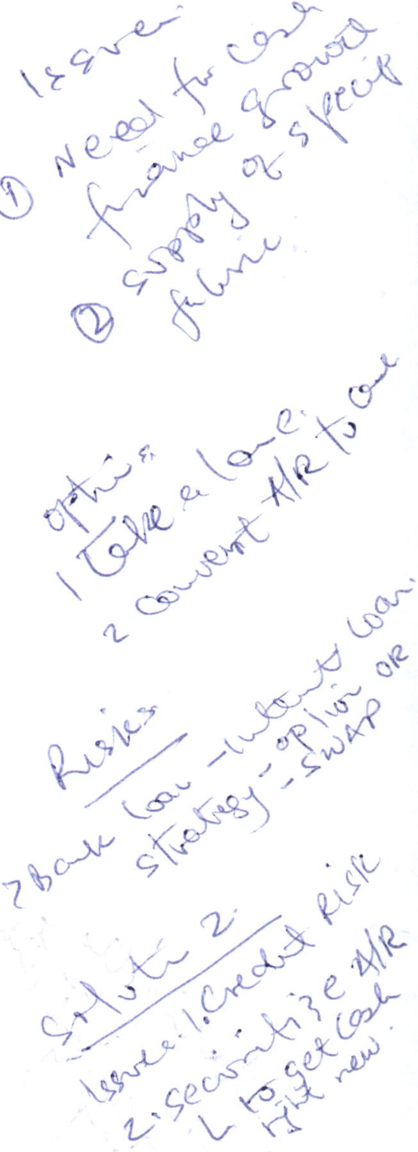

Another concern of WFC management is that it uses a fabric in its products that is, at times, in short supply, causing the cost to purchase the fabric, and in turn the cost to produce the clothing, to vary substantially. WFC needs to secure a more stable cost for the fabric to help the company set consistent prices for its buyers.

Overview of Steps

WFC management should first identify the pertinent financial risks. Second, it should determine a reasonable treatment plan for those exposures.

WFC will create financial risk exposures with the methods it intends to use to raise cash. The first method of raising cash through debt creates financial risk by requiring the company to refinance short term debt at the then-current interest rate. The second method of raising cash—by selling accounts receivable to investors—creates a financial risk of uncertain payment by WFC, to which investors will not likely want to expose themselves. The last financial risk concerns the fluctuating price of the special fabric used to produce WFC's products.

Financial Risk in Raising Cash Through Debt

The first method of raising cash is to take out a loan. However, WFC was only able to obtain short-term financing at a reasonable interest rate and is concerned that when the time comes to refinance the debt, the interest rate could rise, creating an expense it cannot afford. What is the type of financial risk described, and how can this exposure be treated?

The type of financial risk being described is interest rate risk. One possible treatment for it is to use an options contract.

An **options contract** is an agreement that gives its holder (WFC) the right, but not the obligation, to buy or sell an asset at a specific price over a period of time. The **strike price** is the price at which the holder of an option can buy or sell the asset associated with the option. Call options cap or provide a ceiling for interest rates by giving the holder the right to buy an asset—in this case, a lower interest rate.

Option contract
An agreement to keep an offer open for a stated period, supported by consideration.

Strike price
The price at which the stock or commodity underlying a call option (such as a warrant) or a put option can be purchased (called) or sold (put) during a specified period.

If the interest rate at the time WFC refinances its short-term debt exceeds the strike price, the seller of the options contract will pay the difference between the strike price and the interest rate. This option provides an upper limit on the interest expense of WFC as the buyer and holder of the options contract.

Financial Risk in Raising Cash by Selling Accounts Receivable

The second method of raising cash involves converting past sales into cash. Several investors have expressed an interest in paying cash for WFC's accounts receivable as long as the company remains financially solvent and is able to forward retail-store payments to the investors. What type of financial risk is being described, and how can this exposure be treated?

Credit risk is the type of financial risk being described. One possible treatment is to use securitization.

A special purpose vehicle (SPV) is the intermediary that enables WFC to convert its accounts receivable to cash assets. The SPV securitizes the accounts receivable by using them as collateral for securities it sells to investors. The SPV then uses the interest and principal payments on the accounts receivable to fund the interest and principal payments to the security investors. The securities carry the risks of the accounts receivable held by the SPV. These risks include the possibility of default by the retail stores. In essence, securitization transfers the risk inherent in the accounts receivable from WFC to the security investors.

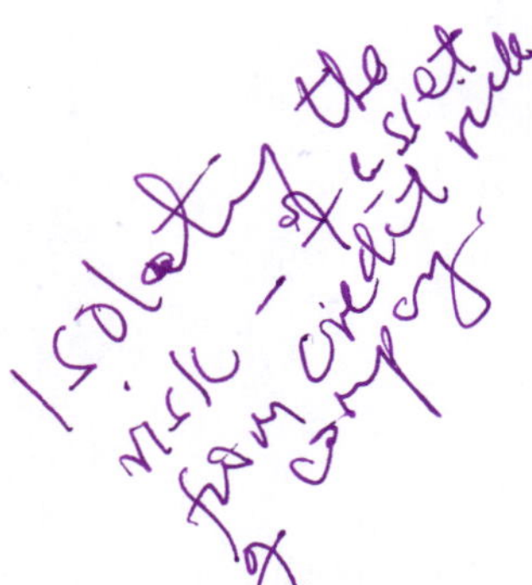

A major benefit of involving an SPV in a securitization transaction is that investors can decide whether to invest in the securities based solely on the risk presented by the income-producing assets held as collateral by the SPV. If WFC directly securitized its income-producing assets without using an SPV as an intermediary, investors would need to consider not only the risks presented by the income-producing assets, but also the overall credit risk of WFC.

Analyzing overall credit risk is complex because WFC may hold many different types of assets and incur many different types of liabilities. Even expert investors have difficulty accurately analyzing the credit risk of an organization such as WFC. An SPV reduces this associated credit risk.

Financial Risk in Fluctuating Price of Special Fabric

WFC uses a fabric in its products that is, at times, in short supply, causing the cost to purchase the fabric, and in turn the cost to produce the clothing, to vary substantially. What type of financial risk is being described, and how can this exposure be treated?

This type of financial risk is called input price risk. One possible treatment for it is to use a forward contract.

A forward contract is the simplest form of derivative for financial risk management. It is a contract that obligates one party (such as WFC) to buy and another party (such as the supplier of the special fabric) to sell at a specified future date and price. Because a forward contract enables a buyer and seller of a commodity, such as a fabric, to know the commodity's price before delivery, it can serve to reduce the risk of price fluctuations of the commodity. Consequently, a forward contract would enable WFC to plan and budget activities with less concern regarding price changes of the fabric.

SUMMARY

Financial risk refers to the uncertainty about the future investment returns of a given asset and can be classified as market risk, credit risk, or price risk. Market risk is the risk that the value of an investment or a portfolio of investments will decrease or increase due to a change in the value of associated market risk factors. Associated market risks include interest rate risk, exchange rate risk, and liquidity risk. Credit risk (which is also referred to as counterparty risk) occurs due to the uncertainty about a party who is obligated to pay money per a binding agreement. Price risk can be due to input price risk or output price risk.

A derivative is a contract that derives its value from another asset. Futures and forward contracts are common financial contracts used in risk management. Two other major categories of derivatives are options and swaps.

An option is an agreement that gives the holder the right, but not the obligation, to buy or sell an asset at a specific price, called the strike price, during a period of time. A swap is an agreement between two organizations to exchange cash flows based on movements in the value of another asset, yield, or index.

Securitization is a means to create a marketable security based on the expected cash flows from a financial transaction. Using an SPV as an intermediary allows investors to decide whether to invest in a security based solely on the risk presented by the income-producing asset and not the credit risk of the organization that owned the asset before transferring it to the SPV. Because some securitizations have been used improperly, utmost care must be taken to meet all regulatory requirements and maintain a high level of disclosure to regulators, auditors, and investors.

You should now be able to identify the types of financial risk, such as interest rate risk, credit risk, and input price risk. You should also be able to recommend ways to address exposures, such as an options contract, securitization, and a forward contract.

Direct Your Learning

10

Transferring Hazard Risk to the Capital Markets

Educational Objectives

After learning the content of this assignment, you should be able to:

- Describe the types of capital market products used for risk financing.
- Explain how insurance-linked securities operate in terms of the following:
  - The use of catastrophe bonds
  - The benefits to investors
  - The advantages and disadvantages
- Explain how insurance derivatives operate, including:
  - The use of swaps
  - The use of insurance options
  - The advantages and disadvantages of insurance derivatives
- Explain how these contingent capital arrangements operate:
  - The use of a standby credit facility
  - The use of a contingent surplus note arrangement
  - The use of a catastrophe equity put arrangement
  - The advantages and disadvantages of contingent capital arrangements
- Analyze the concerns of organizations that use insurance-linked securities and insurance derivatives to transfer risk and the investors supplying capital.
- Describe the regulatory and accounting issues involved with insurance-linked securities and insurance derivatives.

Outline

Transferring Hazard Risk to the Capital Markets

10

CAPITAL MARKET RISK FINANCING PRODUCTS

Organizations use risk financing methods, such as insurance, to obtain funds to offset losses. Rising and unpredictable costs for insurance and reinsurance, particularly for catastrophes, have spurred some organizations to use alternative methods of risk financing.

Some types of risk, particularly **catastrophe** risk (the risk of a large accumulation of losses stemming from one event, such as an earthquake or a tornado), can be difficult to address through traditional risk financing methods.

Capital market products are traded financial instruments (such as stocks and bonds) that mature in more than one year. These products have emerged as tools that organizations can use to finance risk as an alternative to insurance. These instruments were once used only to provide capital to insurers (or reinsurers), who then used the capital to underwrite their customers' risk.

Types of Capital Market Products

The convergence of insurance with other financial services has expanded the capital markets' role in risk financing to include insurance-linked securities, insurance derivatives, and **contingent capital arrangements**.

Some of these capital market products are rooted in the concepts of **securitization** and **special purpose vehicles (SPV)**, which allow organizations to exchange assets for cash. Others are based on **derivatives**. Each of the products involves advantages and disadvantages, many of which relate to risk transfer and retention. In addition to these considerations, risk management professionals must assess the accounting and regulatory ramifications associated with capital market products to determine whether they are appropriate for the organization.

Insurance-Linked Securities

An insurance-linked security is a financial instrument whose value is primarily driven by insurance and/or reinsurance loss events. This marketable instrument is based on the cash flows that arise from the transfer of insurable risks. These cash flows are similar to premium and loss payments under an insurance policy. Investors are attracted to the portfolio diversification aspect of insurance-linked securities, as they constitute a distinct asset class with risk that normally has a low correlation with that of other asset classes, such as

Catastrophe
A single event that causes widespread losses.

Capital market
A financial market in which long-term securities are traded.

Contingent capital arrangement
An agreement, entered into before any losses occur, that enables an organization to raise cash by selling stock or issuing debt at prearranged terms after a loss occurs that exceeds a certain threshold.

Securitization
The process of creating a marketable investment security based on a financial transaction's expected cash flows.

Special purpose vehicle (SPV)
A facility established for the purpose of purchasing income-producing assets from an organization, holding title to them, and then using those assets to collateralize securities that will be sold to investors.

Derivative
A financial contract that derives its value from the value of another asset.

traditional stocks and bonds. To date, insurance-linked securities have been mainly in the form of catastrophe bonds.

For instance, with catastrophe bonds, an SPV "reinsures" the insurer for specific catastrophe losses and in turn funds the coverage by selling bonds in the regular capital markets. The interest and principal on these bonds does not need to be repaid to the capital market investors if the specified losses take place. If the losses do not take place, the SPV pays interest and repays the principal on a schedule, as with most other bonds.

Insurance Derivatives

An insurance derivative is a financial contract whose value is based on the level of insurable losses that occur during a specific time period. An insurance derivative increases in value as specified insurable losses increase, and, therefore, the purchaser of the derivative can use this gain to offset its insurable losses. The buyer of an insurance derivative accepts insurable risk and receives a commensurate return for doing so. The value of an insurance derivative can be based on the level of insurable losses experienced by a single organization or on the level of an insurance industry index of insured losses. Financial contracts based on the insurance derivative concept include forward contracts, swaps, and insurance options.

Contingent Capital Arrangements

A contingent capital arrangement is a pre-loss agreement that establishes terms for an organization to raise cash in the wake of a major loss. The entity that agrees to provide the contingent capital receives a commitment fee in exchange for its promise to reimburse the partner organization for its loss costs. Under a contingent capital arrangement, the organization does not transfer its risk of loss to investors. Instead, after a loss occurs, it receives a capital injection in the form of debt or equity to help it pay for the loss. Because the terms of the capital injection are agreed upon in advance, the organization generally receives more favorable terms than it would receive if it were forced to raise capital after a large loss, when the organization is likely to be in a weakened financial condition. The major types of contingent capital arrangements are standby credit facilities, contingent surplus notes, and catastrophe equity put options.

Value of Capital Market Products

Capital markets offer products to investors who are willing to accept risk. A risk management professional can provide an organization with a competitive advantage by knowing capital market products and their availability, use, and advantages and disadvantages. Capital market products are useful for expanding traditional business and managing financial risk.

Capital market products have evolved from the convergence of insurance with other financial services. Noninsurance financial institutions, particularly investment banks, can expand their traditional business by offering the capital markets' capacity to organizations as an alternative to using insurance to finance losses, thereby allowing these institutions to enter the domain of insurers, reinsurers, and insurance brokers.

Insurers, reinsurers, and insurance brokers can expand their traditional business by using insurance policies and/or capital market products to cover not only losses from traditionally insurable risks, but also losses from other types of risk, such as commodity price risk and interest rate risk.

Theoretically, capital market products can be used to finance any type of insurable risk. Insufficient underwriting data for some categories of risk and regulatory and accounting uncertainty associated with the use of capital market products have limited their market and capacity growth. Each type of capital market product involves a great deal of time and expense to implement. Therefore, relatively few large organizations—mainly insurers and reinsurers—have used them to finance risk. Most successfully implemented capital market products finance catastrophe risk.

INSURANCE-LINKED SECURITIES

Insurance-linked securities created through insurance securitization supplement existing risk-transfer capacity and provide an alternative risk transfer mechanism to traditional insurance and reinsurance.

An insurance securitization is the process of creating a marketable **insurance-linked security** based on the cash flows that arise from the transfer of insurable risks. These cash flows are similar to premium and loss payments under an insurance policy. Risk managers should understand these issues related to insurance-linked securities (ILSs):

Insurance-linked security
A financial instrument whose value is primarily driven by insurance and/or reinsurance loss events.

- Operation of insurance securitizations
- Use of catastrophe bonds
- Benefits to investors
- Advantages of using ILSs
- Disadvantages of using ILSs

Operation of Insurance Securitizations

Insurance securitization can be illustrated through an exhibit. The special purpose vehicle (SPV) is a specialized facility that acts as an insurer (or a reinsurer). Cash is paid by an organization to the SPV in exchange for the promise to pay any losses that occur. The payments are similar to the premium and loss payments under an insurance policy. See the exhibit "Generic Insurance Securitization Model."

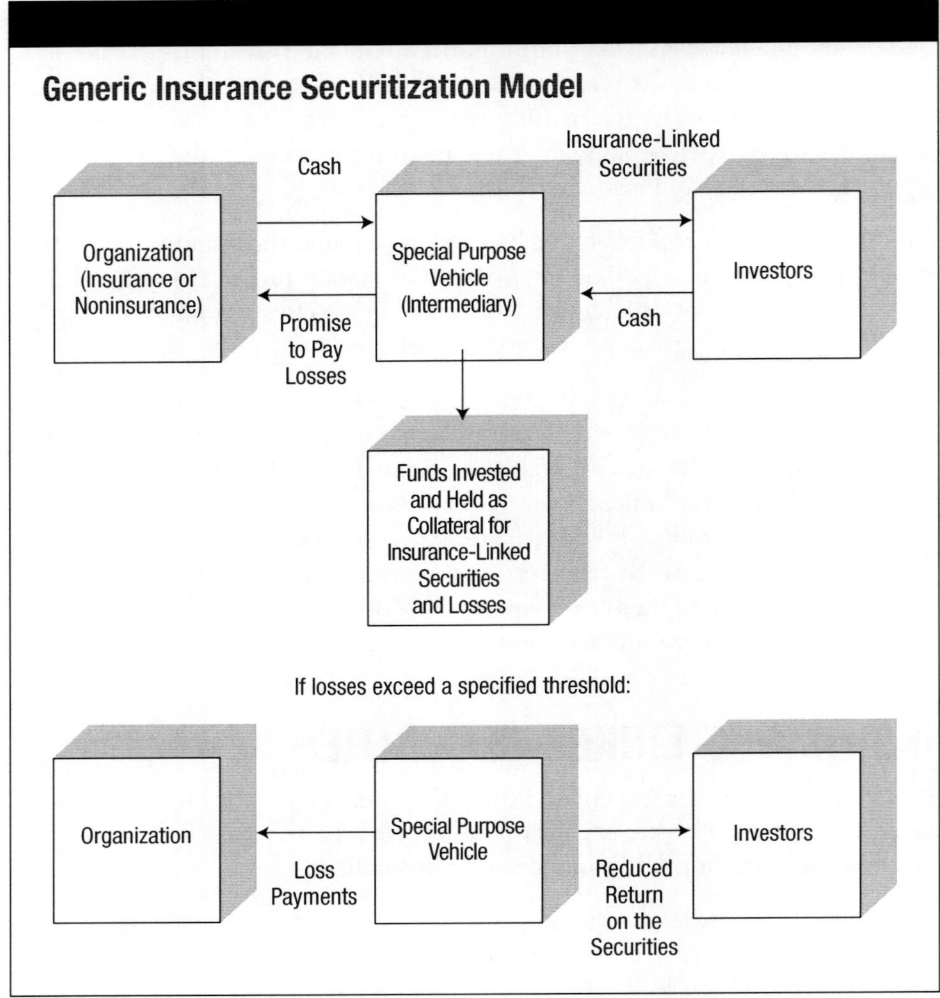

[DA01743]

Insurance securitization differs from most other types of securitization. Instead of selling income-producing assets to an SPV and receiving cash, an organization engaging in an insurance securitization pays cash to the SPV, who sells ILSs to investors on the capital market. The SPV retains the principal from the security sales until the loss threshold specified in the ILS contract is met or the security expires. If the loss threshold is met, the SPV reimburses the organization for qualifying losses that occur, using the principal received for purchase of the securities up to the specified limit. In such cases, at the end of the ILS period, the SPV may withhold from the investor the principal, the interest, or both, depending on the terms of the agreement. If the loss threshold is not met and the security expires, the SPV returns the principle to the investors along with interest earnings.

To determine whether the loss threshold is met, the SPV uses the organization's actual losses or an index of insured losses incurred by a group of insurers (for example, all of the insurers that pay losses for hurricanes that damage properties in the South Atlantic coastal states within the specified period). When the reimbursement is based on the organization's actual losses, the insurance securitization transaction mimics a traditional insurance risk transfer.

An insurance securitization can be designed to cover an organization's losses either on a per occurrence or an aggregate basis. The definition of covered loss (the loss threshold) is specified in the contract between the investors and the SPV and in the contract between the SPV and the organization transferring its risk.

An SPV plays a unique role in an insurance securitization transaction compared with its role in other types of securitization transactions. These differences are notable:

- The SPV transforms insurable risk into investment risk.
- The SPV receives cash from both the investors and the organization that transfers the insurable risk. It holds the cash as collateral for its obligation to repay interest and principal on the insurance-linked securities and its obligation to pay any insured losses that occur.
- Depending on the domicile involved, the SPV may qualify as an authorized insurer (or reinsurer), which enables the organization transferring its risk of loss to treat the transaction as insurance (or reinsurance) for tax and accounting purposes.

Use of Catastrophe Bonds

Even though insurance securitizations, which are also commonly referred to as insurance-linked securities, could, in theory, be applied to any insurable risk, the vast majority of ILSs issued to date are catastrophe bonds, which are a type of ILS specifically designed to transfer insurable catastrophe risk to investors. Catastrophe bonds were developed, in part, in response to the limited availability and affordability of catastrophe reinsurance.

These bonds are issued by SPVs developed and owned by large reinsurers, insurers, or large corporations to serve as catastrophe bond intermediaries and to mimic traditional excess (catastrophe) insurance (and reinsurance). As such, they can be issued for any type of catastrophic insurable risk, including hurricanes, earthquakes, and other adverse weather and environmental risks.

The catastrophe losses that trigger payment under a catastrophe bond can be based on aggregate catastrophe losses over a defined period of time or the occurrence of a single catastrophic event. Losses triggered on an aggregate basis can be measured using an insurance industry loss index for catastrophes or the actual catastrophe losses of an organization, whether for an insurance or a noninsurance organization. Losses can also be measured against a specific standard (such as a Category Four or greater hurricane).

Computer models are used to measure the frequency and severity probabilities that determine the standards used to measure the catastrophic risk embedded in these bonds. Catastrophe bonds are typically structured to provide protection against infrequently occurring (1-in-100-year to 1-in-250-year) events. These frequencies appeal to both the organizations issuing the bonds and investors buying the bonds, because the issuers of the bonds want them to be triggered (and, consequently, priced) at a level that reflects a highly infrequent event. The investors who buy the bonds also want them to respond to highly infrequent events, which lowers the risk of losing money on the investment. See the exhibit "Example of Insurance-Linked Security."

Example of Insurance-Linked Security

A property insurer has hurricane concentration risk in the southeastern and Gulf Coast regions of the United States. The property insurer is financially strong. A Category Three or higher hurricane that affects a densely populated area in the insurer's coverage region (Dade County, for example) could result in over $1.5 billion in paid insured losses for the firm. The insurer, therefore, wants to use a risk transfer mechanism that will reduce the variability of its financial results from one year to the next due to catastrophic events. It determines that traditional catastrophic reinsurance is not the most economically viable option for doing so, because previous hurricane events reduced reinsurer capacity and increased the year-to-year volatility of the cost of reinsurance.

The property insurer uses an SPV to issue $500 million in three-year catastrophe bonds to, in effect, reinsure its Gulf Coast and southeastern hurricane risks. The bond investors lose interest or interest and principal, depending on the bond series, if a Category Three, Four, or Five hurricane causes insured losses to the property insurer in excess of $1 billion during a twelve-month claims period. The property insurer, in turn, receives reimbursement for any catastrophe losses from the SPV. The bond offering is fully subscribed by investors.

The investors purchase the bonds from the SPV because they provide a premium rate of interest (that is, it is higher than that provided by a United States Treasury bond of comparable maturity) based on the expected frequency and severity of the embedded hurricane risk. In exchange for receiving a premium interest rate, the investors' return on the bond is linked to the risk of a Category Three or higher hurricane striking during the term of the bond. The bond investors underwrite the hurricane risk, which is an insurable risk because it could also have been underwritten with a traditional reinsurance policy. Therefore, the bond is an insurance-linked security. It is marketable because a secondary financial market exists, which is a market in which a bond can be sold to a subsequent investor during the bond's term. Therefore, through the process of insurance securitization, the property insurer's risk of a sizable loss due to a major hurricane has been "securitized" by linking it with the returns provided to investors in a marketable security. The securitization solution enables the property insurer to more effectively deploy its capital resources.

[DA01744]

The prevalence of catastrophe bonds is attributable to issuing institutions and underlying catastrophe risks that share these characteristics of successful insurance securitizations:

- A potentially large exposure is needed to make a securitization economically viable because of the significant time commitment and transaction costs it requires. Catastrophe bonds frequently have values in excess of $50 million.
- SPVs with high credit ratings or substantial assets that issue securities receive better pricing and subscription at issuance.
- Loss exposures with independent, accurate loss history data available for analyzing the frequency and severity may be underwritten and priced by investors. For many natural catastrophes, such as hurricanes, over 100 years of historical data are readily available.

Benefits to Investors

Insurance-linked securities differ from most other types of investments because the investor accepts only a specifically defined insurable risk and not the overall risks of an organization, as with investments in traditional stocks and bonds. Because insurable risk has a low level of correlation with the risks of traditional investment vehicles, such as the risk of interest rate or stock market movements, investors achieve the benefit of diversification and additional risk-return options.

ILSs have gained acceptance by investors, and a small secondary market has developed for them. Rating agencies, such as Standard & Poor's, Moody's, and A.M. Best, report on the creditworthiness of many insurance-linked securities. The information contained in these reports is essential for selling these securities to investors. Securities can be invested in pension funds, mutual funds, banks, hedge funds, property-casualty insurers, and life insurers.

Advantages of Insurance Securitizations

Insurance securitizations have a number of advantages and disadvantages. Their advantages include creating additional risk transfer capacity and lowering credit risk.

Create Additional Risk Transfer Capacity

Insurance securitization supplements existing risk-transfer capacity and provides organizations with an alternative to traditional insurance and reinsurance. For example, in 2011, approximately $4.4 billion of the investment capital from catastrophe bond issuances was new to the property-casualty insurance industry, with an average bond size of $123 million.[1] However, the value of new capacity depends on the cost and supply of traditional insurance (and reinsurance), which vary over time.

Lower Credit Risk

The obligations to pay losses to an organization and to pay interest and principal to investors are fully collateralized with investments held by the SPV, which can be readily converted into cash. This feature provides an organization with secure resources equal to the loss limits provided by its contract with the SPV. Some risk management professionals believe that the financial security provided by a typical insurance securitization is higher than that provided by a traditional insurance (or reinsurance) transaction because, in general, insurers (and reinsurers) maintain capital that is only a fraction of the total policy limits they sell.

Disadvantages of Insurance Securitizations

There are several disadvantages of insurance securitizations.

Exposure to the Volatility of the Market's Demand

An insurance securitization exposes an organization to volatility, a potential disadvantage. Insurance securitizations have alleviated reinsurance capacity restrictions in the past; however, there is no guarantee that they will always be an economically effective risk transfer instrument. The relationship between the return demanded by securitization investors and premiums for insurance (and reinsurance) varies depending on two factors: the attractiveness of ILSs to investors when compared with their other investment opportunities and the state of the insurance underwriting cycle—that is, whether it is hard or soft—with its associated fluctuations in insurance (and reinsurance) pricing and market demand.

Opportunity Cost of Collateralized Assets

Organizations that use an insurance securitization incur an opportunity cost for the assets that are used for collateral, because the funds held by the SPV are tied up in liquid assets and, therefore, earn a relatively low rate of return. If held in riskier investments, these funds, on average, would return a higher rate of return, potentially lowering the amount that the organization transferring its risk of loss would pay. Therefore, with an insurance securitization transaction, as with insurance and reinsurance, the insured faces a tradeoff between cost and financial security.

Transaction Costs

The SPV and its business partners commit their time and incur the substantial financial costs associated with risk analysis and modeling, structuring, legal expenses, marketing, and subscribing to the insurance securitization. Analyzing and modeling risk involves gathering large amounts of data and using complex computer simulation programs that project the probability of various loss scenarios. Investors use this information to determine whether

the expected return from an ILS is commensurate with its risk. Additionally, insurance securitization requires compliance with investment and insurance regulations.

Basis Risk

Basis risk is the risk that the amount the organization receives to offset its losses may be greater than or less than its actual losses. For example, an organization is subject to basis risk if it negotiates an insurance securitization transaction to cover its losses from hurricanes, but its contract with the SPV specifies that it will get paid based on the level of an insurance industry index of insured losses from hurricanes. Typically, an organization's actual losses suffered as a result of a hurricane will differ from the amount indicated by the insurance industry index. Although most organizations view basis risk in an insurance securitization to be a disadvantage, basis risk also offers the possibility that the amount an organization receives will exceed its actual losses. See the exhibit "Swiss Re Catastrophe Bond Arrangement."

Swiss Re Catastrophe Bond Arrangement

On January 5, 2011, reinsurer Swiss Re announced that it had placed a catastrophe bond through its special purpose vehicle (SPV), Successor X Ltd., that enables it to receive up to $170 million for its payment of losses if, during a three-year period from January 1, 2011, through December 31, 2013, earthquakes occur in Australia or California or if North Atlantic hurricanes occur. Successor X offered the bonds to investors on the capital market, who will reap the profits from a high rate of return if no earthquakes or hurricanes meet the criteria specified in the bond transaction. Investors seeking diversification are attracted to such a bond because the risk does not correlate with traditional investment risk, and rates of return often exceed those of other investments with comparable risk. Swiss Re incorporates the use of insurance-linked securities into its strategy to hedge catastrophe risk and to minimize its need for capital and its earnings volatility.

Swiss Re, "Swiss Re Concludes $170 Million Successor X Cat Bond Placement," January 5, 2011, www.insurancejournal.com/news/international/2011/01/05/116140.htm (accessed April 10, 2012). [DA08793]

INSURANCE DERIVATIVES

Insurance derivatives provide options for insurers that require additional capacity to manage their potential catastrophic losses.

An **insurance derivative** increases in value as specified insurable losses increase; therefore, the purchaser of the derivative can use this gain to offset its insurable losses. The buyer of an insurance derivative accepts insurable risk and receives a commensurate return for doing so.

Insurance derivative
Financial contract whose value is based on the level of insurable losses that occur during a specific time period.

The value of an insurance derivative can be based on the level of insurable losses experienced by a single organization or on the level of an insurance

industry index of insured losses. An example of the latter is a financial instrument whose value is determined by all insured hurricane losses that occur in the southeastern United States during the third quarter of a particular year.

Two insurance derivatives that may be used for the transfer of financial risk are swaps and insurance options.

Use of Swaps

Insurers can spread their risks through swap arrangements. In such cases, the swap becomes an insurance derivative; the underlying asset is a portfolio of a specific class of insured risks for an individual insurer. For example, one insurer could exchange a portion of the cash flows (premiums and losses) arising from its hurricane exposure in a particular geographic area with a portion of the cash flows arising from another insurer's tornado exposure in another geographic area. A swap arrangement between two insurers produces results similar to a reinsurance arrangement. The majority of swaps have been arranged to mimic reinsurance transactions. See the exhibit "Swap Examples—World Bank and Caribbean Catastrophe Risk Insurance Facility (CCRIF) Swap and Related Swap."

Use of Insurance Options

Insurance option

A specialized type of option that derives its value from insurable losses—either an organization's actual insurable losses or an insurance industry index of losses.

The value of an **insurance option** increases as the underlying insurable losses increase beyond the value of the strike price. Therefore, an organization can use a gain on an insurance option to offset its losses from insurable risk. See the exhibit "Example of an Insurance Option."

Many similarities exist between insurance policies and option contracts. The key features of the two risk transfer mechanisms are outlined in the exhibit. See the exhibit "Insurance Policies Compared With Option Contracts."

Swap Examples—World Bank and Caribbean Catastrophe Risk Insurance Facility (CCRIF) Swap and Related Swap

In June 2006, as part of a regional catastrophe risk insurance pool to protect the Caribbean states against natural disasters (such as hurricanes, earthquakes, floods, and tsunamis), the Caribbean Catastrophe Risk Insurance Facility (CCRIF) established a risk management arrangement that resulted in two catastrophe swaps. The $110 million pool arrangement provides the CCRIF with capacity to serve its claims based on its own reserves and on capacity gained from the international market. The CCRIF arrangement for catastrophe losses consists of four layers. The first layer includes retention of the first $10 million of claims, the second layer is reinsurance of $15 million, the third layer is reinsurance of $24 million, and the fourth layer includes reinsurance of $50 million and a $20 million catastrophe insurance swap between CCRIF and the World Bank through the International Bank for Reconstruction and Development (IBRD). In conjunction with the CCRIF swap, the IBRD established a catastrophe swap with Munich Re Capital Markets to shield its reserves from the catastrophe risk. CCRIF touts its $20 million swap with IBRD as "the first transaction to enable emerging countries to use a derivative transaction to access the capital market to insure against natural disasters."* Participating countries in the CCRIF pool will have immediate access to cash, based on the severity of the catastrophe and its estimated impact on each government's funds.**

*The World Bank News and Broadcast, "First Ever Regional Catastrophe Risk Insurance Pool Up and Running in Time for 2007 Hurricane Season," June 1, 2007, http://web.worldbank.org/WBSITE/EXTERNAL/NEWS/0,,contentMDK:21355052~pagePK:34370~piPK:34424~theSitePK:4607,00.html (accessed March 28, 2012).

**Martin Goddard, Butterfield Business Barbados, "The Evolution of Insurance in Barbados," November 10, 2007, www.businessbarbados.com/industry-guide/financial-services/the-evolution-of-insurance-in-barbados/ (accessed March 28, 2012).

[DA08700]

Advantages of Insurance Derivatives

With the development of the insurance derivatives market, these are some advantages that have emerged:

- Additional risk capacity—Insurance derivatives create additional risk capacity by supplementing existing risk transfer capacity and providing an alternative to traditional insurance (and reinsurance). The degree of the advantage depends on the cost and supply of insurance (and reinsurance). During hard-market periods, derivative markets enable companies to purchase protection for risks when no supply exists for structured insurance markets.
- Lower in cost than insurance-linked securities—Unlike insurance-linked securities, insurance derivatives do not require the establishment of a special purpose vehicle (SPV) for claims settlement, management of cash flows, or collateral maintenance. Consequently, insurance derivative transaction costs are less than costs for insurance-linked securities.

Example of an Insurance Option

Weather options derive their value from a measurement of weather conditions, such as average temperature or cumulative precipitation over a finite period. An organization can purchase these options to transfer weather-related risk.

For example, a midwestern U.S. basement repair contractor is most profitable during unusually wet summers—when cracks in basements are most likely to leak. Therefore, the worst-case weather situation for the basement contractor is a prolonged summer drought. The contractor determines that for every inch of precipitation shortfall below average for the months of August and September, the firm loses $10,000 in net income.

The basement repair contractor purchases a weather put option based on the measurement of rainfall during this period at the nearest weather station. The average precipitation for August through September is seven inches. The insurance option's put strike price is set at five inches. The put option is designed so that for every inch of precipitation below strike value (five inches), the option increases in value by $10,000. The precipitation cover is written as an insurance policy and has a limit of $40,000. If the cumulative precipitation between August and September is only three and one-half inches, the contractor will receive a payout of $15,000 [(5–3.5) × 10,000] from the weather insurer to help offset any lost profit from a reduction in the demand for basement repairs.

[DA08701]

Insurance Policies Compared With Option Contracts

Insurance Policy	Option Contracts—General and Insurance
Premium is paid by the purchaser prior to policy inception.	Premium is paid by the purchaser at the beginning of the contract term.
Deductible of self-insured retention can apply to a single occurrence or to aggregate losses for the policy period.	Strike price can apply to a single event, at regular time periods, or to the average or total experience over the entire contract period.
Purchaser is indemnified by the insurer if the level of insured losses exceeds the deductible or self-insured retention.	An option has value only if the underlying asset or index exceeds the strike price. Only then will the purchaser exercise the option for financial gain.
Has a policy limit.	Theoretically, has no limit of payout.

[DA08702]

- Transparent pricing—An insurance derivative is transparent in pricing when it has an open, high-volume market. Transparency is advantageous because it attracts more potential investors and assures them of liquidity.
- Opportunities for investors to exit during its term—This opportunity to sell the contract in the secondary market during the derivative's term is beneficial when the protection it provides its owner is no longer needed.
- Standardized contracts—Unlike other risk financing techniques, insurance derivatives that are traded on organized exchanges have standard contract terms and conditions. This standardization helps buyers and sellers dealing in multiple contracts to implement and settle them consistently. Even structured derivative transactions retain a significant percentage of these standard terms and conditions.
- Efficient claims and contract settlement—For many insurance derivatives, the final values are readily determined through an independent, publicly available index or an agreed-upon value. Therefore, associated claim administration and end-of-term settlement processes are simpler and more expedient than with insurance.

Disadvantages of Insurance Derivatives

These are some disadvantages associated with insurance derivatives:

- Underdeveloped markets—Because insurance derivatives are sold in markets that are underdeveloped, an organization may be prevented from purchasing the amount or type of coverage it desires. It also results in a small secondary market, which makes it difficult for an investor to exit an option contract during its term.
- Basis risk—Insurance derivatives subject organizations that transfer risk to basis risk. As with insurance securitization transactions, a derivative's structure may result in substantial basis risk for the purchaser. This could result in the payout from the derivative being much lower or higher than an organization's actual losses.
- Credit risk—Insurance derivatives can expose an organization to credit risk. Some insurance derivative transactions are not collateralized, so the degree of credit risk depends on the financial security of the other party to the transaction (the counterparty). However, many swap and option contracts incorporate standardized terms and provide guidelines for recovery in case of default. Therefore, a large portion of the credit risk can be mitigated with standardized contracts, dealings with creditworthy counterparties, counterparty credit monitoring, exchange transactions, or use of an intermediary.
- Uncertain regulatory and accounting treatment—Potential negative regulatory or accounting treatment can outpace the benefits of insurance derivatives.

Apply Your Knowledge

Bellingham Mutual Insurance Company insures a number of properties along the South Atlantic coastline of the United States that are highly susceptible to hurricane losses. Bellingham has reinsurance arrangements to cover much of its risk, but based on estimated losses for the next three years, the insurer needs another $150 million in capacity to meet its potential losses. Westfork Mutual insures a number of U.S. West Coast properties that are subject to earthquake and wildfire risks. Westfork also has reinsurance arrangements to cover most of its estimated loss potential over the next three years, but an additional $150 million would cover its need for capacity. Both Bellingham and Westfork currently have A.M. Best ratings of A+. Describe an insurance derivative that would accommodate the capacity needs of Bellingham and Westfork, and explain how both insurers can mitigate credit risk to which they are exposed as a result of the derivative.

Feedback: Because Bellingham's hurricanes and Westfork's earthquakes and wildfires are risk exposures that are not correlated, the two insurers could enter into a catastrophe swap agreement for their respective catastrophe risks. To mitigate their exposure to credit risk, the insurers could use an intermediary to protect the interests of both, incorporate standardized terms in the swap, and provide guidelines for recovery in case of default by either insurer.

CONTINGENT CAPITAL ARRANGEMENTS

Contingent capital agreements are one of the three major categories of capital market products that are alternatives to insurance for financing losses.

A contingent capital arrangement is an agreement that is entered into before losses occur that enables an organization to raise cash by selling stock or issuing debt at prearranged terms following a loss that exceeds a certain threshold. The loss can arise from insurable risk, such as property damage resulting from an earthquake.

The organization agreeing to provide the contingent capital receives a commitment fee in exchange for its promise to reimburse the organization for its loss costs. The amount of the capital commitment fee is influenced by several factors, including likelihood of loss event, interest rates of alternative investments, and credit risk of the organization trying to arrange for the contingent capital.

Under a contingent capital arrangement, the organization receives a capital injection in the form of debt or equity to help it pay for the loss. Because the terms of the capital injection are agreed to in advance, the organization generally receives more favorable terms than it would receive if it were forced to raise capital after a large loss, when the organization is likely to be in a weakened financial condition and to pose a higher credit risk to potential lenders or investors.

The rate of the guaranteed capital infusion is normally discounted from current market pre-loss values. Investment banks and reinsurers assess the effect a catastrophic event would have on an organization and include in the interest rate on bonds or the agreed-upon stock purchase price the risk that the organization may be financially damaged beyond the contingent capital's ability to assist. Therefore, the organization still is charged an anticipated spread in credit risk, which is the higher interest rate or premium rate the organization has to pay the lender or investor in exchange for their promise to pay the contingent capital when it is needed.

Investors in a contingent capital arrangement become creditors of, or equity investors in, the organization following a loss. A contingent capital arrangement is usually set up as an option. Therefore, the organization that purchases a contingent capital arrangement is not obligated to exercise the option, even if its losses exceed the threshold specified in the agreement. However, the threshold usually is high enough to force the organization to use the agreement to supplement its own resources following the triggering event.

A contingent capital agreement generally falls into one of these categories:

- Standby credit facility
- Contingent surplus note
- Catastrophe equity put option

Standby Credit Facility

A **standby credit facility** is an arrangement in which a bank or another financial institution agrees to provide a loan to an organization in the event the organization suffers a loss. The credit is prearranged so that the terms, such as the interest rate and principal repayment schedule, are known in advance of a loss. In exchange for this credit commitment, the organization taking out the line of credit pays a commitment fee.

Standby credit facility
An arrangement in which a bank or another financial institution agrees to provide a loan to an organization in the event the organization suffers a loss.

Many similarities exist between a standby credit facility and an insurance policy. In fact, these two risk financing techniques are often used together. For example, the owner of a group of fast food franchises may want to self-insure the first $10 million per year of its commercial general liability exposures using a standby credit facility and cover the next layer of $10 million in losses with an excess insurance policy. Alternatively, an organization may want to review the initial costs of making $10 million in funds available for losses with a standby credit facility as compared to insurance. See the exhibit "Standby Credit Facility Compared With Excess Insurance."

At year-end, annual losses determine which of these combinations would have been the most effective. Despite the cash flow advantage of a standby credit facility, the risk management professional should consider the crucial

Standby Credit Facility Compared With Excess Insurance

	Standby Credit Facility	Excess Insurance
Amount of funds available for losses	$10 million	$10 million
Initial cost of making funds available per year—prior to loss payments	$5,000 commitment fee	$200,000 premium
Interest rate on loan—if needed	5%	N/A
Length of loan—if needed	15 years	N/A
Largest possible cost in first year	$700,000 (Repay the loan = $10 million divided by 15 plus 5 percent interest)	$200,000 (premium payment)

[DA01816]

difference between the two risk financing techniques. A standby credit facility obligates the organization to pay back, with interest, a loan it uses to cover losses. Losses paid by insurance, however, do not have to be repaid. Therefore, a standby credit facility entails loss retention, while insurance entails loss transfer.

Not accounting for the claim settlement, risk management, and other services an insurer provides, if an organization's resulting annual losses exceed the insurance premium, insurance is its best option. This underscores the importance of accurate loss forecasts.

Contingent Surplus Note

Surplus note

A type of unsecured debt instrument, issued only by insurers, that has characteristics of both conventional equity and debt securities and is classified as policyholders' surplus rather than as a liability on the insurer's statutory balance sheet.

United States statutory accounting rules allow insurers to issue **surplus notes**, which are notes sold to investors that are counted as policyholders' surplus rather than as a liability on an insurer's statutory balance sheet.

A benefit of surplus notes is that they increase an insurer's assets without increasing its liabilities. (Regular debt increases both assets and liabilities.) Although surplus notes have many of the characteristics of debt, their treatment as equity (policyholders' surplus) on an insurer's statutory balance sheet allows an insurer to increase its capacity to sell business.

Contingent surplus notes are surplus notes that have been designed so that an insurer, at its option, can immediately obtain funds by issuing notes at a pre-agreed rate of interest.

Contingent surplus notes
Surplus notes that have been designed so that an insurer, at its option, can immediately obtain funds by issuing the notes at a pre-agreed rate of interest.

Catastrophe Equity Put Option

Catastrophe equity put options are another way for an insurer or a noninsurance organization to raise funds in the event of a catastrophic loss. Whereas a put option is a right to sell an asset at a predetermined price, a **catastrophe equity put option** is a right to sell equity (stock) at a predetermined price in the event of a catastrophic loss. The buyer of a catastrophe equity put option pays a commitment fee to the seller, who agrees to purchase the equity at a pre-arranged price in the event of a catastrophic loss, as defined in the put agreement. See the exhibit "Catastrophe Equity Put Arrangement."

Catastrophe equity put option
A right to sell equity (stock) at a predetermined price in the event of a catastrophic loss.

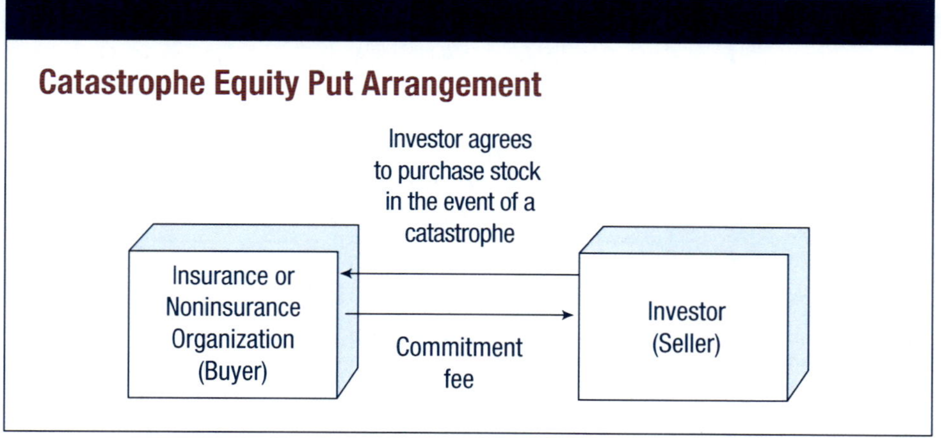

[DA01817]

Advantages of Contingent Capital Arrangements

One advantage of contingent capital arrangements is that the funds it makes available to an organization cost less than funds made available by insurance. The capital commitment fee required by the lender or equity investor is typically much lower than the premium charged for insurance. Although the commitment fee allows the organization to receive a loan on favorable terms, it still must repay the loan because it has retained the risk.

With insurance, however, the organization does not pay back the losses paid because it has transferred the risk. The benefit of the risk retention element of a contingent capital arrangement is a lower initial cost, which lowers the organization's opportunity cost because, instead of using the funds to maintain a reserve fund for losses that may or may not occur, it can use them in production or in another investment opportunity that can earn a higher rate of return. In the event losses exceed an agreed-upon threshold, they will not have to be paid out of the organization's cash flow.

Another advantage of contingent capital arrangements is that they allow an organization to obtain capital infusion at a predetermined price. Contingent capital arrangements enable an organization to obtain funds (either through debt or equity) at a previously set price when it most needs it—immediately following a catastrophe.

If an organization suffers a loss of capital due to a catastrophe, its increased credit risk would likely cause lenders to demand a higher interest rate on a loan. A catastrophe would also likely depress the organization's stock price, lowering the amount it would receive for newly issued stock. Contingent capital arrangements provide instant funds at a predetermined price to help an organization regain its capital following a catastrophe.

Disadvantages of Contingent Capital Arrangements

Funds received from a standby credit facility or contingent surplus note for losses are paid in the form of loans, not equity, and must be paid back to the lender with interest. In contrast, an organization that buys guaranteed-cost insurance pays a set premium that remains constant regardless of losses.

Another disadvantage of a contingent capital arrangement is ownership dilution. The amount of an organization's equity increases when a catastrophe equity put option is exercised, thereby reducing the existing shareholders' percentage of ownership. This dilution may also come at a crucial time in the management of the organization (that is, after a catastrophe).

The additional owners introduced by a contingent capital arrangement, who may be unfamiliar with the issues and causes of the triggering event, may adversely affect the ability of the organization to recover, despite the injection of additional capital.

CONCERNS OF USERS AND SUPPLIERS OF CAPITAL FOR TRANSFERRING HAZARD RISK

The convergence of insurance with other financial services has expanded the capital markets' role in risk financing to include insurance-linked securities and insurance derivatives.

Capital market products for risk financing can be analyzed in terms of various characteristics that determine their attractiveness to the organizations that use them to transfer risk and the investors that supply the risk capital.

Organizations Transferring Risk

The organizations that use insurance-linked securities and insurance derivatives to transfer risk are concerned with cost, the financial security (credit risk) of the parties supplying the risk capital, and the risk that the amount received may not match the amount of their loss (basis risk). The exhibit compares insurance (and reinsurance), insurance-linked securities, and various types of insurance derivatives in terms of financial security and basis risk. See the exhibit "Insurance (Reinsurance), Insurance-Linked Securities, and Insurance Derivatives: Financial Security and Basis Risk."

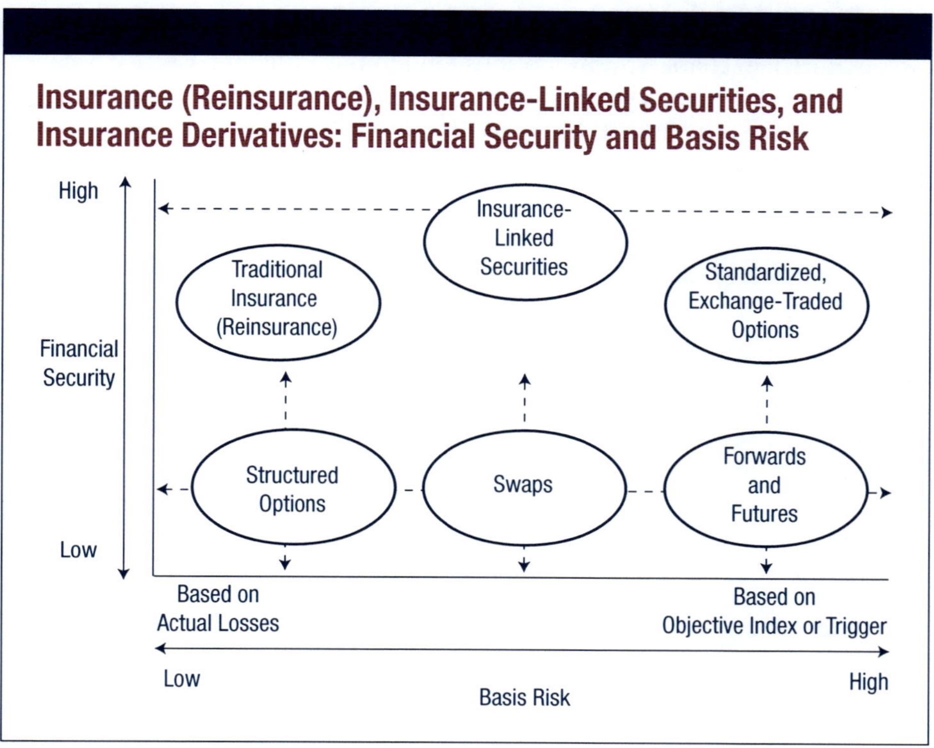

This exhibit is based on an exhibit presented during a lecture on April 28, 1999, given by Neil A. Doherty, PhD, professor of insurance and risk management, The Wharton School of the University of Pennsylvania. [DA01818]

Securities and Options

Insurance-linked securities, insurance (and reinsurance), and exchange-traded options provide a high level of financial security. Insurance-linked securities fall into this category because they are usually fully collateralized. The financial security of traditional and nontraditional insurance, including finite and integrated structures, varies depending on the strength of the balance sheet of the insurer (or reinsurer). The value of standardized, exchange-traded options is guaranteed by the exchange on which they are traded. The financial security of structured options and swaps varies depending on the financial strength of the other party (the counterparty) to the transaction. Therefore, these financial instruments provide a lower level of financial security.

Structured Options and Insurance

Structured options and traditional insurance (and reinsurance) have a low level of basis risk. Structured options, like traditional insurance and reinsurance, are usually tailored to the organization. However, structured options

have slightly higher basis risk than traditional insurance, as options normally settle to an index or are based on an agreed value, rather than providing indemnification for actual losses.

Standardized, Exchange-Traded Options

Standardized, exchange-traded options tend to have higher basis risk because their value is based on a general industry or commodity index. Standardized options also have more rigid intervals of settlement; basis risk exists because the timing of settlement may not match the timing of the organization's actual loss and capital needs. Insurance-linked securities and swaps can be designed to have high or low basis risk, depending on whether their value is based on an index, an organization's expected losses, or actual losses.

Financial Security and No Basis Risk

When using insurance securitizations and insurance derivatives (swaps and options) to offset its losses, an organization must decide on the relative importance it places on financial security and basis risk. Products that provide high financial security tend to cost more than those that provide low financial security. Products that provide a perfect hedge (no basis risk) against an organization's losses tend to cost more than those that do not.

The purchasers of contingent capital arrangements have concerns that include cost, creditworthiness of the party supplying the risk capital, and adequacy and timing of the prearranged capital injection following a loss.

Investors Supplying Capital

The investors that supply risk capital for these capital market products are concerned with moral hazard, which is the degree to which an organization can influence the level of its insurable losses. For example, an organization could decide that, because it has transferred or otherwise financed its risk, it will not diligently prevent or settle its losses.

Objective trigger
A measurement that determines the value of an insurance-related capital market product based on a parameter that is not within the control of the organization transferring the risk.

Some capital market products are based on an **objective trigger**, which is a measurement that determines the value of an insurance-related capital market product based on a parameter that is not within the control of the organization transferring the risk.

Objective triggers such as loss indices or earthquake severity parameters eliminate moral hazard. However, they also introduce basis risk. By contrast, when a transaction is based on an organization's own losses (that is, little or no basis risk exists), a degree of moral hazard could be involved.

Therefore, a tradeoff exists between basis risk and moral hazard. In general, the lower the degree of basis risk, the higher the degree of moral hazard. This relationship helps explain why capital market products that have little or no basis risk tend to cost more than those that have basis risk.

CAPITAL MARKET REGULATORY AND ACCOUNTING ISSUES

A major issue associated with insurance-linked securities and insurance derivatives is whether they can be considered insurance and regulated as such.

Because insurance may be considered a contract that indemnifies an organization for its actual losses, an insured organization must have an insurable interest that is the subject of an insurance contract.

Based on these requirements, insurance securitizations and insurance derivatives (swaps and options) whose value is based on an organization's actual losses may be considered insurance and should be regulated as insurance. However, insurance securitizations and insurance derivatives whose values are based on an objective trigger, such as an index of insurance industry losses, may not be considered insurance and, therefore, should not be regulated as insurance.

If insurance-linked securities (ILSs) and insurance derivatives are determined to be insurance, then the organizations that use them to transfer risk, as well as the investors that supply risk capital, must comply with insurance regulations.

State premium taxes need to be paid when ILSs and insurance derivatives are determined to be insurance. The amount paid (premiums) to transfer risk would probably be tax-deductible to the insured organization. In addition, the organization would not be required to record outstanding losses that are covered by the insurance on the liability section of its balance sheet.

If ILSs and insurance derivatives are determined not to be insurance, then their investors must comply with the requirements of the various regulators of securities and derivatives, such as the Securities and Exchange Commission (SEC) and the Commodities Futures Trading Commission (CFTC) in the United States. An organization may not be able to deduct for tax purposes the amount it pays to transfer risk because that amount would be considered an investment in an asset rather than an insurance premium expense.

In addition, when ILSs and insurance derivatives are not deemed insurance, the organization must record on its balance sheet outstanding losses that are meant to be covered by their proceeds. However, the organization can show a corresponding asset on its balance sheet for the fair value of the ILS or insurance derivative.

Insurance securitization transactions usually use a special purpose vehicle (SPV). For a transaction involving a U.S. organization, the SPV usually qualifies as an insurer or a reinsurer under U.S. state insurance regulations. In this case, the organization that transfers its risk of loss benefits from having the transaction treated as insurance (or reinsurance) because it overcomes the tax and accounting disadvantages. Although most SPVs to date have been formed

in jurisdictions with limited regulation, such as Bermuda, U.S. insurance regulators encourage the formation of SPVs in various states.

In some notable cases, the determination that a capital market product is insurance has been central to corporate finance and accounting scandals. Such cases have contributed to the passage of the Sarbanes-Oxley Act and have resulted in high level scrutiny by various regulatory bodies. This issue is still evolving and will continue to test and refine the current definitions of insurance.

SUMMARY

Capital market risk financing products allow organizations to access the capital markets to offset risks that insurance or reinsurance policies have traditionally covered. These products include insurance-linked securities, insurance derivatives, and contingent capital arrangements. The convergence of insurance with other financial services has spurred the development of these capital market products.

Insurance-linked securities created through insurance securitization supplement existing risk-transfer capacity and provide an alternative to traditional insurance and reinsurance. Catastrophe bonds are issued by SPVs (intermediaries) in the capital market. Losses that trigger payment can be based on aggregate catastrophe losses or a single catastrophic event. Investors accept only a specifically defined insurable risk, and ILSs are accepted in the primary market as well as a secondary market. Advantages of insurance securitization are that it creates additional risk transfer capacity and lowers risk, because SPVs are usually fully collateralized. Disadvantages are that insurance securitizations are exposed to the volatility of the market's demand, incur an opportunity cost for the assets for collateral, incur substantial financial costs in developing and marketing, and may be subject to basis risk.

An insurance derivative obtains its value from the level of insurable losses that occur during a specific time period. Two insurance derivatives that may be used for the transfer of financial risk are swaps and options. Insurance derivatives provide advantages and disadvantages. Advantages include additional risk capacity, lower cost than insurance-linked securities, transparency, ability to exit positions midterm, standardized contracts, and efficient claim and contract settlement. Disadvantages include underdeveloped markets, credit risk, basis risk, and regulatory and accounting issues.

A contingent capital arrangement is an agreement that is entered into before losses occur that enables an organization to raise cash by selling stock or issuing debt at prearranged terms following a loss that exceeds a certain threshold. The major types of contingent capital arrangements are standby credit facilities, contingent surplus notes, and catastrophe equity put options.

Capital market products for risk financing can be analyzed in terms of various characteristics that determine their attractiveness to the organizations that purchase them and the investors that supply the risk capital. The purchaser of insurance (or reinsurance) or a capital market product must determine the relative importance it places on cost, financial security, and basis risk. From the investor's (the capital provider's) perspective, a tradeoff exists between moral hazard and basis risk.

A major issue associated with insurance securitizations and insurance derivatives is whether they are considered insurance and should be regulated as such. If they are determined to be insurance, then the organizations that use them to transfer risk as well as the investors that supply risk capital must comply with insurance regulations. State premium taxes must be paid, and the cash paid (premium) to transfer risk is generally tax-deductible. If ILSs and insurance derivatives are not determined to be insurance, then the investors must comply with the requirements of the various regulators of securities and derivatives and cash paid to transfer risk is not tax-deductible when it is paid.

ASSIGNMENT NOTE

1. National Association of Insurance Commissioners and the Center for Insurance Policy and Research, "Insurance-Linked Securities: Catastrophe Bonds, Sidecars and Life Insurance Securitization," March 13, 2012, www.naic.org/cipr_topics/topic_insurance_linked_securities.htm (accessed April 9, 2012).

Direct Your Learning

11

Allocating Costs of Managing Hazard Risk

Educational Objectives

After learning the content of this assignment, you should be able to:

- Describe the purposes of allocating hazard risk management costs.
- Describe the types of hazard risk management costs an organization may want to allocate.
- Describe the prospective and retrospective approaches to allocating hazard risk management costs.
- Describe the exposure bases and experience bases used to allocate hazard risk management costs.
- Describe the practical considerations when selecting a hazard risk management cost allocation basis.
- Given a case, justify how hazard risk management costs may be allocated among an organization's departments.

Outline

Allocating Costs of Managing Hazard Risk

11

PURPOSE OF ALLOCATING HAZARD RISK MANAGEMENT COSTS

A hazard risk management cost allocation system should focus on these risk management costs:

- Retained losses
- Insurance premiums
- Risk control costs
- Administrative expenses for the risk management function

These hazard risk management costs should be clearly identified and properly attributed to the organization's departments, products, or activities. Effective risk management programs require that most costs be allocated to the departments that generate them.

An effective hazard risk management cost allocation system should serve these purposes:

- Promote risk control
- Facilitate risk retention
- Prioritize risk management expenditures
- Reduce costs
- Distribute costs fairly
- Balance risk bearing and risk sharing
- Provide managers with hazard risk management cost information

Promote Risk Control

The primary purpose of a hazard risk management cost allocation system is to promote risk control throughout an organization by allocating the costs of a loss or potential loss to the responsible department. Therefore, each department is either held accountable or rewarded for its risk control efforts.

For example, a department that effectively controls its property losses will realize a reduction in its allocated property insurance premiums. If a department's risk control measure, such as an investment in risk control equipment, benefits the entire organization, then its cost is allocated across all of the organization's departments.

Facilitate Risk Retention

A hazard risk management cost allocation system implemented by the organization throughout all departments allows the entire organization to benefit from an optimal risk retention level. As a result, individual departments are not unduly exposed to excessive fluctuations in their cost of risk and, consequently, are encouraged to increase their risk retention.

Prioritize Risk Management Expenditures

A hazard risk management cost allocation system, because it assigns responsibility for risk management costs to individual departments, prioritizes risk management expenditures within departments. The method used to allocate risk management expenditures, particularly if the expenditures are allocated to a single department as opposed to all departments within an organization, has a direct bearing on how a department manager determines which risk control measures get funded.

If a department must pay for a risk control measure by itself, it may more carefully scrutinize the measure's cost-effectiveness. The department may also more carefully prioritize among the competing measures to fund those that provide the greatest return on investment.

Reduce Costs

A hazard risk management cost allocation system effectively reduces an organization's costs. As risk control is promoted, losses are prevented or reduced. As risk retention is facilitated, the organization can more easily retain risk at an optimal level, which reduces its cost of risk.

Finally, as risk management expenditures are prioritized in terms of cost-effectiveness and return on investment, an organization's cost of risk is again lowered. This, in turn, allows the risk management professional to apply additional resources to other risk management goals or return funds to the organization's operational budget.

Distribute Costs Fairly

A hazard risk management cost allocation system also should distribute costs fairly. Departmental managers may object if there is no direct correlation between departmental losses and the risk management costs allocated to their units. For example, a manager whose unit has considerably fewer departmental losses than another department may believe it unfair for his or her department to contribute toward high limits of coverage for the entire organization.

As another example, an organization's accounting department may be assigned just one company vehicle, which only the manager uses. The manager has a good claim history but still exposes the company to auto liability. By comparison, the distribution department of the same company uses several dozen long-haul trucks that incur many minor and several severe claims a year.

The company purchases commercial auto liability coverage with high limits that insures all its vehicles. The accounting manager may believe the department should contribute little, if anything, toward the organization's commercial auto liability insurance premium. An effective cost allocation system would address the accounting manager's concerns by reducing the allocated amount charged to the accounting department on the basis of both the amount of the department's auto liability loss exposure and its claim experience.

Balance Risk Bearing and Risk Sharing

A **risk-bearing system** creates a direct correlation between a department's loss exposures and the amount of risk it bears and is therefore responsive to a department's risk control efforts. However, it does not distinguish between risk that is directly attributable to a department's management and risk that is an unavoidable product of a department's function. Additionally, because a risk-bearing system assigns costs only to the responsible department, it can cause fluctuations in a department's financial results from one accounting period to the next, particularly when losses are catastrophic.

Risk-bearing system
A risk management cost allocation system that allocates losses to the individual department that generates them.

A **risk-sharing system** can alleviate individual departments' burdens. Risk-sharing systems stabilize risk management costs across departments but are not as responsive to risk control efforts within individual departments.

Risk-sharing system
A risk management cost allocation system that allocates losses among all of an organization's departments.

Most risk management cost allocation systems are a combination of risk-bearing and risk-sharing systems. Such a balance distributes risk management costs across the organization while also allowing departments to benefit from their own loss experience and other changing conditions.

An effective hazard risk management cost allocation system should balance the two types of plans in a manner that encourages risk control activities (accomplished through the risk-bearing element of a balanced plan) while minimizing departmental cost fluctuations (accomplished through the risk-sharing element of a balanced plan). Because risk control usually takes precedence over cost stabilization, most organizations use risk management cost allocation systems that consist primarily of risk bearing.

Provide Managers With Risk Management Cost Information

Another purpose of a hazard risk management cost allocation system is to provide managers with risk management cost information. Accurate allocation and reporting of cost of risk to the department responsible for the loss generation compels managers to focus on areas in which the cost of risk can

be reduced. Consequently, the risk management cost allocation system may direct managers to address situations in which the cost of risk can be controlled more effectively.

Risk management cost allocation reporting systems that become too complex do not provide clear incentives for performance and cannot be administered easily. Claim runs (detailed listings of incidents causing particular types of losses, the dates and amounts of payments for each loss, and the development of reserves for each loss), loss exposure reports, and other documents providing data for allocating costs should follow a clear format. The system should also be explained in writing by the risk management professional and discussed in presentations to each department's management.

The information generated by a hazard risk management cost allocation system can be useful to an organization only if it can be independently verified and has not been manipulated either within individual departments (internal manipulation) or by an organization's owners or senior management (external manipulation).

Internal Manipulation

Two prevalent examples of internal manipulation are the suppression of claim reporting and the deliberately inaccurate presentation of loss-related facts. The first tactic is effective if the hazard risk management cost allocation system is based on reported claims and does not correct claims based on subsequent reporting.

The second tactic bases the hazard risk management cost allocation system on loss reserves and does not correct for subsequent case valuations in allocating costs. The risk management cost allocation system can discourage or prevent internal manipulation by requiring losses to be reviewed or audited in order to confirm that they were reported in a timely fashion and that subsequent changes to reserve amounts are not attributable to facts that should have been revealed at the time of the loss.

External Manipulation

External manipulation is performed by an organization's owners or senior management and generally occurs when a hazard risk management cost allocation system does not meet the overall financial objectives of the organization's owners or senior management. For example, assume an organization prices its products to reflect production costs, with the exception of one department that produces a loss leader for the rest of the organization. If risk management costs are allocated to that department, senior management might argue that such costs should be absorbed by the rest of the organization, because the department's product is designed and priced exclusively to generate revenue for other departments. Senior management may reason that because the department producing a loss leader is meant to operate at a loss for the benefit of the organization, it would be inappropriate for that department to be allocated part of the organization's risk management costs. To do so would force it to operate at an even greater loss.

The best way to prevent external manipulation is to design the risk management cost allocation system to reflect the organization's overall objectives and to obtain prior approval of the system from senior management.

TYPES OF HAZARD RISK MANAGEMENT COSTS TO BE ALLOCATED

How an organization assigns the costs of its hazard risk management function to individual business units or departments within the organization can significantly affect each department's financial results. An ideal risk management cost allocation system is a balance between departmental risk bearing and risk sharing across all the organization's departments.

A hazard risk management cost allocation system can fully or partially allocate four types of hazard risk management costs, which together constitute an organization's cost of risk:

- Costs of accidental losses not reimbursed by insurance or other outside sources
- Insurance premiums
- Costs of risk control techniques
- Costs of administering risk management activities

Any combination of the preceding costs, or portions of them, can be allocated to any department. Costs that are most beneficial to allocate to a particular department are those that are clearly incurred by and beneficial to a given department and that are wholly within that department's control.

The organization must determine or estimate the value of each hazard cost category for the period for which it is to be allocated and must also determine how to allocate the costs. Consistent costs, such as guaranteed-cost insurance premiums, are more easily allocated than complex costs, such as retained losses, which vary over time.

An organization can assign a different allocation method to each type of hazard cost. For example, it can use distinct allocation systems for general liability, automobile liability, workers compensation, and property losses. Some of these costs can be fully allocated to the department that generated the loss exposure or losses. Other costs can be partially allocated to the department that generated them and partially absorbed by the entire organization. Still other costs can simply be charged as general overhead.

Costs of Accidental Losses Not Reimbursed by Insurance or Other Outside Sources

Most accidental loss costs not reimbursed by insurance or other outside sources are apportioned to the responsible department by the hazard risk management cost allocation system. Other losses, or portions of losses, are charged to the organization as a whole (losses not allocated are treated as overhead).

Losses to be allocated to a department are measured by the dollars incurred as a result of the occurrence. Departments can fund such retained losses with an explicit retention program, alternative risk financing plans, retrospective rating insurance plans, a retrospective rating insurance pool, or any other loss-sensitive risk financing technique.

Allocated and Unallocated Loss Adjustment Expenses

Some costs of accidental losses, such as loss adjustment expenses, can be attributed to a particular loss or claim. Others cannot.

Allocated loss adjustment expenses (ALAE) can be specifically related to and/or identified with a particular loss or claim. Such expenses include investigation, negotiation, and legal costs, as well as salvage, debris removal, and similar costs associated with administering claims. If retained by the organization, the ALAE should be allocated either within the responsible department or to the organization as a whole.

Some retrospective rating insurance programs and pools do not handle ALAE through the general risk management allocation system but instead treat them as part of the program's or pool's overhead cost. Normally, to be included in an organization's hazard risk management cost allocation system, a loss adjustment expense should be identified as being incurred to adjust a particular claim.

Unallocated loss adjustment expenses (ULAE) are not easily identified with a particular claim; however, they should be charged to a particular department. For example, an organization that retains its workers compensation losses may pay a third-party administrator to handle claims. The administrator's fee may be charged to each department that generates claims handled by the administrator.

Allocating Retained Losses

To determine how much of each retained loss to allocate, it is important to first select an appropriate basis for calculating the values and loss costs. Loss costs can be calculated by one of three bases:

- Incurred loss basis—The calculation of loss costs by adding the amounts paid for losses to reserves for pending claims, to the additions to those reserves and to the estimated amount of incurred but not reported losses.
- Claims-made basis—The calculation of loss costs by adding the actual payments to changes in reserves for claims made during the accounting period.
- Claims-paid basis—The calculation of loss costs using the amount paid on losses during the accounting period, regardless of when the losses were incurred.

Risk Charges

Each basis for calculating losses can include a risk charge. A risk charge is an amount added to an organization's expected losses to cover potential adverse fluctuations in experience. If an organization's loss experience is worse than expected, the risk charge will help pay for those additional, unexpected losses.

Some organizations accumulate a risk charge for the organization as a whole, and others establish annual department risk charges for each accounting period. During an accounting period, if a department does not have worse than expected losses and, consequently, does not require the risk charge, the risk charge amount is returned to the organization.

According to generally accepted accounting principles (GAAP), an organization should indicate on its financial statements its incurred but unpaid liabilities, which are those liabilities that reflect both the reserve amount of reported losses and the incurred but not reported losses that the organization anticipates financing through retention. A risk charge, however, is not a liability and should not be shown as such on financial statements. The risk charge should be shown as a segregated part of the organization's equity.

Insurance Premiums

Insurance premiums are payments made to an insurer to transfer risk. Premiums are generally fixed for a policy year and can usually be attributed directly to a department. For example, aircraft product liability premiums can be allocated directly to a department that manufactures aircraft or aircraft components. In contrast, certain coverages, such as directors and officers liability insurance, provide a more general benefit for the entire organization.

Costs associated with such coverages do not have a specific source of exposure and therefore are usually allocated equally across the whole organization.

Costs of Risk Control Techniques

Costs of risk control techniques include either long-term capital investments (such as a fire detection and suppression system) or expenditures to purchase less expensive loss control measures (such as safety shoes or driver-training instruction). Capital investments create or add to depreciable assets; occasional expenditures are usually charged against the accounting period in which they produce services or other benefits for the organization.

In either case, most loss control expenditures are clearly allocable to a particular department. When a risk control expenditure is not closely linked to a particular department, the cost is usually treated as part of administrative overhead for the risk management function.

Costs of Administering Risk Management Activities

These are among the costs of administering risk management activities:

- The operating budget of the risk management department
- Cost of executives' time from other departments
- Other resources from other departments devoted to hazard risk management

Some organizations allocate all operating costs of some or all central departments, such as risk management, to other departments. Other organizations allocate to other departments only those costs associated with certain types of loss exposures clearly attributable to those departments.

Costs can include the salary and benefits for people working in workers compensation claim administration departments and the cost of their furniture, supplies, and other needs. Allocated costs can also include the portion of the risk management professional's salary and benefits that represents the time that person spends on the workers compensation program for each department.

Other administrative expenses are not so easily attributable to a particular department or departments and therefore are often not charged as such. Examples include a consultant's audit of the entire hazard risk management program, an actuarial evaluation of a risk retention proposal, and management services for the organization's captive insurer.

PROSPECTIVE AND RETROSPECTIVE COST ALLOCATION

After an organization determines which hazard risk management costs to allocate and to whom they will be allocated, it must then decide the allocation method it will use. There are many approaches to risk management cost allocation. This section discusses two widely used, but mutually exclusive, approaches.

The first approach to hazard risk management cost allocation, prospective cost allocation, is one in which estimated costs are allocated at the beginning of the accounting period during which they are expected to be incurred. Once they are allocated, costs are not changed for that period, regardless of actual losses incurred. The second approach, retrospective cost allocation, is a cost allocation approach in which estimated costs are allocated at the beginning of the accounting period during which they are expected to be incurred but can then be reallocated one or more times during or after the close of the period, with payments or returns made retrospectively according to changes in loss experience.

Both systems seek a balance between loss experience and loss exposure. In a prospective system, costs are allocated primarily on the basis of potential exposures to loss and secondarily on the basis of recent actual loss experience. In a retrospective system, the opposite is true; actual loss experience is the primary basis for allocation, and potential loss exposures are the secondary basis.

Prospective Cost Allocation Approach

The primary advantage of prospective hazard cost allocation is a stable budget in which costs are assumed to be known before the beginning of the accounting period and are not changed. The corresponding disadvantage is that actual costs can differ substantially from those allocated. Although the differences can be corrected in subsequent periods, the corrected costs are not associated with the output of the period to which they are charged.

Another disadvantage of prospective allocation is that an increase (or a decrease) in risk control activity can be separated by several accounting periods from the corresponding reduction (or increase) in allocated costs, which can delay the positive influence a cost allocation system may have on a departmental manager's risk control efforts.

Retrospective Cost Allocation Approach

The primary advantage of retrospective hazard cost allocation is that costs are more accurately attributed to the period and the department with which they are associated. Consequently, an increase (or a decrease) in risk control activity and a corresponding reduction (or increase) in loss costs are immediately recognized in terms of allocated costs, facilitating the evaluation of the risk control program's effectiveness.

The corresponding disadvantage is that final allocated risk management costs are not determined until well after the end of the period during which the losses were incurred, which complicates risk management budgeting.

BASES FOR ALLOCATING HAZARD RISK MANAGEMENT COSTS

After an organization determines the types and amounts of its costs of hazard risk, which it may approach prospectively or retrospectively, it must determine the bases on which it will allocate the costs among its departments.

Exposure-based system

A system that allocates costs to departments on the basis of their exposures, regardless of their loss experience.

Experience-based system

A system that allocates costs to departments according to their pro rata portion of past losses.

Hazard costs can be allocated based on loss exposure or loss experience. An **exposure-based system** is a system that allocates costs to departments on the basis of their exposures, regardless of loss experience. Under such a system, the proportionate costs charged to any department do not change as long as its loss exposures do not change.

An **experience-based system** is a system that allocates costs to departments according to their pro rata portion of past losses. This system can subject small departments to significant fluctuations in costs from one accounting period to the next if their loss experience fluctuates significantly.

Allocating Hazard Costs

Rather than exclusively relying on one system or the other, many organizations use a combination of loss exposure and experience to allocate costs of hazard risk throughout the organization's departments, a practice known as blending allocation.

Generally, systems for allocating costs for loss exposures that generate frequent claims (such as workers' compensation) rely more on loss experience than on loss exposures. Furthermore, managers of larger, more financially capable departments generally want their costs to be allocated by experience rather than by loss exposures because loss experience can decrease their allocated costs to an amount less than what their department's size alone suggests.

For example, consider an organization composed of two departments, one that generates $100 million in revenues and another that generates $50 million in revenues. Hazard risk management costs associated with property can be allocated to both departments, based 90 percent on their loss exposure and 10 percent on their loss experience. In contrast, workers compensation costs can be allocated 75 percent on experience (25 percent on exposure) for the larger-revenue department and 50 percent on experience (50 percent on exposure) for the smaller-revenue department.

Percentages should reflect the relative degree of confidence placed in the organization's past experience as a predictor of its future experience. The greater the correlation between past losses and future losses, the more closely the loss experience approaches 100 percent credibility. In practice, credibility is often determined by judgment or by actuarial calculations.

The costs of loss-sensitive insurance (such as a retrospective rating plan) can be apportioned not in percentages, but in layers. For example, in a system

that allocates the costs of insuring liability loss exposures, each department can be responsible for paying all relatively small losses within its individual deductible. Costs for losses above the deductible, but within the organization's overall retention, can be allocated to each department, based 50 percent on experience and 50 percent on exposure. The costs for liability insurance above the organization's retention can be allocated wholly on the basis of each department's loss exposure.

Exposure Bases

The bases for determining and allocating hazard risk management costs differ by type of loss exposure. For example, different bases are used to allocate general liability costs than are used to allocate workers compensation costs. Each basis selected should, to the extent practical, reflect the underlying loss exposures.

For each risk management cost category, loss exposure can generally be measured by size, nature of operations, and territory, which, in turn, can be measured by some easily verified gauge. Size, for example, can be measured by revenues, number of employees, or square footage. A department with twice the revenues of another with identical operations can be considered to have twice the loss exposure and, thus, twice the allocated costs.

The nature of a department's operations also determines the extent of the loss exposure. A department making pharmaceutical products has a greater products liability exposure than one that manufactures soap because of the greater risk of health complication for consumers from pharmaceutical products. Therefore, the products liability risk management charges per dollar of revenue that are allocated to the pharmaceutical department should be greater than the risk management charges for each dollar of revenue allocated to the soap-manufacturing department.

The geographic location of the loss exposure can also be used to estimate the cost of risk for the exposure because it can reflect the difference in benefit levels and expected legal costs to be incurred. For example, a person injured in the United States would probably receive greater compensation than a person similarly injured in Brazil. Consequently, general liability risk management charges for each dollar of an organization's output in the U.S. should exceed charges for revenues generated in other countries.

Another type of loss exposure basis is rate per unit of exposure. Insurance premiums for guaranteed-cost coverages for a particular department are usually calculated on a rate per unit of exposure. The rate for each department can differ substantially from the premium rate that an insurer charges the organization as a whole because each department's degree of hazard differs from the organization's composite rate.

The exposure bases used by the insurer are usually helpful in determining an appropriate exposure for the type of risk management cost being allocated.

These types of costs are common to many organizations and require a variety of exposure bases:

- General liability
- Automobile liability
- Workers compensation
- Property
- Other exposures

General Liability

General liability loss exposures vary widely among different types of organizations. For some organizations, general liability exposure arises primarily from premises and operations. For others, it comes primarily from products or the activities of independent contractors.

Commonly used bases for measuring an organization's dominant general liability exposure and for allocating general liability costs include square footage of floor space, annual budget, payroll, full-time-equivalent workers, and sales. If an insurer charges an extra premium for a special exposure, such as mobile communication systems, the premium is usually charged directly to the department responsible for it.

At times, an organization may have to modify an insurer's exposure basis to better reflect the degree of exposure associated with a particular department's activities. For example, department budgets can indicate the premises liability exposure for each department. However, if a department has extremely high research and development costs, and those costs generate no significant premises liability exposure, the department's budget (which is large) does not accurately reflect its exposure (which is small). For cost allocation purposes, the department's research and development costs may be excluded from its budget because they do not increase the department's premises liability exposure.

Automobile Liability

Automobile liability loss exposures differ by departments and by types of vehicles operated by those departments. Some departments use small trucks; some, large trucks; some, only passenger vehicles; and some, essentially no vehicles at all. The most commonly used exposure basis for allocating automobile liability costs is the number of vehicles used, with some adjustments for differences in types of vehicles.

For example, a department operating both private passenger automobiles and delivery trucks might assign to private passenger automobiles an exposure basis, which is also referred to as a relativity in this circumstance, of 1.00, and to delivery trucks a relativity of 5.00 (if, hypothetically, it is assumed that the trucks typically generate five times the losses of an equal number of the private passenger automobiles). Therefore, the number of vehicles serving as the allocation basis for the department would be computed as the number of private passenger automobiles plus five times the number of trucks.

Workers Compensation

Workers compensation loss exposures differ by department and by job classifications within departments. A workers compensation loss exposure can involve highly hazardous mining operations or much safer office operations, for example. The two most common exposure bases for allocating workers compensation costs are payroll and full-time-equivalent number of employees. For both, rates are commonly adjusted for differences in loss exposure by job classification.

For example, office workers might have a payroll relativity of 1.00, and firefighting personnel might have a relativity of 12.00. Therefore, a department that employs fifty office workers and two firefighters would be shown as having a total of seventy-four employees in the organization's workers compensation cost allocation system. The National Council on Compensation Insurance provides exposure bases, called "rate relativities," which can be modified for particular departments.

Property

Property loss exposures vary by organization and by type of building and occupancy within an organization. For some organizations, manufacturing plants are the dominant property exposure; for others, office buildings.

The two most common exposure bases for allocating risk management costs for property are square footage and property values (either replacement cost or actual cash value). When an insurer charges an extra premium for a particular loss exposure, such as a chemical mixing operation, the premium is often charged directly to the department responsible for it.

The exposure basis for property must often be modified to accurately reflect the associated loss exposure.For example, although property values are good general indicators of exposure, one department might operate in a building containing inflammable chemicals. The property values for that department, when used in the cost allocation system, should reflect the degree of hazard created by the presence of the chemicals.

The effects of location, such as a building located in a hurricane zone, should also be considered. Again, the relativities used by property insurers are often germane but are usually modified for each organization.

Other Exposures

Activities within the hazard risk management program related to other loss exposures, such as crime and fidelity, should have corresponding exposure

bases for cost allocation, to the extent practical. For example, risk management department overhead can be allocated in different ways, including these:

- In proportion to the total of other risk management department costs allocated for particular loss exposures
- As a fixed percentage of some other basis, such as sales
- As a combination of a flat fee per department (to cover fixed costs) and a percentage of some base, such as sales (to cover variable costs)

Using the most desirable exposure basis in all situations might not be possible because of one or more of these problems:

- The data that form an exposure base, such as the number of full-time equivalent employees for allocating workers' compensation costs, are not available readily or at a reasonable price.
- Department managers disagree on how to calculate a particular exposure basis (for example, total operating expenditures excluding capital investments).
- Desired data, such as replacement cost property values, cannot be calculated each year in time to be used in a prospective cost allocation system.

However, in situations that effectively prohibit using the desired exposure base, finding an adequate, practical alternative is usually possible. For the three preceding problems, acceptable alternative exposure bases are payroll for workers compensation, payroll for general liability, and replacement cost property values for the previous year. For building values, it may be necessary to adjust for more recent building acquisitions and disposals (again valued at the previous year's replacement cost).

Experience Basis

Loss experience is another basis that has been used effectively to allocate hazard costs among departments within an organization. Loss experience is also often used as an indicator of the success of a risk management program and is measured by frequency or aggregate severity limited to some dollar amount. Frequency of losses indicates the quality of most loss control programs better than severity of losses because frequency is usually easier to control than severity.

Aggregate severity, which is the cumulative losses for a given period, is commonly used to indicate each department's claim experience. Each loss charged to a department is limited to a certain amount. The amount—for example, $25,000 per occurrence—is often meant to be high enough to include the majority of a department's losses but low enough to prevent a rare large loss from detrimentally affecting a department's loss experience that otherwise was good. Each loss, up to the limit, is added to the department's loss experience. All claims reported for a given period are then accumulated to determine the department's experience.

Once a department's claim experience has been measured by severity, its future losses and related costs can be projected. These three primary criteria are used:

- Changes in claims paid
- Changes in payments plus loss reserves
- Changes in projected ultimate incurred losses

When cost of risk allocations are made according to changes in claims paid, the costs to a department tend to fluctuate by accounting period. Allocations based on changes in payments plus loss reserves typically fluctuate less (assuming the individual incurred losses are limited) than the most recent claim payments. However, loss reserves may be poorly estimated, which can artificially influence a department's allocated costs. (But if that artificial influence is uniform across departments, the cost distribution among departments will not be altered.) Also, using payments plus loss reserves avoids difficulties that can arise because of different reporting and payment patterns for claims that are characteristic of different departments.

In such situations, estimated ultimate incurred losses, which are estimated total payments for open claims, could be a better choice. If presumably incurred but unreported losses are allocated to departments in proportion to reported claims (as measured by payments plus case reserves), allocations based on payments plus cash reserves and allocations based on projected ultimate losses will produce the same results.

Regardless of the experience criteria used, these considerations are useful in calculating the aggregate severity of a department's claims:

- Per occurrence limit
- Aggregate limit
- Experience period

Per Occurrence Limit

Effective hazard risk management programs work to reduce both the number of occurrences that result in claims and the amount of each claim that arises. As mentioned, claim frequency is usually easier to control than claim severity. Consequently, most hazard risk management cost allocation systems are designed to be more sensitive to loss frequency than loss severity. By limiting losses to a specified amount per occurrence, the cost allocation system directs management's attention to where frequency of losses is a problem rather than to a department that has incurred a large loss that may never reoccur.

The amount of each loss and related allocated loss adjustment expenses (ALAE) in excess of the per occurrence limit can be allocated among all departments based on their loss exposures, rather than experience, to reflect the fortuitous nature of catastrophic events and losses. Alternatively, the excess amount of losses can be absorbed by the organization as a whole rather than by its departments.

Aggregate Limit

In addition to capping per occurrence limits, some hazard risk management cost allocation systems further cap annual losses by using an annual aggregate limit. Aggregate limits should be set high enough so that a manager is directly penalized for poor aggregate loss experience. A high aggregate limit ensures that more costs can be allocated to each department.

Experience Period

Any experience-based cost allocation system distributes current claims and related ALAE among departments proportionally to each department's claims and related ALAE experience. For prospective plans, loss costs are collected over the **experience period**, usually ranging from two to five previous years. For retrospective plans, the allocation is based on the losses for the current year.

Experience period
The length of time available to collect loss costs.

The shorter the experience period, the more responsive the cost allocation formula is to changes in recent past loss experience. Consequently, a short experience period more quickly reflects the results of recent changes in risk management activity. However, a short experience period also tends to subject individual departments to more widely fluctuating charges resulting from unusually good or bad claim experience.

That fluctuation can be mitigated by placing maximums and minimums on the claim amounts that can be included in any one department's experience base. Furthermore, multi-year experience periods can be weighted to more heavily count recent experience. Therefore, experience accumulated over five years can be used to develop a weighted average in which each of the two most recent years is weighted by 30 percent, the third year 20 percent, and each of the two most distant years 10 percent.

RISK MANAGEMENT COST ALLOCATION—PRACTICAL CONSIDERATIONS

Many practical considerations affect selection of a hazard risk management cost allocation basis and the actual or perceived fairness of that allocation.

These considerations pertain to selecting a hazard risk management cost allocation basis:

- An organization's accounting system
- The tax system for each of the organization's operations
- A minimum charge amount for risk management services for each department
- A determination as to whether cost allocation is insignificant
- Penalties or rewards for department managers

- Inclusion of managers in development of the risk management cost allocation plan
- Use of risk management information systems (RMIS)
- The consistency of the cost allocation system
- Any changes in the organization's structure

One practical consideration is that an organization's accounting system can influence cost allocation. Exposure bases often rely on exposure-based data, such as sales and payroll, which are maintained as part of the organization's overall accounting system. However, the desired data may not be readily available per department or activity.

Also, the data may be available but unusable by the risk management professional to allocate costs because they were collected for purposes other than hazard risk management cost allocation. For example, the organization's accounting system must follow certain statutory and regulatory guidelines when collecting and reporting the data.

Another practical consideration is that some of an organization's operations may be subject to more than one tax system, such as when an organization operates internationally or with foreign subsidiaries. Allocating costs among internationally operating departments and subsidiaries can have unfavorable tax consequences for the organization as a whole. Consequently, hazard cost allocation systems must consider tax implications on an aggregate basis.

In some organizations, each department should be charged at least a minimum amount for risk management services, regardless of its loss exposures or claim experience. Charging a minimum amount incorporates an exposure basis within the hazard risk management cost allocation system. For example, when allocating costs associated with a workers compensation retention program, each department may have the following as a minimum charge:

- Risk control costs
- Risk management department overhead
- Excess insurance premiums

These costs could be allocated by payroll and adjusted for differences in job classifications. The services and protection afforded by excess insurance benefit all departments, regardless of loss experience. Similarly, it may be appropriate to establish a maximum that a department can be charged despite the worst possible experience.

The usual purpose of establishing a maximum charge is to reduce the fluctuations in allocated costs from one accounting period to the next. Such a maximum is often expressed as a percentage of the prior year's allocated hazard risk management costs.

An additional practical consideration is that if an organization is highly decentralized, department managers may be allowed to purchase their own

insurance rather than participate in a centralized hazard risk management cost allocation system. This is likely not to be as cost-effective as buying insurance for the organization as a whole because it does not leverage the combined purchasing power of all the departments to negotiate lower expense factors and service fees from an insurer. Gaps in coverage or duplications of coverage also may result. Consistent application of umbrella or excess liability insurance policies also presents a challenge when departments are allowed to purchase their own coverage.

Also, for an organization with a small aggregate cost of hazard risk relative to its total budget, the results of cost allocation can be insignificant. In this case, a hazard risk management cost allocation system is probably not needed at all. For instance, a $10,000 or $25,000 charge for workers compensation coverage will have little effect on a department with a $10 million budget.

Another practical consideration is that a hazard risk management cost allocation system should penalize or reward each department manager according to that department's risk management costs. This can be accomplished if managers' bonuses reflect their allocated hazard risk management costs as well as other operating results. Moreover, a department's total budget should not be adjusted to compensate for changes in risk management results; doing so tends to cushion or cancel the manager's penalty or reward. For example, if a department's workers compensation cost allocation increases from $1 million to $5 million because of its deteriorating experience, increasing its total budget by $4 million does not penalize its manager appropriately and fails to motivate improvement of the department's workers compensation results.

Department and senior managers should support the hazard risk management cost allocation plan that is selected. Having the support of department and senior managers is necessary to collect the data for cost allocation and to foster cooperation. Cooperation can also be encouraged by including managers in the development of the risk management cost allocation plan.

An additional practical consideration is that the use of computerized risk management information systems (RMIS) has become standard in many industries, particularly in the application of experience-based hazard risk management allocation systems. Many RMIS gather cost information and allocate costs among departments, products, or functions. Department and senior managers should agree in advance, if possible, on the allocation bases, formulas, and limits of the RMIS.

Another practical consideration when selecting an allocation basis is that hazard cost allocation systems should remain as consistent as possible from year to year. Risk management cost allocation systems usually use past loss and claim data as a benchmark to evaluate current performance. Consequently, changes in the underlying data may make the current performance evaluation meaningless.

Changes in hazard risk management cost allocation systems can be necessary, however, because the organizations they monitor are dynamic. The ramifications of any changes in the organization's structure should be considered and communicated to the affected managers. These situations typically trigger system changes:

- Material shifts in the organization's operations (for example, purchasing a large subsidiary, discontinuing operations, or deciding to make one product a loss leader)
- Change in expected losses because of change in legal climate, inflation, or some other factor, which can create the need to change the per occurrence limit
- Restructuring of the organization's departments or lines of authority

ALLOCATING COSTS FOR HAZARD RISK MANAGEMENT

This section presents an example of how a hypothetical organization, Lorac Management Corporation (Lorac), might apply the appropriate steps when developing its hazard risk management cost allocation system for its general liability risk financing program. The case illustrates the need for an organization-specific system and demonstrates that no right or wrong approach to risk management cost allocation exists, only one that makes sense for a given organization within the guidelines.

Effective hazard risk management cost allocation systems require that most costs be allocated to the departments that generate them. A properly designed risk management cost allocation system meets these goals:

- Promotes risk control
- Facilitates risk retention
- Prioritizes risk management expenditures
- Reduces costs
- Distributes costs fairly
- Balances risk bearing and risk sharing
- Provides managers with hazard risk management cost information

Case Facts

Lorac Management Corporation (Lorac) is a privately held organization that owns and manages five commercial properties located in three United States cities, as shown in the "Listing of Lorac Properties" exhibit. Each property is treated as a profit center, and each maintains separate accounting information in the form of profit and loss statements. Each property manager is on an incentive compensation system that reflects the profitability of each property and that takes into account all expenses, including hazard risk management expenses. See the exhibit "Listing of Lorac Properties."

Listing of Lorac Properties

Location	Occupancy
Los Angeles	Hotel
Los Angeles	Apartment building
Denver	Hotel
Denver	Office building
Houston	Hotel

[DA01914]

Last year, Lorac purchased guaranteed-cost, occurrence-basis, primary general liability insurance for a premium of $300,000. The premium had been allocated as shown in the "Allocation of Costs Based on Square Footage" exhibit. Using square footage as an allocation basis limited fluctuations in allocated costs to the changes in annual premiums because the square footage at each property remained fairly constant. See the exhibit "Allocation of Costs Based on Square Footage."

Allocation of Costs Based on Square Footage

(1) Location	(2) Occupancy	(3) Square Footage	(4) Percentage of Total	(5) Cost Allocation
Los Angeles	Hotel	200,000	20%	$ 60,000
Los Angeles	Apartment building	300,000	30	90,000
Denver	Hotel	200,000	20	60,000
Denver	Office building	100,000	10	30,000
Houston	Hotel	200,000	20	60,000
Total		1,000,000	100%	$300,000

[DA01915]

After last year's allocations, some of Lorac's property managers complained about general liability insurance costs. The manager of the Houston hotel, which had a significantly lower occupancy rate than the other two hotels, believed that the Houston property was subsidizing the cost of hazard risk for the hotels in Denver and Los Angeles. In contrast, the managers of the apartment and office buildings, which historically had fewer claims, believed that they were subsidizing the hotels.

Case Analysis Steps

Applying a hazard risk management cost allocation system to a specific organization requires the risk management professional to perform these six steps:

1. Review the attributes of an effective hazard risk management cost allocation system and determine the organization's objectives for such a system.
2. Identify the costs that will be allocated by the risk management cost allocation system.
3. For each category of cost, determine whether a prospective or retrospective allocation would best show where risk management techniques should be used.
4. Determine the value and the way each cost will be allocated based on one or more of these issues: exposure basis, experience basis, per occurrence limit, aggregate limit, and experience period.
5. Consider the opportunities and challenges of each of these factors when implementing a hazard risk management cost allocation system: accounting system, each organization's tax system, minimum and/or maximum limits on costs to be allocated for each accounting period, decentralized departments, significance of risk management costs to each department's budget, ways in which cost allocations may penalize or reward a department manager according to that department's costs to influence motivation and performance, level of support and cooperation from management, risk management information systems (RMIS) used, and consistency of allocation system.
6. Perform trial calculations to determine whether the proposed system meets the organization's needs. If it does not, make adjustments and repeat this step as necessary.

Determining an Effective Hazard Cost Allocation System

For the forthcoming renewal, Lorac's risk management professional realizes that, because of market conditions and deteriorating claim experience, Lorac's guaranteed-cost general liability premium will probably increase from $300,000 to $500,000. The risk management professional considers these factors:

- Allocating costs according to square footage may not encourage risk control activities at the properties.
- Senior management would support a risk management cost allocation process that influenced property managers' bonuses so that each manager

would have a personal incentive to reach the goals of the new risk control program.

- The risk management professional worked with an outside consultant to develop a basic risk control program that addresses many of the causes of past accidents, which may reduce future losses.

Identifying the Costs to Be Allocated

The program recommended by the outside consultant includes a $10,000 per occurrence liability deductible for the general liability coverage. Lorac's acceptance of the deductible induced the underwriter to lower the guaranteed-cost premium for the coming year to $250,000. The risk management professional determines that annual losses within the $10,000 per occurrence deductible could be expected to aggregate to $150,000. She consequently estimates that the total primary general liability risk financing cost for the coming year would be $400,000, consisting of $250,000 in premiums and $150,000 in retained losses (including loss adjustment expenses for both insured and uninsured claims).

Choosing Between Prospective and Retrospective Allocations

The risk management professional also concludes that maintaining a prospective cost allocation system is important because the property managers want hazard risk management costs that can be determined in advance. As a result, changes in loss experience for each year will influence only cost allocations for the next year. The risk management professional evaluates how costs would be allocated for the coming year and decides that the projected $150,000 in retained losses should be allocated by the last three years of losses, up to $10,000 per occurrence. In contrast, the guaranteed-cost insurance premium should be allocated principally on relative exposure, with some adjustment for large losses. She believes this blended approach should reflect her contention that the frequency of losses within the $10,000 deductible is controllable.

Determining the Value and Method for Allocating Costs

The risk management professional next performs cost allocation calculations to develop a table. See the exhibit "Allocation of Retained Claims by Three Years' Cumulative Claim Experience Capped at $10,000 per Occurrence."

For the $150,000 projected annual losses within the $10,000 per occurrence deductible, she calculates by location the past three years of paid and reserved losses, which were increased to reflect inflation and were capped at $10,000 per occurrence. The calculations are shown in Columns 3, 4, and 5 of the table.

The sum of those three columns appears in Column 6. The amounts in Column 6 have been used to calculate the percentages in Column 7. Each

Allocation of Retained Claims by Three Years' Cumulative Claim Experience Capped at $10,000 per Occurrence

(1) Location	(2) Occupancy	(3) Least Recent Year 1	(4) Year 2	(5) Most Recent Year 3	(6) Total Claims (Col. 3 + Col. 4 + Col. 5)	(7) Percentage of Total	(8) Cost Allocation (Col. 7 × $150,000)
Los Angeles	Hotel	$ 75,000	$ 75,000	$40,000	$190,000	47.5%	$ 71,250
Los Angeles	Apartment building	30,000	25,000	15,000	70,000	17.5	26,250
Denver	Hotel	40,000	40,000	20,000	100,000	25.0	37,500
Denver	Office building	8,000	2,000	0	10,000	2.5	3,750
Houston	Hotel	2,000	10,000	18,000	30,000	7.5	11,250
Total		$155,000	$152,000	$93,000	$400,000	100.0%	$150,000

[DA01916]

percentage in Column 7 has been computed by dividing the total losses at each location by the $400,000 of losses at all locations.

The allocated costs in Column 8 apportion the $150,000 of projected retained claims by the percentages in Column 7.

Identifying Challenges and Opportunities

Next, the risk management professional develops a table showing the allocation of insurance premium based on the square footage of Lorac's properties. She notes that the Los Angeles hotel has generated a large portion of the claims that would have fallen within the $10,000 deductible. Although the hotel represents 20 percent of Lorac's total square footage, it sustained 47.5 percent of all inflation-adjusted claims capped at $10,000. The risk management professional believes that square footage does not sufficiently indicate exposure. Although square footage represents size relativities, it does not reflect differences in the operational exposures of hotel, apartment, and office occupancies. Furthermore, square footage does not account for territorial relativities—for example, the differences in the legal environments of Los Angeles, Denver, and Houston. See the exhibit "Allocation of Insurance Premium Based on Adjusted Square Footage."

The risk management professional, therefore, develops a table showing the allocation of insurance premium based on Lorac's past five years of claim experience. She relies on insurance premium rates for different occupancies in the states in which Lorac's buildings are located to reflect the relativities shown in Column 4 of the table. (Notice that those relativities are weighting factors that, unlike percentages, need not add up to 1.00.)

Allocation of Insurance Premium Based on Adjusted Square Footage

(1) Location	(2) Occupancy	(3) Square Footage	(4) Rate	(5) Adjusted Square Footage (Col. 3 × Col. 4)	(6) Percentage of Total	(7) Allocation of Insurance Premium
Los Angeles	Hotel	200,000	0.225	45,000	30%	$75,000
Los Angeles	Apartment building	300,000	0.100	30,000	20	50,000
Denver	Hotel	200,000	0.200	40,000	27	67,500
Denver	Office building	100,000	0.050	5,000	3	7,500
Houston	Hotel	200,000	0.150	30,000	20	50,000
Total		1,000,000		150,000	100%	$250,000

[DA01917]

Applying the relativities to the square footage in Column 3 of the table enables the risk management professional to adjust square footage so it more closely reflects exposure, as shown in Column 5. Column 6 shows the resulting changes in the percentage of the total premium allocated to each location. The actual cost based on those percentages is shown in Column 7. The calculations conclude the exposure-based allocation of retained losses. See the exhibit "Allocation of Insurance Premium Based on Five Years of Claim Experience Between $10,000 and $50,000 per Occurrence."

To build an experience-based allocation of the guaranteed-cost insurance premium, the risk management professional decides to use large losses (that is, inflation-adjusted claims between $10,000 and $50,000) as the allocation basis and five years of experience because of the low frequency of large claims. The results are shown in the table. Column 8 totals the relevant claims from Columns 3 through 7. Column 9 indicates the experience basis for each location as a percentage of their $400,000 total. The allocated insurance premium in Column 10 is based on those percentages.

The risk management professional next considers the amount of loss experience that should be reflected in hazard cost allocation figures to motivate division managers to improve loss control. A high percentage based on losses could lead to fluctuations in divisional costs that would not always reflect the long-term effects of loss control. The risk management professional thus develops a table showing allocation of insurance premium based on experience and exposure, in which she allocates 80 percent of the $250,000 premium by exposure and 20 percent by the claim experience from the table. See the exhibit "Allocation of Insurance Premium Based on Experience and Exposure."

Allocation of Insurance Premium Based on Five Years of Claim Experience Between $10,000 and $50,000 per Occurrence

(1) Location	(2) Occupancy	(3) Least Recent Year 1	(4) Year 2	(5) Year 3	(6) Year 4	(7) Most Recent Year 5	(8) Cumulative Total Claims	(9) Percentage of Total	(10) Allocation of Insurance Premium
Los Angeles	Hotel	$0	$60,000	$60,000	$30,000	$30,000	$180,000	45%	$112,500
Los Angeles	Apartment building	20,000	0	10,000	10,000	40,000	80,000	20	50,000
Denver	Hotel	40,000	10,000	20,000	40,000	10,000	120,000	30	75,000
Denver	Office building	0	0	0	0	0	0	0	0
Houston	Hotel	10,000	0	0	0	10,000	20,000	5	12,500
Total		$70,000	$70,000	$90,000	$80,000	$90,000	$400,000	100%	$250,000

[DA01918]

The results shown in the "Allocation of Insurance Premium Based on Experience and Exposure" table were obtained by taking the exposure percentages from Column 6 of the "Allocation of Insurance Premium Based on Adjusted Square Footage" table and multiplying them by 80 percent. The risk management professional then uses the experience percentages from Column 9 of the "Allocation of Insurance Premium Based on Five Years of Claim Experience Between $10,000 and $50,000 per Occurrence" table and multiplies them by 20 percent. The sum of the two percentages, the overall allocation percentage, is shown for each property in Column 7 of the "Allocation of Insurance Premium Based on Experience and Exposure" table. Applying those percentages to the $250,000 premium generates the insurance costs allocated to each location, as shown in Column 8 of the experience and exposure table.

Performing Trial Calculations

The risk management professional develops a table to compare the final cost allocation to the initial cost allocation. She decides to use the costs in Column 6 of this table as a first approximation of the final allocation for the coming year. She knows that a lively discussion will ensue concerning the significant shifts in cost, particularly toward the Los Angeles and Denver hotels. The risk management professional considers this the ideal means to draw senior and operating management attention to the costs of claims as well as to the new risk control measures to reduce those claims. Although the

Allocation of Insurance Premium Based on Experience and Exposure

(1) Location	(2) Occupancy	(3) Exposure Percentage	(4) Exposure Percentage (80% of Col. 3)	(5) Experience Percentage	(6) Experience Percentage (20% of Col. 5)	(7) Total Percentage Allocation (Col. 4 + Col. 6)	(8) Premium Allocation (Col. 7 × $250,000)
Los Angeles	Hotel	30%	24.0%	45%	9%	33.0%	$ 82,500
Los Angeles	Apartment building	20	16.0	20	4	20.0	50,000
Denver	Hotel	27	21.6	30	6	27.6	69,000
Denver	Office building	3	2.4	0	0	2.4	6,000
Houston	Hotel	20	16.0	5	1	17.0	42,500
Total		100%	80.0%	100%	20%	100.0%	$250,000

[DA01920]

final hazard cost allocations may not represent such a dramatic departure from the previous year, they should improve and justify Lorac's hazard risk control efforts and overall risk management program. See the exhibit "Comparison of Final to Initial Cost Allocation."

Comparison of Final to Initial Cost Allocation

(1) Location	(2) Occupancy	(3) Final Premium Allocation	(4) Final Retained Claim Allocation	(5) Final Total Cost Allocation (Col. 3 + Col. 4)	(6) Initial Cost Allocation	(7) Percentage Change
Los Angeles	Hotel	$82,500	$71,250	$153,750	$60,000	156%
Los Angeles	Apartment building	50,000	26,250	76,250	90,000	(15)
Denver	Hotel	69,000	37,500	106,500	60,000	78
Denver	Office building	6,000	3,750	9,750	30,000	(67)
Houston	Hotel	42,500	11,250	53,750	60,000	(10)
Total		$250,000	$150,000	$400,000	$300,000	33%

[DA01921]

SUMMARY

Effective hazard risk management cost allocation systems require that most costs be allocated to the departments that generate them. A properly designed risk management cost allocation system promotes risk control, facilitates risk retention, prioritizes risk management expenditures, reduces costs, distributes costs fairly, balances risk bearing and risk sharing, and provides managers with cost information.

The four types of hazard risk management costs that can be fully or partially allocated, which together constitute an organization's cost of risk, include the costs of accidental losses not reimbursed by insurance or other outside sources, insurance premiums, costs of risk control techniques, and costs of administering risk management activities. Any combination of these costs, or portions of them, can be allocated to any department. Costs that are clearly incurred by and beneficial to a given department, or wholly within that department's control, are easily allocated to that department.

The two widely used approaches to hazard risk management cost allocation are prospective and retrospective. The distinction refers to differences in determining both the initial allocation and the final payment of losses and other risk management costs.

The initial step in the hazard risk management cost allocation process is to determine the types and amounts of an organization's risk management costs. The next step is to decide the basis on which they should be allocated to each department. Costs can be allocated by loss exposure or loss experience.

Each basis selected should reflect the underlying exposures. Exposure can generally be measured by size, nature of operations, and territory. Loss experience is often used as a direct measure of a risk management program's success. It is measured by frequency or aggregate severity limited to some dollar amount.

Several practical factors affect the design of a hazard risk management cost allocation system. The risk management professional should consider that an organization's accounting system can affect the plan's design and that some of an organization's operations may be subject to more than one tax system.

A hazard risk management cost allocation system may not be necessary for an organization that has an insignificant aggregate cost of risk relative to its total budget. If a risk management cost allocation system is needed, the plan may charge each department at least a minimum amount for risk management services, and it may penalize or reward each department manager according to that department's risk management costs.

All managers should be included in developing the risk management cost allocation plan and should agree on the extent to which RMIS should be used. Finally, the hazard cost allocation systems should remain as consistent as possible from year to year; however, adjustments may be needed to accommodate any changes in the organization's structure.

A risk management professional performs six steps when developing a hazard risk management cost allocation system. These steps include reviewing the attributes of an effective hazard risk management cost allocation system, identifying the costs to be allocated by the hazard risk management cost allocation system, choosing between a prospective or retrospective allocation, determining the value and the way each cost will be allocated, considering the opportunities and challenges of the cost allocation system, and performing trial calculations as part of the analysis of a proposed cost allocation system.

Index

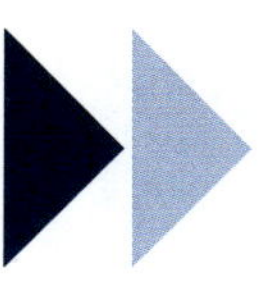

Page numbers in boldface refer to pages where the word or phrase is defined.

D

E

F

Q

R

S

T

U

V

W